Blue Blood:

The History of the Indianapolis Colts

Second Edition

Nate Dunlevy

Published by Madison House Publishing
www.madisonhousepublishing.com

ISBN 978-0-9966556-2-0

Under the Title: "Blue Blood: Tales of Glory of the Indianapolis Colts"

Edited by Kyle David Torke

Second Edition Edited by Jessica Flaherty

Cover Design by Matt Hasenbalg

Table of Contents

Preface to the Second Edition

In the original edition of this book, I wrote two sentences that I've regretted many times since. They are exactly why a second edition of *Blue Blood* is necessary.

About the 2009 Colts, I wrote:

"The decade is done. The dominance is not."

Man, did I ever blow that.

As I write this, Peyton is preparing for his retirement press conference in Denver. The man who shaped the destiny of the Indianapolis Colts left the game as a Denver Bronco.

History is wet cement. What is written can be smoothed over and re-written. This new edition will be honest to that process.

The goal of this second edition is not only to present the 2010 through 2016 seasons in context and to introduce new "characters" like Andrew Luck and Chuck Pagano to the stage, but also to provide a final word on the Manning Era.

The radical developments of the last few years have forced me to do rewrites to various sections of this book. Whenever possible, I have preserved key passages that are no longer relevant via footnotes. I have no interest in making myself look prescient after the fact, but I do want this edition (and any future editions) to represent the most up-to-date interpretation of past events.

Additionally, I have fixed innumerable errors and annoyances that have haunted me for better than five years now, as well as expanded the roster of Classic Colts and Games We'll Never Forget.

The appendix has swelled as well, as I have included a pair of pieces that were well-loved and enthusiastically received at the time of their original publication.

The outpouring of affection for the original edition of this book was amazing. I cannot adequately thank those of you who have gone out of your way to encourage me over the years.

Once again, thank you for reading and for loving the Colts as much as I do.

Go Horse,

-DZ

Acknowledgements

I wish to thank the following people for their inspiration and help in making this book a reality:

- My wife, Deborah, for her patience and countless good ideas.
- My brother Luke for starting 18to88.com.
- My parents and grandparents for all the tickets through the years.
- My friends at Madison House for their years of support and friendship.
- Neil Salkind for inspiring me to take on this project.
- Nathan Brown, my tireless research assistant.
- Bob Mangino for his constant support and advice.
- Matt Hasenbalg for his contribution to the cover design.
- John Oehser and Paul Kuharsky for their support of 18to88.com and of me personally.
- Phil B. Wilson and Bob Kravitz for their encouragement.
- Mike Chappell and Phil Richards for years of outstanding football coverage.
- Kerry Byrne (coldhardfootballfacts.com) and Mike Tanier (footballoutsiders.com) for the opportunity to contribute to their fine sites from time to time.

- Derek Schultz, Jake Query, Kent Sterling, Greg Rakestraw, Dan Dakich, Eddie White, and John Michael Vincent for helping 18to88.com and Colts Authority on the airwaves.
- Mike Tanier, Nate Miller and Will Carroll for the advice.
- Collin McCollough for being a great editor at Bleacher Report.
- Kyle Rodriguez, Marcus Dugan, and Josh Baker for their many efforts.
- Indiana Humanities for their promotion of my work.
- Pat Maier for his work on the second edition.
- My friends at Art Fight Club for their critique.
- Jessica Flaherty for her editing prowess.

Jim Irsay for being the best owner in football.

18 and 88. We'll never see the likes of you again.

And finally, special thanks to the community of readers at 18to88.com, ColtsAuthority.com, and Bleacher Report, who have made writing about the Colts a thrill for the past decade.

This book is dedicated to Ellie, Scott, and Lucy, and to the second generation of Indianapolis Colts fans everywhere.

The Kickoff

For Felix,

Merry Christmas 2018!

With love,

Uncle Pete

March was madness in Indiana.

Hoosier Hysteria was a yearly illness that afflicted tens of thousands across Indiana. The high school basketball championship gripped the state while simultaneously, people kept one eye glued to the NCAA tournament. The name Hoosier was synonymous with basketball. Basketball was Indiana. Basketball was king.

In 1984, I played my first organized sport. I was just eight when my father registered me to play elementary-school basketball. Everyone in my class signed up. It was basketball after all, and in 1984 basketball ruled Indiana with an iron fist. Indiana returned the favor by ruling basketball as well.

At the highest level, a Hoosier legend named Larry was about to win his first of three-consecutive NBA MVP awards. Bob Knight was breaking in a freshman guard by the name of Steve Alford at Indiana University. In the tournament, Knight devised a way to shut down Michael Jordan as the Hoosiers toppled the top-ranked Tar Heels. That summer, Knight took both Alford and Jordan to Los Angeles where the USA won the gold medal in the Olympic Games. In high school ball, Warsaw High won their first and only Boys State Title.

All of it washed over me. At that age, I had no ability to process or understand the significance of the basketball universe aligning. I just knew that all anyone talked about was basketball, and by playing hoops, I was part of that conversation.

In March of 1984, I had no idea that my world was about to be invaded. An alien presence descended on my hometown of Indianapolis. It was called the NFL, and men in pads changed everything.

Over the next quarter century, a team and a sport that was foreign to us took root and grew. Though in 1984 no one would ever have believed it, the Colts transformed Indiana into a football state. That year, the high school basketball finals outpaced the football finals by 9,000 fans.[1] Twenty-six years later, those numbers have flipped. Attendance at the IHSAA football finals has nearly doubled, while it has fallen off at the basketball championships. The result is that in 2009, football beat basketball by nearly 17,000 fans.[2] [3]

Growing up in Indianapolis, basketball was an important part of our family life. I played; my brother played. My sisters played. My father coached us. I never played organized football at any level. Two-and-a-half decades later, my brother and I spend the vast majority of our free time watching, analyzing, and writing about the NFL. I rarely ever watch my once beloved Hoosiers play round ball, and the NBA has been cut out of my life entirely.[4]

I am not alone in my defection. Attendance at high school basketball games has been falling for years in Indiana. It has been more than 30 years since Indiana University won an NCAA national title. The Pacers' crowds have dwindled. Such changes are about more than a rough patch for the local teams or even a dip in the economy. They represent a tide that rolled into Indiana on March 29th, 1984.

---

[1] Roughly 23,200 people attended the four IHSAA football championship games, while 32,508 people attended the basketball championships. The 1983 football championship numbers are composed of four games with eight teams. The basketball numbers for 1984 represent just three games and four teams.

[2] Attendance at the football championships would nearly double from '84 to 46,162. The basketball tournament did not fare as well. Only 29,250 patrons came to the games of the basketball finals. The 2009 football numbers are composed of five games and ten teams. The 2009 basketball numbers represent four games and eight teams. Despite the differences in the number of games, it is easy to see how football attendance has spiked, while the basketball championships added teams and games, yet saw a decline in their total attendance.

[3] In 2017, fewer than 25,000 people attended the two-session, four-game event.

[4] I've come back to the pro game since the time of the original writing, but I don't follow it with the zeal of my youth.

Here is the history of the Indianapolis Colts, of how they remade the face of Indiana sports. Here is the story of what the Colts mean to their fans, of what they mean to me. The Colts franchise has

another history in a different city, but that is a story for a different book and a different author. The other city can keep its history and its memories. We have our own now.

In 1984, basketball was king.

The king is dead. Long live the king.

Chapter One
1984-1986
C.O.L.T.S.

Record: 12-36

Highest finish: 4th in AFC East (1984, 1985)

Head Coaches (wins): Frank Kush (4), Hal Hunter (0), Rod Dowhower (5), Ron Meyer (3)

Leading Passer: Mike Pagel

Leading Rusher: Randy McMillian

Leading Receiver: Matt Bouza

March 29th, 1984, was "one of the greatest days in the history" of Indianapolis,[5] though you could forgive anyone who might have had doubts. At a ceremony in the brand-new Hoosier Dome, Mayor Bill Hudnut welcomed the Colts owner, Robert Irsay, to town, and professional football in Indiana had a pulse.

The Colts' arrival has become a notorious part of NFL history. Baltimore was long one of the NFL's flagship franchises, but the stadium situation in Baltimore had become untenable. Irsay shopped the team to multiple cities including Jacksonville and Phoenix while trying to secure a new stadium in Baltimore. Talks broke down, and the Maryland legislature took steps to wrest ownership of the team from Irsay.

By forcing his hand, the legislators ran him straight into the waiting arms of Indianapolis, which had a new, empty dome all ready for the team. Irsay and representatives of the city signed a hasty contract. He then ordered the physical belongings of the franchise loaded into Mayflower moving vans. They literally escaped Baltimore in the dead of the night, breaking the hearts of Baltimore fans.

---

[5] William Hudnut, "RCA Dome nears last game," *WTHR.com* January 4, 2008, http://www.wthr.com/article/rca-dome-nears-last-game.

Though the story of the midnight move was full of excitement and intrigue, the story of the team on the field was not nearly as entertaining. Unfortunately, by the time the first training camp in Anderson rolled around, it was clear that the team Indianapolis inherited was not going to be competitive.

The Colts were not a talented group. The franchise was still smarting from the refusal of John Elway to sign with the team the year before. The trade of the rights to Elway eventually brought two important players to the Colts (Chris Hinton and Ron Solt), but a couple of good, young offensive linemen were not nearly enough to turn around a team that had won just nine games in the previous three seasons combined.

The 1984 Colts did manage a signature win over the Steelers in the inaugural season, but offered little hope on either side of the ball. The Colts scored the fewest points in the NFL in 1984 and allowed the fourth-most. Things got so bad that Head Coach Frank Kush quit before the final game of the season, going on to coach in the fledging USFL. The Colts finished 4-12 and in fourth place in the AFC East.

Nothing improved in 1985. The team eked out only five wins, though they did split their home games at the Hoosier Dome. The Colts developed an effective rushing attack with a variety of backs, but lacked any downfield passing game whatsoever as quarterback Mike Pagel averaged just 6.1 yards-per-pass-attempt,[6] and the team's leading receiver was Wayne Capers who caught 25 passes for a measly 438 yards. The only bright spot was rookie Duane Bickett, who won the Defensive Rookie of the Year award with six sacks and a pick from the linebacker spot.

1986 was the darkness before the dawn for Colts fans. The draft after the 1985 season brought important future starters like Jon Hand, Jack Trudeau, and Bill Brooks to the Colts. Despite an impressive debut season from Brooks (65 catches, 1,131 yards, 8 TDs), Trudeau struggled mightily, and the Colts dropped their first 13 games of the season. Only two of the games were even close, and they lost by

---

[6] Yards-per-attempt, or YPA, is one of the most important statistical measures of a quarterback. A good passing attack gets above 7.0 YPA.

8

an average of more than 14 points a game. Coach Rod Dowhower was fired after 13 games.

As a kid, it was hard to take the Colts seriously. The Bears were all the rage, what with their sunglasses, and their rap videos, and their "actually winning football games." The Colts were a local punch line. Everyone called them "the Dolts." The joke around Indianapolis was, "What does COLTS stand for? Count On Losing This Sunday."

Just in time, the storms broke. Ron Meyer was brought in to finish the 1986 season. He was a former Coach of the Year award winner, and the team responded to the hire by winning their final three games of the year. One of those games included the last home game of the '86 season with the Buffalo Bills. The Colts won for the only time all year, and a certain 10-year-old happened to be in attendance for his first ever game.

There was something thrilling about being in the Hoosier Dome. My grandfather took me to the game, and we sat in his seats at the 50-yard line in the second row of the second deck. They were perfect. Whatever lingering loyalties I felt to Chicago were killed that day as I watched *my* team win.

The jokes did not stop because the Colts won a few games to finish the year. In fact, many people mocked the Colts for missing out on the first-overall pick in the 1987 draft, which would have brought Vinnie Testaverde to Indy. The only difference was that now I wasn't laughing along with the crowd.

Understanding 1984-1986

Bill Hudnut

I love Indianapolis. It is a beautiful, thriving city with plenty to do for anyone looking to have a good time. Having spent my teenage years in Indianapolis, I can attest that Indy was a great place to live. It always bothered me to hear people call it "Indiana-no-place" or "Naptown" as if it was among the most boring cities in America.

However, the history books attest and my parents confirm that those disparagements once rang true. The Indianapolis I can't remember and never knew began to disappear in the early 1980s. One man more than any other was responsible for shoveling dirt on the image of Indy as a glorified farm town that "watched the [Indianapolis 500 Mile] race one day a year and [slept] the other 364."[7] Mayor Bill Hudnut had the vision to transform the image of the city from a cow-town to a vibrant hub of sporting life.

Capitalizing on Indy's central geographic location, Hudnut, along with other city leaders, devised a plan to position Indianapolis as the "Amateur Sports Capital of the World." They convinced countless athletic organizations and competitions to come to Indiana to hold national and world championship-level events. Among the crown jewels of their plan was the construction of the Hoosier Dome. It was a bold move, considering that Indianapolis was building a partially-publicly-funded stadium with no promise of a cornerstone occupant to make use of it, but the brain trust was desperate to show that Indianapolis was more than just The Race.

What could have become Hudnut's Folly is one of the greatest triumphs in his 16 years as mayor. When Robert Irsay became serious about moving his Colts franchise out of Baltimore, Hudnut lost little time in wooing him. Over a period of six weeks, the ground work was

---

[7] Bill Hudnut, *The Hudnut Years*, (Bloomington, IN: Indiana University Press, 1995), 96.

10

laid for the Mayflower Escape. The Mayor had done it. He had secured an NFL team and brought them to Indianapolis.

Nationally, he took considerable flak for the move. Baltimore considered Hudnut a thief who stole a part of their civic identity. He defended himself against such charges, saying that he was just trying to do what was best for his city and the people who elected him. "What am I supposed to do?" he said, "Sit on the sidelines and watch the river of history flow by and eat bonbons? Of course I'm going to compete. Any mayor worth his or her salt is going to be a fighter for their city and do what they can to attract jobs and economic development."[8] While Hudnut was reviled in Maryland, he was a hero in Indianapolis. Indy had hit the big time. The NFL was coming to Indiana.

The Colts' move set things in motion. Indy was on the front of every sports page in the country. The city extended its reputation by bringing the Pan American Games to Indianapolis in 1987. The plan to make our town a sports Mecca was working. The attention Indy received as a hard charger on a national level brought continued investment from other businesses. During the next decade after the arrival of the Colts, the entire downtown was transformed. Downtown Indianapolis became a place people wanted to visit.

The plan laid out by Hudnut in the late 1970s continues to unfold to this day. Indy is now home to the NCAA Headquarters, has hosted the World Basketball Championships, and is in the permanent rotation for the NCAA Final Four. The NFL Scouting Combine takes place in Indy each February, and the city even hosted the Major League Baseball Winter Meetings in 2009. In 2012, the crown jewel of American Sports, the Super Bowl, was played in Indianapolis.

The plan did more than just affect the businesses and buildings in Indianapolis; it changed the culture as well. Growing up in the city, it was impressed on all of us that we were making a collective effort to be a sporting center. We placed a high value on sports on all levels. Every Little League game, every high school contest, every Sunday

---

[8] Hudnut, 104.

11

afternoon in the Dome felt like a subtle declaration of who we were as a city.

Mayor Hudnut had a vision to give Indianapolis an identity and a reputation as a major player on the national scene. Today his vision has become reality, and none of it could have happened without the Colts. In 2009, the *Toronto Star* declared Indianapolis The Best Sports City in North America.[9]

More than just the Race indeed.

Dome Sweet Dome

We parked on Capital, just north of the State House. The foot traffic would pick up as we passed down Market to look at Monument Circle decorated for Christmas.

It was five or six blocks to the Dome, and the walk was a thrill. The sax player on the corner was belting out the theme to the Muppet Show, and everyone was wearing blue.

As we approached the Dome, the architecture towered over us, and we marveled at the giant images of our heroes that bracketed the doors. We marched up the stairs, packing in as hundreds struggled to make it to their seats by kick off.

After the game, we held our hats as the wind from inside the building hurtled us into the streets where we reveled in the bells from St. John's announcing a Colts' victory as we walked through the snow falling over downtown.

The Hoosier Dome never quite fit in Indianapolis. It was a crazy endeavor to begin with. City leaders spent nearly $80 million with no assurance that they would ever get a team to play in it.

---

[9] Robert Cribb, "Best Sports City Contest Draws Fans Worldwide," *The Star.com*, May 16, 2009, https://www.thestar.com/sports/2009/05/16/best_sport_city_contest_draws_fans_worldwide.html.

Construction began in 1982, and citizens of Marion County began paying an extra penny on the dollar each time they ate out to pay for it.

Its completion altered the skyline. Local residents joked that a flying saucer had landed on Capital Avenue. The building itself was not unique. It was modeled after other domed stadiums like the Metrodome in Minneapolis. It was built to be a multi-use stadium of sorts, but those plans never panned out. For a time, some thought it could be adapted for baseball, but the plan was impractical. People complained endlessly about the dome. They said it was too small, too big, not right, too modern, too plain, too expensive, too much. Everyone had an opinion, but most of them centered on building a stadium without a team to play in it.

When the Colts agreed to be the anchor resident, the building named after the people of Indiana finally had a clear purpose. The team spent more than twenty seasons there, and the Dome itself became part of the fabric and culture of the Colts. It was small. It was loud. It had a "fast track."[10] The Colts became the kind of team that played to the strengths of their building. When the team was doing well, I felt like I was surfing a wave of sound as the throats of 55,000 reverberated all around. The Dome became one of the most difficult and intimidating buildings in the NFL.

The Colts posted a record of 107-85 (.557) over the years. The building was so loud that at times you could still hear the crowd all the way down at the State House. It was perhaps the best, truest home field advantage in football.

Though the Colts were the primary occupant, basketball became an important part of the stadium's identity. It was the Hoosier Dome after all, and Hoosier meant basketball. The first event ever hosted in the Dome was in July of 1984 when a then-record crowd of more than 68,000 came out to watch the US Men's Olympic Team (coached by Bob Knight) play a squad of NBA All Stars led by Larry Bird. In 1990, the IHSAA began to hold the boys high school finals there. Tens of thousands filled the building to watch the legendary

---

[10] The type of turf used in the Dome was suited to sprinting, which accentuated the speed of faster players.

Damon Bailey and the famous clash of Alan Henderson and Glenn Robinson. The NCAA held the Men's Final Four there in 1991, and it proved a major step forward for the city as everyone raved about what a great site Indianapolis was.

The Dome was a gift that kept giving to the city. As the decrepit Bush Stadium crumbled around the AAA Indians, the city needed a way to pay for a new park. They sold the naming rights to the Dome to RCA for $10 million for ten years. Essentially, the dome paid for the beautiful new Victory Field that was built next door. Calling the building the RCA Dome never felt right, but Hoosiers are a thrifty people, and the chance to build a new ball park without raising taxes appealed to everyone.

Once it was finally time to replace the Dome, the city still owed money on it. The bill for the stadium had never been paid. Considering how much the city grew and changed because of the Dome, however, it could be argued that it had more than paid for itself. The Colts played for the last time there in January of 2008. Even though they lost that day, I kissed the wall of the building as I left. The Dome fit in Indianapolis just fine, after all.

The roof was deflated for good on September 25th, 2008. The RCA Dome was no more.

The Hoosier Dome? That will live forever.

Bob Irsay

Robert Irsay remains a controversial figure in NFL history. There is little to be gained by sugar coating most people's opinion of the owner of the Baltimore Colts who up and pulled his team out of town in the middle of the night. The popular narrative device is to paint Irsay as the grand villain who rashly robbed a city of its beloved team.

There is certainly ample evidence to portray him in that light. His drunken press conference with the Baltimore media is infamous, and witnesses will freely line up to testify that he was mean, abusive,

14

and a liar. Few people associated with him in Baltimore have anything nice to say about him. Even his own mother called him "the devil on earth."[11]

Such characterizations are to be expected, I suppose. Loss is easier to swallow when there is an arch villain to blame. Baltimore and Indianapolis were involved in a tug-of-war for NFL membership and all the benefits it offered. The side that lost chose to vilify the man because he promised a last phone call to the mayor of Baltimore before moving the team. When it came time to pack up the vans and go, Irsay misplaced his dime and never made the call. I know all the stories. I have heard all the evidence, but I also know that one man's villain is another man's hero.

Indianapolis never had the misfortune of seeing the inebriated, belligerent Robert Irsay. We saw the smiling man with his arms raised in victory who brought a team and big-city respectability to our once sleepy Midwestern town. The Bob Irsay that Hoosiers knew was a free-market hero who whisked his property away from a greedy government eager to seize what did not belong to it.

While Mayor Schaefer[12] wept over the call that never came, Hoosiers knew the other side of the story. Had Irsay placed that call, the cops would have stormed the facility to enforce the state's recently passed decree giving the city the right to seize the team by eminent domain; they intended to offer a fraction of the team's real value as payment.

We all felt bad for Irsay. Indiana is a conservative state by nature, and the story of the government threatening to take control of a man's property by force chilled everyone. Irsay represented the potential of the individual against the state, and in Indiana that is a powerful story. He *had* to sneak the team out of town in the middle of the night. They *forced* him to send the moving vans in every direction

---

[11] EM Swift, "Now You See Him, Now You Don't," *Sports Illustrated*. December 16, 1986, https://www.si.com/vault/1986/12/15/106777270/now-you-see-him-now-you-dont#.
[12] Mayor of Baltimore in 1984, William Donald Schaefer.

out of the state until they met at the Indiana border where a friendly escort of Indiana State Troopers was waiting to guide them to their new home.

It was an idealistic view of the man and the situation, to be sure, but it was no more slanted than the version the jilted Colts lovers of Baltimore still sell. Irsay was a complicated and tortured man, but he did two great favors for the people of Indianapolis. This first was bringing the team to town, and the second was the way he involved his son Jim in every level of the operation of the team.

He named Jim the general manager of the team in 1984, and the son later grew into the kind of owner the father could never quite manage to be: successful and beloved. In Indianapolis, we rarely saw the meddling, over-the-top Bob Irsay. Instead, he largely stayed out of team affairs and lived a quiet and generous life quite unlike the nasty image he had obtained in Baltimore. He was not a simple man and was certainly not the caricature that others had made of him.

The Colts never won consistently in Indianapolis while the senior Irsay lived, and tragically he suffered a stroke late in 1995 just as the team was about to have its first brush with greatness. He was never again in good health and passed away 14 months later. Control of the team rested with Jim, whom he had prepared so well to take his place. His son would later rightly install him as the first name in the Colts Ring of Honor.[13]

It was a fitting tribute because without Bob Irsay there would be no Indianapolis Colts.

One city's villain.

Our city's hero.

---

[13] The Ring of Honor is a list of names that runs along the upper deck of Lucas Oil Stadium. It recognizes significant figures in Indianapolis Colts' history, and does not include Baltimore Colts.

The 1985 Bears

My first item of NFL team apparel was a Chicago Bears jacket. There, I've confessed it, and I feel better.

For most Hoosiers, the Chicago Bears were the football team of choice before the Colts came to town. In fact, the arrival of the Colts did little to affect the rooting interests of North and Central Indiana. The simple reason was that in the mid-80s, the Colts were awful and the Bears were legends.

The Colts won just 12 games in their first three seasons in Indianapolis while the Bears hit upon an historic run of dominance in which they won 39 games during the same span. The Bears were everything the Colts weren't. They were big. They were brash. They were winners.

Arguably the greatest team of all time, the 1985 Bears cast a massive shadow over Indiana. They had the bad-boy quarterback, the fiery Hall-of-Famer turned coach, the greatest runner in history, and a big fat guy named the Fridge. In a day when most homes just had three networks on TV, Bears sucked all the oxygen out of sports coverage. They were the hottest flame in the nation, and they burned brightly just three hours away from our hometown. Their ascendency, at the exact moment the Colts stumbled into Indianapolis with a series of bad teams, hurt the Colts' efforts to win the hearts of Hoosiers. The kind of glory and attention the Bears received felt impossible for the Colts to attain.

As hokey as it is to watch now, the Super Bowl Shuffle video made the Bears the most popular team in America among children. The Colts may have been the big story in town to adults, but kids all loved the Bears. The first generation of Colts fans all started their sports awareness cheering for the navy and orange of Chicago. When the Bears finally visited the Hoosier Dome for the first time in 1988, the fans were decidedly pro-Chicago. Lots of people had some allegiance to the Colts out of civic duty, but when push came to shove, they were Bears fans.

By the mid-90s, Indianapolis had fully embraced the Horse, but Northern Indiana was still solid Bears country[14]. The Colts had yet to penetrate places like South Bend, Lafayette, and Fort Wayne. Any town north of Kokomo was still pulling for the Bears. Colts fans were few and far between.

In the end, it took a Super Bowl to change loyalties. When the Colts finally made it to the top of the NFL world, it was fitting that the last team they had to beat was the Bears. Before the Super Bowl in 2007, CNN did a story in which reporters traveled down I-65 from Chicago to find out where Bears Country ended and Colts Nation began. Until they reached the Purdue campus, it was still solid Bears' territory and did not become fully Colts-centric until Lebanon, just 30 miles outside of Indy.

In one memorable night, everything changed. The Colts made all the big plays and came back with the Lombardi trophy and the hearts of Hoosiers in tow. A whole new generation of kids who had no memory of McMahon, Perry, Singletary, or Dent celebrated the accomplishments of Manning, Harrison, Freeney, and Sanders. Their first jerseys, caps, and jackets would be blue and white and emblazoned with horseshoes.

Finally, 22 years after coming to Indianapolis and 21 years after the Bears shuffled their way to glory, the Colts grabbed hold of Hoosierland for good. The franchise took advantage of their victory and paraded the Lombardi Trophy to all corners of the state, even holding a rally in Warsaw. Today, the Colts are easily the most popular team in Indiana, not just in Marion County.

It wasn't time that did the trick.

It was beating the Bears.

---

[14] I attended college near Warsaw, just two hours north of Indianapolis, and in 1995 I was known as "the Colts fan." Considering that most of the students were from Indiana, it was shocking that no one on campus cared about the team.

Classic Colts

Rohn Stark: Punter 1984-1994

During their early years in town, the Colts were bad, but if not for Rohn Stark, they might have been even worse. Stark was the last of the Baltimore Colts to play in Indy and lasted a remarkable 13 seasons (11 in Indianapolis). Stark had punted for more total yardage than anyone in NFL history when he retired. He was voted to four Pro Bowls as a Colt.[15]

Stark was a great punter because he could do all aspects of the job. He led the league in net average four times in his career, but in 1990 he also led the league with a ridiculous 24 punts inside the 20-yard line. Seven times in his career he managed to stick more than 20 punts inside the 20. He also was the holder on kicks. On a bad team, you had better have a good punter. Stark was it. He also spelled his name with an extra H. Three letters just were not enough to contain his ghreatness.

Duane Bickett: Linebacker 1985-1993

Bickett burst onto the NFL map with a stellar rookie campaign for the otherwise moribund defense in 1985. The linebacker out of USC brought a physical presence to the Colts, and he tallied more than 140 tackles each of his first two years. He excelled at getting pressure on the quarterback, and his 50 total sacks were the club record until Dwight Freeney broke it in 2005. In six of his nine years with the Colts, he had at least five sacks and was selected to the Pro Bowl in 1987. It would be 18 years before another Colt linebacker would be selected.

---

[15] 1985, 1986, 1990, 1992

19

Bill Brooks: Wide Receiver 1986-1992

No player from the early days in Indianapolis is deserving of more honor or recognition than Bill Brooks. From his first games in Colts uniform during the tumultuous 1986 season, Brooks showed he was special. The 86 Colts had a terrible offensive team, but Brooks shined all season, posting Colts rookie records for catches, yards, and touchdowns. He was a steady presence for the Colts, catching at least 50 passes each of his first six years with the team.

Brooks came back to Indianapolis to work for the Colts after his retirement and was named to the Colts Ring of Honor.

Chapter Two
1987-1989
The Big Deal

Record: 26-21

Highest finish: 1st in AFC East (1987)

Head Coach: Ron Meyer

Leading Passer: Jack Trudeau

Leading Rusher: Eric Dickerson

Leading Receiver: Bill Brooks

By winning the final three games of the 1986 season, the Colts deprived themselves of the first-overall pick in 1987. Instead of Vinnie Testaverde, they acquired the rights to a dynamic linebacker named Cornelius Bennett. The choice of Bennett was an inspired one. He became a three-time All Pro, five-time Pro Bowler, played in five Super Bowls, and was named a member of the All-Decade Team for the 1990s. The only problem is that he did none of that in a Colts jersey. Bennett and the Colts never agreed to a contract, and he held out into the start of the season.

Still, years of bad teams and high draft picks left the Colts with a steadily improving base of talent. Young players like Ron Solt, Chris Hinton, and Duane Bickett provided reason for optimism for Colts fans. In fact, the biggest concern heading into the 1987 season was bigger than the Colts.

The NFL Players Association wanted to obtain true free agency for the players and threatened the owners with a strike. Once the players walked, the owners used replacement players to fill the squads. One week of the season was canceled, but the replacements played three games before the union finally broke. Not every player honored the strike, however, and the Colts benefitted greatly from quarterback Gary Hogeboom's decision to cross the picket line. The Colts won two of their three strike games including a 6-0 eye-bleeder over the New York Jets. A win over the Patriots after all the players returned pulled the Colts' record to 3-3.

The defining moment of not only 1987, but also the first decade of the Colts in Indianapolis was approaching. Jim Irsay, still unable to reach an agreement with Bennett, pulled off a stunning three-team trade that sent Bennett's rights to Buffalo, a bevy of draft picks to the Los Angeles Rams, and star running back Eric Dickerson to the Colts. Dickerson brought instant credibility to the Colts and created a buzz that just a year before was unthinkable.

The Colts responded well to the addition of the All Pro. As they worked Dickerson into the offense, they won five of their final seven games. Dickerson rushed for over 1,000 yards in just nine games with the Colts, and Indianapolis won the AFC East division. Just one season after losing 13-consecutive games, the Colts were headed to the playoffs. Even so, the road to postseason glory was a dead end. The Colts lost to the Browns in the first round.

The postseason loss in Cleveland was disappointing, but the arrow was pointing up on the Colts. Head Coach, Ron Meyer, described by many people as a sort of "used-car salesman," had everyone convinced that the Colts could be Super Bowl contenders. It was all sleight of hand. The team surrendered their first two picks in the 88 draft in the Dickerson deal, so there was no way to fill the still numerous holes the team had.

The 1988 season was turbulent in part because the Colts never settled on a quarterback. The Colts used their third-round pick on Chris Chandler, and the rookie started 13 games. Veteran Gary Hogeboom also played and Jack Trudeau even got a couple of starts. At one point, the Colts brought in a wishbone quarterback, Ricky Turner, and experimented with the run-heavy offense.[16] The old saying

---

[16] The wishbone is an option formation that was popular in college football in the 70s and 80s. It did not work well in the NFL because the speed of the defense makes it impractical.

is that a team with two quarterbacks really has no quarterback at all. The Colts had four.

The team was rife with constant locker-room tension; the Colts still managed a successful season anyway. Dickerson shouldered the burden, leading the league with 1,659 yards rushing and more than 2,000 total yards from scrimmage to go with 15 touchdowns. The Colts overcame a 1-5 start to win eight of their final ten games. Though they beat the Bills on the final Sunday of the season to finish 9-7, the Colts missed out on a playoff berth. Still, the positive momentum gained at the end of the season raised expectations.

The addition of Andre Rison via the draft should have elevated the offense to new heights. Rison was productive in his rookie year (820 yards and four touchdowns), but his impact did nothing to solve the still unsettled quarterback controversy. Once again, the Colts started three different QBs as the offense muddled through the season. Dickerson showed troubling signs of wear. His yards-per-carry dropped for the fourth-straight year; he scored only eight touchdowns and fumbled ten times.

Despite the ups and downs, the Colts entered the final week of play at 8-7. All they needed to clinch a playoff spot was to beat the New Orleans Saints in the Super Dome. Backup quarterback John Fourcade of the Saints threw two touchdowns as the Saints trounced the Colts 41-6, ending any dreams of a second postseason appearance for the Horse.

Jim Irsay's bold trade for Dickerson made the Colts relevant, but the team still lacked a galvanizing figure for the fans to rally around. Dickerson was too mercurial and sullen for the fans to embrace him. What the Colts needed was a quarterback, a young, dynamic talent to transform them into perennial contenders.

They had just the guy in mind, too.

Understanding 1987-1989

The First Age of Jim Irsay[17]

The Indianapolis Colts as we know them now exist because Jim Irsay was not a successful general manager.

From 1984-1993, Irsay called the shots for the Colts as general manager of the team. During that ten-season stretch, Indy lost 100 games. In comparison, the franchise has only lost 90 this century.

While it's reasonable to look at Irsay's tenure as GM and cry nepotism, there was a great good achieved. The appointment of one of the league's least-effective general managers was just one more step in the cultivation of one of the league's most successful owners.

The son of Bob Irsay grew up around football. The senior Irsay bought the team when his son was just 12 years old and required his son to work his way up through nearly every level of the organization. From the ticket window to the front office, Irsay the son had the privilege of learning football from the ground up. His father was a wealthy man who happened to buy a football team, but Jim Irsay grew up a football man who understood what makes a franchise tick.

Fresh out of college, he was handed the reigns to the newly-minted Indianapolis Colts. After his father named him general manager of the team in 1984, Jim struggled to find his footing. Of course, it is easy to criticize him for some of the early failures on the field, but the roster he took over was already in shambles. Irsay led several effective drafts before the Colts were finally on the cusp of playoff contention in 1987.

---

[17] This section originally encompassed the entirety of Jim Irsay's involvement with the Colts. Events of the last five years have made it impossible to break him down in the binary way he was originally presented. I have preserved the original essay on Irsay in an appendix at the end of this book.

One thing has always marked Jim Irsay, regardless of his role with the team: he does what it takes to win. As an owner, he has always been willing to spend money to improve the roster. Perhaps that's the result of seeing the damage that trades can do.

His most high-profile move, the trade for Eric Dickerson, instantly transformed the Colts into a playoff team and made the team relevant to Indianapolis. Perhaps buoyed by that short-term success, Irsay just kept wheeling and dealing away draft picks.

Over the next few years Irsay traded away three more first round selections, netting Fredd Young[18] and Jeff George. But even the George trade was meant to be part of the bigger picture. Irsay was committed to the Colts staying in Indianapolis and becoming part of the local fabric. That deal for a local hero was not just an attempt to give the Colts a franchise quarterback, but was also about giving the people of Indianapolis an icon who would help the city take emotional ownership of the team.

These high-profile moves backfired one by one. Irsay agreed to give Dickerson a new contract after his best days were behind him. Young proved to be a bust. The Jeff George Experiment ended in acrimony. The results speak for themselves. Irsay was the general manager for ten seasons, posting just three winning records, one playoff appearance, and never more than nine wins.

In the end, it was the failures of the First Age of Irsay that laid the foundation for the Second Age of Irsay, a golden age if there ever was one.

Eric Dickerson

I walked into the library of my elementary school and stopped in my tracks. There on the magazine rack was a copy of Sports Illustrated *with a picture of a Colts player.*

---

[18] Young played three seasons with the Colts, collecting just two sacks and two interceptions.

I had never looked twice at a magazine like that before. I walked straight to it and picked it up.

They were talking about my team. I had to find out why.

Few players have ever done as much for or to a franchise as Eric Dickerson did with the Colts. The move to attain Dickerson was an early turning point for the team. In just four seasons in the NFL, he had already rushed for an astounding 55 touchdowns and 6,968 yards including an NFL-record 2,105 in his second season in the league. In four years, he had already been named an All Pro three times.

The deal to acquire him was complicated. On Halloween in 1987, The Colts gave up the rights to Cornelius Bennett to the Bills. The Bills sent running back Greg Bell and first-round picks in '88 and '89 as well as a second in '89 to the Colts. Indy then sent Bell, those three picks, and three more picks (another first in '88 and the '88 and '89 second-round selections) as well as running back Owen Gill to the Los Angeles Rams for Dickerson. All told, four players and six draft picks changed hands with the Rams getting all of it except for Dickerson and Bennett.[19] It was a king's ransom, but the result was instant success.

Trades are not made in a vacuum, and for every person who questions the logic of dealing so many picks, not to mention a dominant linebacker, for a running back, it is important to understand the emotional significance of bringing Dickerson to Indianapolis.

The trade for Dickerson established the Colts as a serious team on the rise. His arrival created a buzz. Seeing an Indianapolis player on the cover of Sports Illustrated was a watershed moment for young fans. The move assured the ticket-buying public that, if nothing else, the Colts were trying to win, and win immediately.

For his part, Dickerson cooperated magnificently, at first. He ran hard with the Colts, topping 1,000 yards in his first nine games,

---

[19] Only one of the picks the Rams received would ever reach the Pro Bowl. Running back Gaston Green, selected with the Bills' 1988 first-round pick, would play two seasons for the Rams, making one Pro Bowl.

26

lifting them to the playoffs. Considering the team's instability at the quarterback position, his 1987 numbers were remarkable.

He shouldered the burden in 1988 as well, giving the franchise a signature moment with four first-half touchdown runs against the Broncos on Monday Night Football. He led the league in rushing and yards from scrimmage as the Colts narrowly missed a second-consecutive trip to the postseason.

Through two years, no one could have asked for more from Dickerson. The Colts had no passing game to speak of, and he continually faced a stacked box.[20] He carried the ball more than 600 times in his first 25 games with the Colts. Through his first six years in the NFL, he had already rushed for 9,915 yards and was on a pace to shatter the all-time rushing record held by Walter Payton. Dickerson WAS the Indianapolis Colts, and no one doubted the trade was a success. Had his career in blue and white finished the way it started, Dickerson would be remembered as one of the greatest Colts ever.

Unfortunately, things started to unravel during the 1989 season. Though still productive on the field (1,311 yards rushing), Dickerson began to gripe incessantly. He was unhappy with the Colts offensive line, calling them "awful," "terrible," "pathetic," or "pitiful."[21] He was unhappy with the offensive system. He was unhappy with the lack of a passing game. He was just flat unhappy. Despite making the Pro Bowl, Dickerson's penchant for fumbling wore on the fans. No one realized at the time it would be the last 1,000-yard season in his career.

Over the next two seasons, both his play and his attitude deteriorated. He insulted Jim Irsay, the man who had brought him to Indianapolis, saying he was qualified "about as much as Daffy Duck"[22] to be an NFL GM. The ingratitude displayed by savaging the man who traded for him was lost on Dickerson. Ultimately, his complaining was

---

[20] A stacked box refers to a defensive strategy of placing safeties close to the line of scrimmage in an effort to stop the run. Such a strategy is risky if the offense is adept at passing the ball. The Colts were not.
[21] Terry Hutchings, *Let 'Er Rip* (Dallas: Masters Press, 1996), 27.
[22] Hutchins, 27.

motivated by the same thing that had led to his departure from Los Angeles. He wanted more money.

Dickerson held out of camp in 1990, reaping hundreds of thousands of dollars in fines, a suspension, and, stunningly, a new contract that would make the nearly 30-year-old Dickerson the highest-paid running back in the league.

Dickerson was wise to hold out for every dollar. As with most NFL runners, his best years had passed before he turned 30. After the 1989 season, he had already amassed 11,226 rushing yards, better than all but five players in history. He only needed another 5,500 yards to challenge Payton's record. He would not get even halfway there. E.D.'s antics had secured him one last pay day. He did what was best for him, and the fans and the franchise never forgot.

After a lackluster 1991 season, the Colts had finally had enough. They sent Dickerson back to Hollywood. A trade with the Raiders netted the Colts two low-round draft picks.[23] It was a good haul considering how little Dickerson had left to offer. He was slow and lacked the power of his youth. Not even five full seasons after acquiring him, the Colts and their fans were more than happy to be rid of him.

In hindsight, the trade should not be criticized. Dickerson gave the Colts a jolt of credibility. He gave young fans a name they could latch on to and root for. He helped put Indianapolis on prime-time television and lifted the Colts to a playoff berth. The cost was Cornelius Bennett, who turned in a highly-decorated career. It was a steep price, but worth it.

The real mistake by the front office was not coming down harder on Dickerson when he began to act out. His petulant displays soured both fans and other players. Fortunately, the Colts would not make the mistake of coddling an unhappy star again. They would also never again pay an aging running back a big, new contract, as players like Marshall Faulk and Edgerrin James would later learn.

---

[23] A fourth- and an eight-round pick. Long-time Colt defensive tackle Tony McCoy was selected with one of the picks.

Ultimately, the franchise made peace with the first Hall of Fame player to play in Indianapolis. Dickerson was invited back to town and honored with a half-time ceremony. Later in 2013, he was honored with a spot in the Ring of Honor.

If only for putting Indianapolis on the map, he deserved that much.

The Monday Night Massacre

Monday Night Football was the crowning glory of every week in the NFL. For years, it was the spotlight game that everyone waited for. There was a Sunday night game on ESPN starting in 1987, but it was new, and cable had not penetrated American homes as deeply as it does now. Most people were treated to just one nationally-televised game a week, and it was on Monday night.

In 1988, the Colts were finally slated to host a Monday night game. For the first four years the team was in town, the Colts had not had a good enough squad to merit any prime-time games. Finally, in 1988, they had two. The first was a road game in Cleveland, but the second was the plum Hoosiers had been waiting for. Monday Night Football was coming to Indianapolis.

It was a major-league event for the team and the city. The hope was that the entire broadcast would serve as a three-hour commercial for Indy. The master plan of using sports to promote the city and encourage businesses to relocate to Indianapolis depended on such events.

The game was scheduled for Halloween night, and the team pulled out all the stops. At the time, Monday Night Football had a three-man booth featuring Al Michaels, Dan Dierdorf, and Frank Gifford. Masks of the three announcers' faces were passed out to the patrons who then donned them for the opening sequence where the cameras showed the crowd. The message was sent: Indianapolis is smart, playful, and thrilled to have Monday Night Football in town.

The opponent that night was symbolic as well. The Denver Broncos were the reigning AFC Champions, and they featured 1987 MVP John Elway. Elway's decision not to sign with the Colts still resonated in Indianapolis, even though when it happened the team was still in Baltimore. On top of everything else, the Colts were trying to save their season after a 1-5 start. They had pulled their record to 3-5 but needed more wins in a hurry.

When it finally came time to play the game, the Colts dominated. Eric Dickerson had a spectacular night, scoring three touchdowns in the first quarter and another in the second. The Colts opened up a 31-0 lead as Dickerson rumbled for 159 yards in the game. The Colts constantly harassed Elway as they held the MVP to just 158-yards passing before he gave way to backup Gary Kubiak.[24] The Colts' lead swelled to 45 points and by the end of the night, they had slaughtered the Broncos 55-23.

The Monday Night Massacre had a profound effect on Indianapolis. First, it signaled to the casual fan that the Colts were a legitimate team. Those who did not follow football heard about how the Colts had blown out a Super Bowl team on national television. It forced everyone to take the Colts seriously. For younger fans, it was a source of tremendous pride. There were not many Colts fans in those days. Kids follow winners, and a win on Monday Night Football helped to validate the team and made it acceptable to cheer for the home team.

Furthermore, the team had done so well and the city came off so beautifully, that it created a sort of civic debt. Everyone was grateful to the Colts because they made Indianapolis look good. It helped the city embrace Dickerson. His performance was so breathtaking that even his sharpest critics had to admit that he was a force of nature carrying the ball.

Unfortunately, Monday Night Football would not be a regular visitor to Indianapolis for years. Despite the convincing win, the Colts appeared on the big show just five more times in the next 12 years. It

---

[24] Yes, that Gary Kubiak. Weird, huh?

was not until Peyton Manning was firmly established as a major NFL star that the Colts became a prime-time fixture. For the next decade, fans eagerly awaited the Monday Night schedule to be released, hoping they could relive their memories of the Monday Night Massacre.

Classic Colts

Albert Bentley: Running Back 1985-1991

In the fall of 1987, the Colts featured one of the league's top running backs. That was *before* they traded for Eric Dickerson.

Albert Bentley was never fully appreciated during his time in Indianapolis, but he definitely qualifies as a Classic Colt. Albert posted strong numbers during six of his seven years in blue and white. He averaged a franchise record 4.5 yards-per-carry during his tenure and was a serious threat catching the ball out of the backfield. In 1990, he had a tremendous year with the Colts, posting 556 yards rushing and 664 yards receiving on 71 catches.

Among his claims to fame are his touchdown late in the Colts 1987 playoff loss to Cleveland and the fact that he, not Dickerson, was the Colts' running back on the original NES *Tecmo Bowl*.[25] Bentley finished first in the AFC with 1,578 all-purpose yards in 1987, and the Colts won their first division title of the Indianapolis era.

Ray Donaldson: Center 1984-1992

Ray Donaldson played 13 seasons with the Colts (nine in Indy). During his tenure as center, Donaldson, along with Ring-of-Honor inductee Chris Hinton, anchored an offensive line that blocked

---

[25] *Tecmo Bowl* was the first video game to use "real" players. It is considered one of the most ground-breaking video games ever, the forerunner to today's wildly popular Madden franchise.

for Hall-of-Famer Eric Dickerson. The first African-American center in the NFL, he played in four of his six Pro Bowls as a Colt and would later win a Super Bowl ring with the Dallas Cowboys.

Donaldson was durable and is among the all-time leaders in games played as a Colt.

For many years, the offensive line was one of the strongest aspects of the Colts, and Donaldson was one of the men who kept the team competitive in the late 80s, despite instability at quarterback. Donaldson, a Georgia native, was elected to the Georgia Sports Hall of Fame in 2006.

Dean Biasucci: Place Kicker 1984-1994

Dean Biasucci had a live leg and anchored the special teams for the first decade of football in Indianapolis. An original Colt, he made the Pro Bowl after the 1987 season, scoring ten points in the game. He retired as the leading scorer in franchise history with 783 points.[26] In the 1988 season, he made a stunning 6-of-8 field goals from beyond 50 yards, earning him a spot on *The Sporting News'* All NFL First Team. Biasucci was a tremendous kicker from long range, and in many seasons he was one of the few bright spots on a struggling team.

"Deano" is also an actor. Once, during the off-season, he starred as Mark Antony in the Indiana Repertory Theater's production of *Julius Caesar*. His acting credits also include such heights as "Man" in the West Wing pilot, "Rick" in an episode of ER, and "Himself" in Jerry Maguire.

---

[26] He has since been passed by Mike Vanderjagt and Adam Vinatieri.

Chris Hinton: Left Tackle 1984-1989

Few Colts have been as decorated as Chris Hinton. Originally obtained as part of the trade that sent John Elway to Denver, Hinton did as much as any player could to help the Colts get reasonable value from trading a legend. Manning the all-important left tackle position,[27] Hinton starred during his tenure with the Colts. He was selected to seven Pro Bowls (five while in Indianapolis). To this day, only four Indianapolis Colts have been to more.[28] He was traded in his prime to Atlanta as part of the Jeff George exchange.

With Hinton leading the way, the Colts rushed for more than 2,000 yards in four of their first six seasons in Indianapolis.[29] He became the first Indianapolis Colt selected to the Ring of Honor.

---

[27] The left tackle is considered a critical position because he protects the back of a right-handed quarterback.

[28] Peyton Manning (11), Marvin Harrison (8), Dwight Freeney (7), and Reggie Wayne (6). Robert Mathis and Jeff Saturday also appeared in five each.

[29] They have accomplished it only once since (1994).

Chapter Three
1990–1993
You Can't Go Home Again

Record: 21-43

Highest finish: 3rd in AFC East (1990, 1992)

Head Coaches (wins): Ron Meyer (7), Rick Venturi (1), Ted Marchibroda (13)

Leading Passer: Jeff George

Leading Rusher: Anthony Johnson

Leading Receiver: Jesse Hester

Three moderately-successful seasons in a row created an appetite for more. Despite the advances of the run game, the Colts still lacked a true franchise quarterback.

The 1990 draft changed that. Illinois junior and Indianapolis native, Jeff George, declared for the draft, forgoing his senior season. Despite affording scouts just three weeks to evaluate him, George shot up many draft boards. The Colts were interested. The chance to draft a big-armed local hero was too attractive to pass up. They swung a massive trade with the Atlanta Falcons, sending off Chris Hinton and Andre Rison for the rights to the signal caller.

The move was unpopular with fans and the locker room. Dickerson slammed the deal and started the 1990 season on the wrong foot with a contentious hold out. The Colts got off to a rocky 2-6 start as George eased into the starting job with two touchdowns and six interceptions. He gained rhythm as the season wore along, however, and the Colts briefly flirted with another .500 season before finishing 7-9. George's season was a successful one as he accomplished the then-rare rookie feat of throwing more touchdowns (16) than interceptions (13). It was early, but there was every reason to think George would be the man in Indianapolis for a long time.

Whatever hope fans harbored of a new age of perfectly-thrown deep balls evaporated in 1991. The Colts were a mess.

Years of trading away top draft choices took their toll. Coach Ron Meyer did not make it through the season, getting fired after five losses to open the season. The Colts won only one game the entire season as they plummeted to the bottom of the league.

Without question, the 1991 Colts were the worst team in franchise history. At one point, they failed to score a touchdown for an inconceivable 21 consecutive quarters. The culprits were the injuries and the offensive line. An aging Dickerson had become a liability on the field and in the locker room as the team averaged just 3.3 yards-per-carry for the season. Meanwhile, George absorbed a franchise-record 56 sacks. The season was capped by a loss to the 2-14 Buccaneers, which cemented Indy as the worst team in the NFL.

Wholesale changes were needed. Jim Irsay's first move was to bring on Ted Marchibroda. Marchibroda had been the offensive coordinator for division rival Buffalo and had coached the Baltimore Colts in the 70s. He was seen as the perfect coach to mentor a battered Jeff George. George was a star on the rise, and with the right coach, he could break through as a major figure in the league.

The Colts needed help, and fortunately, the 1992 draft promised to bring it. By virtue of the worst record in the league, the Colts had the first-overall pick. The Colts also had acquired the second pick in the draft by trading Chris Chandler to the Bucs two years before.[30] On draft day, they swung a trade to divest themselves of Dickerson, netting two more picks. Despite hiring the offensively-minded Marchibroda, the '92 draft produced five eventual defensive starters for the team, including lineman Steve Emtman and linebacker Quentin Coryatt with the first two picks.

The '92 Colts rebounded with a respectable 9-7 season, but failed to make the playoffs for the fifth straight season as a four-game losing streak proved too much to overcome. Despite the wins, there

---

[30] Chandler went on to have a successful career, but not before being outright released by Tampa Bay.

were warning signs that all was not right. The team was outscored by nearly 100 points on the season, and the offense ranked just 26th out of 28 teams in the league.

George's lack of development was the most troubling aspect of the season. Instead of taking a leap forward under Marchibroda, the quarterback continued to struggle. Most of George's statistics dipped even below 1991 levels as he battled injuries all season. When Marchibroda benched him against the Jets in December, George reacted with petulance, refusing to congratulate his teammates on a come-from-behind win. After three years in the NFL, George was going backward.

The relationship between George and the Colts continued to unravel throughout the off-season as he engaged in an ill-advised holdout designed to force a trade. The temper tantrum cost George dearly, and when he returned to the starting job six games into the season, the fans had completely turned on him. The turmoil never subsided all season as the team stumbled to a 4-12 record. It was clear that the match made in heaven between the hometown boy and the team who needed a superstar was going to end in a bitter divorce.

The Jeff George Era began with great promise, but ended with the Colts right back at the bottom of the NFL. Fans wondered if the Colts would ever find a quarterback who could lead the team to victory and inspire the players around him.

Understanding 1990-1993

Jeff George

We arrived at the pre-season game two hours early and made our way down to the tunnel through which the Colts would walk after their pregame work out.

Several Colts came over to sign our football cards. Jeff Herrod and Dean Biasucci both took the time for all the kids lined up.

The big fish we were all waiting for was Jeff George. After his rookie year, we expected big things from our hometown hero.

He came over and signed my football card. I was the happiest kid in town.

I thought Jeff George was the nicest guy in Indianapolis.

It never worked out between Jeff George and Indianapolis. There are a million reasons why, but none of them tell the whole story.

On paper, it should have worked. All the Colts needed was a quarterback. Once George, a junior, declared for the draft, the football community was instantly split. Draft experts like Mel Kiper Jr. considered George an average player, but everyone who saw his legendary pre-draft workouts was in awe of his NFL-ready arm. He had complete command of every throw a pro quarterback needs to demonstrate.

He was talented, but there were plenty of red flags with George. After transferring from Purdue, jilting the University of Miami, and leaving Illinois early for the draft, many questioned whether he had the necessary character to stick out difficult situations. When the Colts traded up to snag George, one expert said,

> "I can't stress enough what a major mistake Indianapolis has made. George emerged because he was like the new girl on the block. Everybody fell in love but they didn't check with the old neighbors to see what a bad girl she was. The Colts better make sure they have got a big stock of Excedrin because they're going to need it."[31]

The trade for George rubbed many fans the wrong way. Public opinion polls showed the fans felt the Colts had weakened the team by surrendering Chris Hinton, Andre Rison, and the 1991 first-round

[31] Douglas Looney, "Suddenly No. 1," *Sports Illustrated.* April 30, 1990, p 51.

pick. On top of everything else, George scored a huge rookie contract that made him the third-highest paid player in the NFL.[32]

The move was controversial but easily understood given the larger context. The Colts needed an identity. The Dickerson situation was already showing signs of deterioration both on and off the field, and the Colts lacked a quarterback in order to become a legitimate threat in the AFC. George's prodigious talent was obvious, and his habit of jumping ship could be explained away by extenuating circumstances. He was too talented to ignore.

While his own immaturity sabotaged his career in Indianapolis, it was not as if the locker room he joined was a united front. During George's first training camp, Dickerson began his lengthy and acrimonious hold out. Though the running back paid thousands in fines, he got what he wanted from the team in the form of a new contract. One can only wonder what terrible lessons George absorbed by watching the situation up close. Had the Colts franchise running back at the time been a player like Edgerrin James who was an exemplary teammate and hard worker, perhaps George's entire career would have played out differently.

The firing of Ron Meyer five games into the 1991 season did not help George either. The dissolution of the offensive line, coupled with the coaching turmoil, left George unprotected on the field and in the locker room. George absorbed a savage beating at the hands of opposing defenses in his second year and would feel the effects in following seasons. He never gelled with Ted Marchibroda, creating tensions that would not be resolved until his eventual departure from the team.

Colts fans never fully embraced George. Once the crowds began to turn on George, it was only a matter of time before he would have to be traded. Many were still bitter over his departure from Purdue. Boiler fans are fiercely loyal and viewed George's flight to Illinois as a betrayal.

---

[32] Behind Jim Kelly and Randal Cunningham.

In the end, even George's status as a home-town boy worked against him. Everyone had an opinion about George or knew someone who knew him. Fans decided that George was "spoiled," and there was nothing he could do to convince them otherwise.

We can argue about the self-fulfilling nature of the prophecies about George, but there is no denying that they proved true. After just three seasons in Indianapolis, everyone had had enough. In the '93 off-season, George marched into Jim Irsay's office and demanded a trade out of Indianapolis. Irsay called the stunt "insulting" and warned George that demanding a trade would be "disastrous."[33]

He was right.

The trade George wanted never materialized, and neither his teammates nor the city would ever forgive him.

Fortunately, the Colts learned their lesson from the Dickerson nightmare. There was no trade that season. There was no truck full of money to reward George for holding out. He suffered through the '93 season before being shipped off to the Atlanta Falcons, the very team that had traded his rights to the Colts originally. The Falcons gave up three picks for George, the last of which was the Falcons' first-round selection in the 1996 draft. The Colts eventually used that pick on a slender kick returner and wide receiver out of Syracuse named Marvin Harrison.

George spent most of his career bouncing from one unhappy situation to another. Every couple of years or so, *Sports Illustrated* would do an obligatory story about how George was misunderstood and how "this time it will work out" and how his new teammates loved him. In some ways, George proved everyone wrong. The scouts loved his talent, and they were right to. He never made a Pro Bowl, but was far more successful in the NFL than the "draft experts" who hated him foresaw.

In the end, however, his sense of entitlement and inability to handle criticism drove him from one starting job to another. George

---

[33] Bruce Newman, "AWOL and Unlamented," *Sports Illustrated*, August 9, 1993, 28.

became a cautionary tale for teams enamored with big-armed young quarterbacks. He was Ryan Leaf and Jay Cutler before the world had heard of either.

George proved the old saying true, "You can't go home again." His talent was wasted in Indianapolis, leaving nothing but broken promises and a stack of what-ifs.

The Top Two Picks

There was no way to screw up two top picks. Thanks to a miserable 1991 season and a well-timed trade, the Colts managed to secure the first two picks in the 1992 draft. It was the ultimate motherlode. By adding the two top college players to the team, the Colts had a chance to get better fast.

The first-overall pick was an easy one. Steve Emtman was a massive defensive end. The junior from the University of Washington towered over opponents standing 6'6" tall, weighing a svelte 290 lbs. Emtman won virtually every award a defender could win in college football. He was an All American and a national champion. He won the Outland Trophy as the best interior lineman. He was the Pac-10 Defensive Player of the Year and even finished fourth in Heisman balloting, a remarkable accomplishment for a defensive player. During pre-draft workouts, Emtman was spectacular. He was fast. He was strong. He was the unquestioned best player in the country.

Faced with the unique luxury of having not only the first pick, but the second pick as well, the Colts had to decide how they wanted to reconstruct a roster in desperate need of repair. The draft was top heavy with elite defenders as five of the first seven players selected were defensive players.

Indy could have selected Heisman Trophy winner Desmond Howard or standout corner Terrell Buckley, but they settled on a ferocious linebacker out of Texas A&M named Quentin Coryatt. Coryatt was a heavy hitter known for his violent collisions with pass catchers over the middle of the field. He was a highly-decorated junior, and, combined with Emtman, Jim Irsay saw a chance to instantly turn around a defense that had languished at the bottom of the league in 1991.

The only question was which of the two players would be selected first. Emtman coveted the honor and obviously deserved it. The Colts saw a chance to hold the salaries of both players down by selecting Coryatt first. He was the easier of the two to sign, and if they took him before Emtman, they could pay Emtman less.

As the draft approached, the situation grew tense. Irsay wanted both players inked before the draft, but Emtman wanted to be the number-one overall pick. Finally, a compromise was reached. Emtman took less than he was looking for, but was chosen first and still received the largest contract for a defender in NFL history. With Emtman signed, the Coryatt negotiations came easily. Irsay got the job done, selecting and signing the two best players available before the draft ever took place.

I wish the story had a happy ending. Emtman's career started off with a bang as he played wonderfully during his rookie season. The Colts moved him to end, and in half a season he had three sacks, an interception, and 49 tackles. He was a force on the field and showed every indication that he would live up to his incredible potential. But it was not to be.

In his ninth game, he crumpled to the Hoosier Dome turf. He had blown his anterior cruciate ligament in his left knee. Through vigorous rehab, he managed to come back for the 1993 season. His comeback lasted just five games before his right knee exploded. As he lay on the field, some fans openly wept. He represented hope, but in Indianapolis, hope had two bad knees.

Some players are forever known as draft busts, but that word is rarely used about Emtman in Indianapolis. He was a draft tragedy. He worked hard. He was talented. He was cursed.

He played just 18 games in his three years as a Colt. He was released after the 1994 season. He bounced around the league for a couple of years, but would never become an impact player. Steve

Emtman is the greatest example of why the tag "can't miss prospect" is the most foolish phrase in sports.

It is not fair to label Quentin Coryatt a bust either, but he never became the impact defender the Colts dreamed of when they drafted him. He was a fixture of the Colts defense that led to the resurgence of the team in 1995 and 1996. His work was effective but never spectacular. In six mediocre seasons with the Colts, he collected just 8.5 sacks, three interceptions, and six forced fumbles. Only once did he ever top 100 tackles for a season.[34]

Coryatt was serviceable but not a game changer. The play that best summarized his career with the Colts occurred in the final moments of the 1995 AFC Championship Game in Pittsburgh. With the Colts clinging to the lead, Neil O'Donnell fired a pass right at Coryatt. The ball hit him in the hands, face high. Had he secured the interception, Indianapolis would have gone to the Super Bowl. Instead, the pass bounced off his hands, falling incomplete. The Steelers went on to win the game.

It is easy to second guess the picks now, but the Colts had an excellent draft in 1992. Several starters like Jason Belser, Tony McCoy, Stephen Grant, and Ashley Ambrose were taken. Overall, it's hard to point to anyone the Colts passed over and say they should have been selected over Coryatt.

The first fifteen picks of the draft produced only six Pro Bowl players, and there were several busts much more egregious than Coryatt, including quarterback David Klingler. Ten players taken in the first round served as starters for two years or less. Dallas cornerback Darren Woodson, a second-round pick, was the only player in the 1992 draft selected to multiple All Pro teams.

It was bad luck more than bad drafting that did in the Colts. It was bad luck that Emtman, a player with no history of injury, blew out

---

[34] After a brief switch to middle linebacker, Coryatt recorded 150 tackles in 1993. He then moved out of the position and only topped 60 one other time.

both knees. It was equally bad luck to have the top two picks in one of the thinnest drafts in history.

Bob Lamey

Once upon a time, sellouts were rare in Indianapolis. We spent many a cold fall Sunday sitting in our living room with the radio on, listening to Bob Lamey give us the blow-by-blow of another frustrating game.

My dad would grumble about Bob yelling too much, but I loved him. He felt about the Colts the way I felt about the Colts.

Every Indianapolis Colts game has been televised for more than a decade. The team has become appointment television in Indy, but that was not always the case. For many years, fans had to rely on the radio play-by-play to follow the team at home. Virtually from day one, Bob Lamey has been "The Voice of the Colts" and is as much a part of the team's identity in Indiana as any player or coach.

"Hockey Bob" was a fixture on Indiana radio well before the Colts came to town. He broadcast the Pacers starting in 1977 and called games for the Racers and Checkers hockey clubs. Later in his career, he was also a fixture in Indianapolis 500 coverage, working the turns. Despite his deep roots in Hoosier sports, it is Lamey's work as the play-by-play announcer for the Colts that has earned him a place in the hearts of central Indiana sports fans.

Lamey took over the play-by-play for the Colts after the first game in Indianapolis and held that spot for the next eight years. Suddenly, in 1992, the Colts switched stations. They were no longer on 1070 WIBC, jumping instead to 1260 WNDE. The move was a frustrating one to local fans for two reasons. The first was that WNDE did not have nearly the signal strength of WIBC, and the second was that Lamey, a WIBC employee, was replaced behind the microphone. Joe McConnell, an excellent broadcaster in his own right, took over.

McConnell's work was fine, but it felt wrong to listen to the Colts called by someone other than Lamey. In less than a decade, Lamey had already put his stamp on the consciousness of Indiana fans. Bob was a homer. He screamed and yelled and bitched about the game. His was not the classic detached style favored by many in the media. It was a more personal method that drew fans into the action. Bob was a fan first, and fans could relate to his pain and his ecstasy.

For three long years, the games were called by someone else, but Lamey never stopped being The Voice of the Colts. His absence made the Colts feel foreign. The dark 1993 season was darker because he was not around to share our pain.

He finally returned for the 1995 season, and all was right with the world again. His comeback came at the perfect moment as he captured the rapture and shock that was the Cardiac Colts of 1995. Even as the Colts moved into the Manning Era and every game was televised, turning on the postgame shows to listen to replays of Bob calling the key moments of the game became a weekly ritual.

Hockey Bob's most famous moment coincided with the Colts' greatest triumph. After a Dominic Rhodes fumble in the fourth quarter of the 2006 AFC Championship Game, Lamey despondently declared, "He fumbled the fricken' football!" Then he erupted with glee as Jeff Saturday fell on the ball. The clip was replayed ad nauseum by ESPN the following day.

When I think of Lamey calling that game, that isn't my first memory. Though I saw Marlin Jackson intercept Tom Brady to send the Colts to their first Super Bowl, it did not feel real until after the game when I heard him proclaim, "INTERCEPTED! MARLIN JACKSON! MARLIN'S GOT IT! WE'RE GOING TO THE SUPER BOWL! WE'RE GOING TO THE SUPER BOWL!"

Lamey is not everyone's idea of the perfect broadcaster. He can be irrational. He makes mistakes. He yells too much. He gets too high on a great play and too low when the team does not play well. He gripes about the officials and often openly criticizes the team's performance.

In other words, Bob Lamey is just like us.

Classic Colts

Eugene Daniel: Defensive Back 1984-1996

Eugene Daniel was a solid corner for the Colts for more than a decade. Daniel had a strong start to his career, picking off 14 passes in his first two seasons before teams started to throw away from his side of the field. Daniel retired with more interceptions than any Indianapolis defender and played more games on defense than any other Indianapolis Colt. His 97-yard interception return for a touchdown against the Jets is still the longest in franchise history.

An original Colt, he managed to last through the first renaissance that ended with the playoff loss in Pittsburgh in 1996. In that game, his last as a Colt, he picked off Neil O'Donnell just before halftime and ran it back for a touchdown. That score gave the Colts a virtually miraculous 14-13 lead in a game that the Steelers had dominated. Three Rivers Stadium was stunned to deathly silence until the Steelers put the game out of reach in the second half. The game ended in defeat, but it was a memorable farewell for the classy veteran.

Jeff Herrod: Linebacker 1988-1996, 1998

Jeff Herrod was a fixture at linebacker for the Colts for ten seasons, serving as a team captain for nine of them. Though lightly regarded out of college,[35] he played his way into the starting lineup and started all 16 games his rookie year. His signature moment with the team was his interception return for a touchdown against the Ravens in 1996. The score sealed a win for the Colts and gave them a 5-1 record. After streaking down the sideline for 68 yards, he dove head-first into the end zone, flying through the air like Superman.

---

[35] He was a ninth-round choice.

Herrod spent one year in Philadelphia before returning to Indianapolis for a final season. When asked to explain why he would retire at the relatively early age of 32, Herrod said,

"I can actually come out some days and feel like I'm 20 years old," he said at the time. "Some days, I come out and I feel like . . . 'wow.' I don't think I want to go anywhere else and play. This is my home, and I've been part of this team, this community, for so long. Last year, being away (with Philadelphia), I really don't want to experience again."[36]

Herrod retired as the Colts' all-time leading tackler, and was the team's most valuable player in 1991. He was voted the Colts' defensive player of the year in 1989, 1990, and 1992. He is a member of the Ole Miss Hall of Fame.

Jon Hand: Defensive End 1986-1994

Jon Hand was the Colts' first-round draft pick in 1986 and part of the first good teams in Indianapolis. He was an immediate starter with the team, playing in 15 games his rookie year, racking up five sacks and 82 tackles as one of the lone bright spots on a team that started 3-13. Three times in his career, Hand led the Colts in sacks, including posting 10 in 1988. He was a key cog in a solid defense that was first in the NFL in 1987 and 11th the next two years.

Injuries ended his career at 31 years old after nine seasons, all with the Colts. He still ranks sixth on the Colts all-time sacks list after retiring in third. A high character player, Hand now runs a local construction firm.

---

[36] Quotation from Colts.com. Page subsequently removed.

Chapter Four
1994-1997
Captain Comeback and the Cardiac Colts

Record: 29-35

Highest Finish: 2nd AFC East (Wild Card 1995)

Head Coaches (wins): Ted Marchibroda (17), Lindy Infante (12)

Leading Passer: Jim Harbaugh

Leading Rusher: Marshall Faulk

Leading Receiver: Sean Dawkins

If there was any bright side to the mess that was the 1993 season, it was that the Colts were once again picking near the top of the draft. The Jeff George Era was over. Just as significantly, Jim Irsay stepped aside from running the football side of the show as the elder Irsay brought ex-Bears' boss Vince Tobin in to run the team as Vice President and Director of Football Operations.

Tobin made most fans feel good about the direction of the team. That was a small miracle considering how horrible 1993 was both on and off the field. He quickly ingratiated himself to Colts fans by bringing some of the "Bears' spirit" south to Indianapolis. The Bears were not exactly world beaters under Tobin, but it did not matter to Colts fans. They were the Bears!

He managed to swing a trade with the Falcons, sending George out of town in exchange for the seventh pick in the draft.[37] It was depressing. For young fans, George represented an identity, and the trade closed the door on our dreams of a "Larry Bird in cleats." Tobin filled the void at quarterback by signing ex-Chicago starter Jim Harbaugh. It seemed like an insignificant move at the time, but it changed the fate of the franchise.

---

[37] There was another important pick that came out of that trade that would change the franchise forever.

49

Tobin's maneuvering, coupled with the team's awful 1993 season, left Indy with two of the first five picks in the draft once again. This time, however, the Bengals drafted first and in typical "Bungal" style, they botched the pick by selecting Big Daddy Wilkinson, leaving Marshall Faulk sitting on the board. Oddly enough, Tobin's pick of Faulk is not what everyone remembers about that day.

With the fifth pick, Tobin took Trev Alberts and touched off a firestorm that gets replayed every April. ESPN draft expert Mel Kiper Jr. crushed Tobin, mocking him for passing over celebrated quarterback Trent Dilfer. He disparaged Tobin's decision to go with Harbaugh as a starter and declared the pick of Alberts to be exactly why the Colts were always drafting at the top of the first round.

Tobin was furious, famously screaming, "Who the hell is Mel Kiper Jr.?" He was an instant hit in conservative Indiana where people were none too keen on slick-haired, east-coast, talking-heads with bogus job descriptions like "NFL draft analyst." Tobin struck a blow for all of us that day by ripping Kiper on the air. The Colts had a new direction.[38]

That new direction was straight up, all the way to the middle of the pack. 1994 was an up-and-down year, but it saw the Colts finish 8-8, which felt like improvement. Harbaugh proved to be exactly what everyone expected. He was a competent, but not spectacular, quarterback. He battled injuries, however, so the Colts decided to make a bold move to acquire their next franchise signal caller. They surrendered their first-round pick to trade for Craig Erickson of the

---

[38] Ironically, both men were wrong. Kiper loved Trent Dilfer, but he never materialized as a top-flight NFL QB. He was a solid-enough player, going to one Pro Bowl and winning a Super Bowl title as caretaker of the Baltimore Ravens offense, but was certainly never the great player that Kiper envisioned. Moreover, Jim Harbaugh became a signature player for the Colts. Tobin's selection of Alberts rates as one of the worst picks in history, however. Alberts hid an injury from the Colts, later claiming that at no time was he ever healthy. He retired after just three seasons, totaling four sacks in his career. He remains among the least-popular Colts of all time.

Bucs. They signed him to a long-term deal and handed him the starting job. That decision stood for all of two games.

It didn't take Marchibroda even a whole game to sour on Erickson. After three picks in the season opener, Erickson was pulled in favor of Harbaugh who helped the Colts overcome a 21-10 deficit before the Bengals won in overtime. The very next week, Erickson was pulled yet again as Harbaugh led a 21-point comeback over the Jets. There would be no need to pull him off the bench a third time. Jim Harbaugh had won the job.

It was a turning point for the Colts, though no one knew it at the time. Harbaugh went on to lead three more comeback wins and take the NFL Passer Rating title for 1995. The '95 Colts had a dynamic running back in Marshall Faulk,[39] a quarterback who did not make mistakes, and a stout defense that ranked fifth in the NFL in points allowed. The end result was a wild-card berth and a trip to the playoffs for just the second time in Indianapolis history.

The run through the playoffs was as electrifying as it was improbable. The city rallied behind the team, and for the first time since coming to town, there were more Colts' jerseys on people's backs than there were for sale in the stores. The Colts charged through to the AFC Championship game, and it was clear that a corner had been turned among the fan base.

The Cardiac Colts' miracle run ended in heartbreak as a million little things conspired to keep them out of the Super Bowl. Still, optimism was high after the season. Both coordinators were hot commodities, and the franchise had a tough decision to make. Faced with the threat of losing both offensive coordinator Lindy Infante and defensive coordinator Vince Tobin, the team only offered Marchibroda a one-year contract. It was seen by many around town as a slight and an indication that the team really wanted to go in another direction. Marchibroda refused the deal, and the team promoted Infante to head coach. It was not a popular move among fans,[40] but

---

[39] Faulk missed the playoffs after being slowed by injuries late in the season.

[40] Or with Jim Irsay. Chappell and Richards, 24.

the team had a real superstar in Faulk, a viable identity built around their defense, and a quarterback who had the respect of the locker room and the fans.

The 1996 draft brought one more key piece to the puzzle: a marquee wide receiver. The Colts finally managed to cash in on the final piece of the Jeff George disaster. They had acquired Atlanta's number one pick in the 1996 draft, which completed the trade they had made two years earlier. With the 19th-overall pick, the Colts took Marvin Harrison. No other player taken that year by the Colts would play more than two years with the team, but you won't hear anyone complaining about the class of '96.

The '96 Colts stood for many years as my personal favorite edition of the Horse. They started the year as world beaters, ripping off four consecutive wins including a thrilling road upset of the world-champion Dallas Cowboys. The Colts had it all working and even began to top NFL power rankings for the first time.

The glory was short lived, however. A brutal Week 5 loss in overtime to the Bills left the Colts with a pile of injured players. They did manage to win the first-ever matchup with the Ravens of Baltimore the next week,[41] but wins would soon be hard to come by.

Despite the 5-1 start, Indy dropped five of the next six contests. With the season hanging in the balance, the team got hot once again and ripped off three-consecutive wins including another nail-biter in Kansas City that all but assured the Horse a playoff spot.

The Colts managed to qualify for a second-consecutive postseason with a 9-7 record, which earned them a rematch with the Steelers. There would be no opportunity for last-second heroics that year, however. The Steelers throttled the Colts 42-14. It was a

---

[41] The worst-behaved visiting fans I've ever seen were the Baltimore fans during the 1996 game. They had effigies of Bob Irsay and spent the entire game with their backs to the field chanting expletives at the home fans. Similar incidents occurred all over the Dome. There was a lot of bitterness to say the least. Fortunately, the Colts won the game and shut them up — at least for that night.

disappointing end to the season. The Colts had been a walking MASH unit all season but had managed to make it back to the postseason.

Young stars like Faulk and Harrison, two of the greatest players in NFL history, made the team an easy sell around town. During the '97 offseason, our family bought four additional season tickets to go with the four we had been purchasing from my grandparents. The Colts were going places, and we all wanted to be along for the ride.

Little did we know that the road was about to get rough. The injuries and age that had doomed the '96 team didn't get better in the offseason. Harbaugh's mileage caught up to him. He took a beating in '97, absorbing 41 sacks in just 350 drop backs, which is more than once every nine times he tried to throw. The team floundered, and injuries relegated Captain Comeback to the bench. The Colts lost the first 10 games of the season before pulling off a miraculous upset of the defending-champion Packers. Three wins in the final six games was not nearly enough to raise anyone's spirits. The only bright side was that the losses secured the first-overall pick in the 1998 draft for the Colts.

With two hot-shot young quarterbacks expected to go in the first two picks, we all knew that the Harbaugh Era had come to a close in Indianapolis. Harbaugh had won us playoff games. He had made believers out of a city of doubters. Personally, I was distraught about Harbaugh moving on.

After all, how often do first-overall quarterbacks work out, anyway?

Understanding 1994-1997

Marshall Faulk

Marshall Faulk was the best athlete to ever wear the horseshoe on his helmet.

In terms of pure, raw ability, I'd take Faulk over any Colt including Unitas, Dickerson, Harrison, James, Freeney, or even Manning. He was breathtaking right from the start. From the moment that Faulk was drafted by the Colts, he could do things with the ball in his hands that were unthinkable. He represented the future of the NFL, but no one knew it. He was the perfect blend of running and receiving and helped herald a new style of offense in the league.

In his rookie year, he rushed for 1,200 yards, caught 52 passes, and scored 12 touchdowns. He was named Offensive Rookie of the year. He went to the Pro Bowl and won the game MVP award with a monster rushing day, posting a record 180 yards rushing. Despite so many top-of-the-draft picks, the Colts hadn't had many all-star caliber players other than Dickerson. It was clear from the go that Faulk was a special talent.

Despite his ability to run and catch, he was unpopular in Indianapolis. Though he made three Pro Bowls in five seasons with the Colts, there was always a subtle drumbeat to get rid of him.

Most of that had to do with injuries he suffered in his second season. He got off to a blazing start to the 1995 season, including an eye-popping game against the Rams where he posted 177 yards rushing and three touchdowns. He was scary fast, and his moves were electric. But a toe injury slowed him down. His production fell off, and he missed all three playoff games. He still made the Pro Bowl, but many saw the Colts have playoff success without him and assumed he was overrated.

Toe injuries are serious, especially for a running back, but the fans in Indy reacted as if Faulk was soft. He continued to be hampered in 1996, posting just 587 yards rushing at just three yards-per-carry.

54

Many assumed that Faulk was done and saw his 22-game streak without 100 yards rushing as confirmation.

Faulk was far from finished, however. Once he got healthy, he returned to form, playing great football behind two of the worst offensive lines in history. The 1997 and 1998 Colts went a combined 6-26 with the 1997 Colts allowing 62 quarterback sacks. Still, Faulk's numbers rebounded, and he posted a 1,000-yard season in 1997.

The Colts took Peyton Manning first overall in the 1998 draft, and Faulk was his go-to security blanket. This led to one of the greatest seasons by a running back in history. Marshall Faulk posted 2,227 total yards from scrimmage (1,319 rushing, 908 receiving). He caught 86 passes in 1998 and scored 10 total touchdowns.

Despite the incredible rapport he was developing with Manning, we never got to see what year two of the combo would bring. Faulk wanted a badly-deserved new contract, and new Colts' GM, Bill Polian, would have none of it. The Colts as a franchise had already suffered through an acrimonious hold out and an ill-advised extension with Eric Dickerson.

Indy had a high pick in the draft, and Polian was determined to move Faulk. I was irate. My only hope was that no one would want him. As crazy as it sounded, it was almost the case. The best offer Polian could score for a guy with 1,300 yards rushing and 900 yards receiving were second- and fifth-round picks.[42] He took the offer, and Faulk was gone.

It did not take long for everyone to realize how wrong they were about Marshall. He was never the problem in Indianapolis. The Colts were suffering behind a degenerating line for the better part of three seasons. Faulk went to the Rams and instantly turned them into one of the greatest offenses in the history of football. The 1999 Rams won the Super Bowl, and Faulk was named the Offensive Player of the

[42] Years later, news leaked out that Polian was offered first-round picks by the Dolphins, but didn't want Faulk to play in the AFC East. This begs the question as to why he wanted to trade Faulk at all if he knew how dangerous he was. Money and power are often the best and worst answers to questions.

Year each of the next three seasons while also winning the 2000 AP MVP award. Just one season after leading the league in yards from scrimmage with the Colts, Faulk posted a 1,300-yard rushing, 1,000-yard receiving season. He is now universally acknowledged to be one of the most special and complete backs ever to play in the NFL.

And we got Mike Peterson for him.

And everyone was happy about it.

Jim Harbaugh

For Christmas in 1995, my dad gave me a present that was as exciting as any I had ever received.

It was a blue jersey with the number four on the back. It was the hottest gift in town and downright impossible to find.

It was also my first Colts jersey.

Normally, 32-year-old quarterbacks with barely 2,500 yards passing don't qualify for hero worship, but Jim Harbaugh was special. He took the Colts to the playoffs for just the second time. He was a superhero. He was Captain Comeback.

Everyone knows that Peyton Manning has taken the Colts to new levels of local devotion and national attention, but outside of Central Indiana, few understand the impact that Harbaugh had. Harbaugh taught local fans to believe. By the time Manning arrived in town, we all had a sense that the Colts could be competitive in the playoffs.

Considering the impact he had, Harbaugh's tenure was surprisingly short. He led the team through a nondescript 8-8 season in 1994, but had a lot of fans in town thanks to his days as a Bear and because of Mel Kiper Jr.'s criticism of him. After the miraculous comeback over the Jets early in 1995, Harbaugh engineered a series of other dramatic wins, including victories over the defending-champion 49ers and a 21-point comeback against the Dolphins.

56

Harbaugh was unflappable down the stretch in 1995 and put together his finest NFL season, leading the league in passer rating. At the time, I didn't fully understand the statistic, but it was my favorite. The fact that Joe Montana always led the league made me think it must be the best way to judge a quarterback. For our guy to post a rating of 100.7 was incredible. He was named to the Pro Bowl and was the most popular man in town. Before each game, Coach Marchibroda would come up to Jim and tell him, "Just let 'er rip." His confidence in the quarterback spread to the entire city.

Harbaugh had an easy charm and in-command tone. He spoke of his recent "born again" experience with Christianity. It's impossible to overestimate how far such things go in Indiana. Captain Comeback was already the big man in town before the 1995 playoffs, but it was his performance in three games in January 1996 that made him an Indianapolis legend.

After scoring two upset wins on the road and getting the Colts to within a dropped Hail Mary of the Super Bowl, Harbaugh had fans believing the team was a legitimate Super Bowl contender. 1996 got off to the kind of start that confirmed those beliefs. Jimmy pulled off an all-time-great upset off the world-champion Cowboys in Texas stadium, again rallying the Colts for a comeback victory. Indy started the season 4-0.

Greatness was fleeting in Indianapolis back then, however. Injuries piled up in waves, and even Harbaugh was hurt. Harbaugh missed two games in the 1996 season (both Indy wins), but his play dropped off precipitously as his mobility was greatly affected. The effect of 72 sacks over two seasons took its toll. Harbaugh rallied the Colts into the 1996 playoffs, but the team was a shell of the promising squad that started off so well. In the playoff loss against the Steelers, Harbaugh suffered a broken tooth and a cut in his mouth that required 20 stitches.

He did not come out of the game.

1997 was a disaster. Harbaugh was a skeleton of his former self. He only played in 11 games, taking 41 sacks behind the worst offensive line in football. It felt like the life was beaten out of him, and the team stumbled to 10 straight losses to open the season and finished with a 3-13 record. After the season, there was a regime change in Indy as Bill Tobin was ousted in favor of Bill Polian. The Colts had the number-one pick in the draft, and with Manning and Leaf on the board, the handwriting was on the wall.

Captain Comeback wasn't coming back.

In four seasons with the Colts, Harbaugh was just 20-26. He threw only 49 touchdowns, as many as Peyton Manning would later have in a single season.

Recently, I read a writer who mocked the Colts[43] for putting Harbaugh in the Ring of Honor. I suppose if you weren't there in 1995 and 1996, it wouldn't make sense why a man with such mediocre numbers would be honored so highly.

Those of us that were there understand. He laid the ground work. Peyton gave us something to believe in, but it was Harbaugh who taught us belief was something that could exist in Indianapolis at all.

Good to the Last Drop

No game has ever hurt as much as the 1995 AFC Championship Game in Pittsburgh. It's been 20 years since the Colts made their last stand in Three Rivers, but I can barely think about the near miss.

We were so close.

Needing just one win to go to the Super Bowl, the Colts went up against heavily-favored Pittsburgh and hung right with them. The game was back-and-forth all day, and just before the half, the Steelers scored the first touchdown to take a 10-6 lead into the half. That touchdown was scored by Kordell Stewart, who in later years would become the Steelers quarterback. Stewart ran across the back of the

---

[43] Who was it? I don't know. Why don't you Ask Vic?

58

end zone, famously stepping out of bounds twice in the process. The back judge, who is supposed to be positioned on the end line specifically to make that call, stepped back to allow Stewart to run in front of him. Instead of an illegal touching call and a field-goal attempt, the Steelers had taken the lead.

Still, the Colts had at least three chances to win the game in the final minutes. First, Indy attempted to run out the clock, needing to convert a third-and-one. They ran the ball with Lamont Warren, and a massive hole opened up on the left side. A Steeler defender got his hand on Warren's foot and tripped him, dropping him just shy of the first. The Colts punted. It was up to the defense to hold the lead.

Neil O'Donnell responded on the game-winning drive for Pittsburgh by throwing a ball right at linebacker Quinten Coryatt. The ball hit Coryatt face-high in the hands. He had an easy pick six, but he dropped the pass, giving the Steelers new life. Then the defense got the Steelers to fourth down, but could not make the one final play necessary to win the game. The Steelers took the lead on a short touchdown run just a few plays later.

Just when it seemed all hope was lost, Captain Comeback went to work, driving the Colts down to the Pittsburgh 29 with just enough time left for a final toss. His last pass was batted around in the end zone, and Aaron Bailey jumped off the ground holding the ball high above his head.

It was a miracle! We were going to the Super Bowl!

I ran around the room screaming, yelling, hugging everyone. Then I saw the official waiving incomplete. The replay confirmed it. The ball landed squarely on Bailey's chest. All he had to do was squeeze it.

He couldn't hold on. It dribbled onto the ground. Incomplete. Pittsburgh had won the AFC.

There was solace in the final moments as Jim Harbaugh was interviewed on television. He was classy and congratulatory to the Steelers, and then he celebrated what a great game it had been, thanking God he got to be a part of it. His were the most gracious, warmest comments I've ever seen from the loser of a heartbreaking game.

The loss was scarring. The game seemed won many times, but the Colts lost. We had never dreamed of going to the Super Bowl before in Indianapolis, let alone to have been so close that it seemed real. Before we even realized what was happening, the opportunity had all come and gone.

I was in college at the time, and for weeks afterward, everyone who saw me gave condolences and said how impressed they were with the team. The first seeds of loyalty to the Horse were sown in Bears' Country that January, and while they wouldn't fully take root for several more years, change was coming to Hoosierland.

Marvin Harrison

He had just made another outstanding catch. He shoulder-shimmied his man, burst past him, and caught a deep ball along the sidelines, just barely tapping his feet before tumbling out of bounds.

I turned to my brother and said, "Do you have any idea how lucky we are to watch this guy play every week?"

Marvin Harrison came to the Colts with the 19th pick in 1996. The selection was immediately hailed as an excellent one by major media sources as Harrison was a fine receiver and kick returner at Syracuse. The selection of Harrison was the final punctuation on George's career with the Colts. In the end, Harrison made George worth all the headaches along way.

Harrison was an impact player from his first game. It has become fashionable in recent years to attribute Harrison's success to playing with Peyton Manning, but it is only because people have forgotten how well Marvin played before Manning arrived.

In the first game of his career, he caught six balls for 85 yards and a score. He had a strong rookie season, and in a virtual playoff

60

game against the Chiefs, he was simply marvelous. He burned the Chiefs secondary to the tune of 103 yards and three touchdowns. He followed up his rookie campaign with a strong second season. Harrison was known around the league as one of the top young receivers in football before Manning was ever drafted.

Once Manning came on board, Harrison's potential was instantly obvious. Manning threw his first pass in a Colts uniform to Harrison in the preseason. He broke the short toss for a 48-yard touchdown. It was only the beginning.

Over the course of the next decade, Manning and Harrison would come to own every tandem passing-receiving record in football. Together, they dominated the Teflon skies of the RCA Dome. Harrison went to his first Pro Bowl in 1999, the first Indianapolis receiver ever to earn that honor. He represented the AFC each of the next eight seasons, posting at least 1,100 yards and 10 touchdowns every year.

His list of career accomplishments is staggering. He was a first-team All Pro three times. Five times he was in the top five in receptions, leading the league twice (including an NFL-record 143 in 2002). He was top-five in the NFL in touchdown catches for eight-straight years. He finished with more yards and receptions than any receiver in history not named Jerry Rice. He is fifth all-time in touchdown catches. He caught a pass in every game he ever played-all 188 of them.

Numbers do not begin to describe Harrison's play. He had the best feet in football. He ran the best routes in football. He was precise. He would catch a handful of little hooks or slants, and just when the defender bit on one too many, he would shake his shoulders and fly right past him for a long score.

He had possibly the best hands in NFL history and had the ability to snatch balls that other wideouts couldn't handle. His highlight reel includes some of the most breathtaking catches ever made including a one-handed diving grab against the Titans and a touchdown in New England when he tapped the ball to himself, spun, and got his feet in bounds for a critical score.

Once the Colts drafted Edgerrin James, the triplets were born. The trio of James, Manning, and Harrison did all the heavy lifting for the Colts until the 2003 season when Reggie Wayne finally emerged as the first real second receiving option of Harrison's career. People often forget that for the first half of his career, Harrison was more than just the Colts' first option at wide receiver; he was the only option. From 1998-2002, no Colt wideout other than Harrison caught more than 50 passes in a season.

The threat of James created the amazing play action that embodied the triplets. Its most memorable incarnation was when Manning would fake a stretch handoff to James and drop back to hit Harrison on a deep ball as he flew down the right sideline. It was a devastating play that summed up the ability of the Colts to strike at any time.

Harrison was the opposite of every other premier wideout in the game. He was quiet. He never called attention to himself. He worked hard in the off-season, spending hours with Peyton each spring in the early years as the two worked to build on their now legendary link that bordered on telepathy. He was the archetype for the new Colts: efficient, tenacious, quiet, and devastatingly talented.

Though there was a brief window of time where it appeared that Harrison would challenge some of Jerry Rice's untouchable records, the end came quickly. Early in the 2007 season, Joseph Addai fell on the back of Harrison's leg at the end of a play. At the time, none of us knew that it would be the last time we'd ever see the real Marvin Harrison. His status remained a mystery through most of the 2007 season, and when he returned for the playoff game against San Diego, it was clear he was not himself. He languished all day, even fumbling after his first catch. By the end of the game, he was not even on the field for the Colts' final drives.

He was back for 15 games in 2008, but he wasn't the same. He could no longer get the same separation. It was difficult for the fans to accept what they were seeing. He still had a couple of classic moments left in him, but it was clear something would have to be done after the season. His yards and yards-per-catch represented career lows. There would be no more Pro Bowls. After the season, the Colts tried to renegotiate his contract, but Harrison was unwilling to play for the reduced salary the team was offering. After 13 brilliant seasons, Marvin Harrison was no longer a Colt.

It was a bitter moment. No one questioned that the team had done right by Marvin, and everyone wished him the best, but neither did any of us want to see him in another jersey. The off-season came and went, and Harrison did not sign. We never had to endure the sight of the second greatest Indianapolis Colt wearing the helmet of another team.

Already there have been efforts in some circles to reinterpret Harrison's career. Whereas, for years, many pundits questioned Manning's true ability because he got to throw to Harrison, now there are those that would question Harrison because he got to catch passes from Manning. Though during his career he was known as quiet and humble, some in the media now classify him as standoffish or selfish because behind the scenes he wanted the ball. Such attempts to reinterpret Harrison are disappointing because they twist what really happened.

Elite wideouts always want the ball; that is what makes them great. Whatever grievances Harrison may have had were always aired behind closed doors, where they belonged, instead of in the press. His individual brilliance became collaborative because he had the good fortune of playing with one of the great passers in history, but it was also uniquely his own as he repeatedly made plays and catches that few others could ever hope to make.

Some wondered if these issues, combined with unsubstantiated rumors involving Philadelphia street violence,[44] and increasingly inflated career totals for receivers, might keep Harrison out of the Hall of Fame. In the end, none of it mattered. After a politically-driven[45] three-year wait, Harrison was selected for induction to the Hall of Fame in 2016. Though Richard Dent, Bill Polian, Eric Dickerson, and Marshall Faulk all had significant Indianapolis ties, Harrison is the first true all-Indianapolis Colt to be enshrined.

If there was a Mount Rushmore of Indianapolis Colts, Marvin Harrison's face would be carved on it.[46] He is the greatest receiver Indianapolis will ever see and one of the greatest players in the history of the NFL.

Classic Colts

Jason Belser: Safety 1992-2000

Often the players who hit the hardest and give the most are too quickly forgotten by fans. Jason Belser is one of those players. For nine seasons, Belser anchored the secondary. He was a hard-hitting, run-stuffing safety. He was Bob Sanders before there was a Bob Sanders. Belser was part of the first renaissance of the Colts D that went to the AFC title game after the 1995 season. He suffered the lean

---

[44] Harrison was accused of participating in a gun fight with a dangerous ex-con in Philadelphia. The dispute allegedly began when the perpetrator attempted to bring a weapon into Harrison's bar and culminated with an attack on Harrison in a nearby neighborhood days later. No charges were filed. The gunman was later killed in a different incident causing some, including the victim, to speculate as to Harrison's involvement.

[45] A backlog of excellent receivers was broken by an agreement to support players in succession to ensure all qualified players gained election to the Hall. Harrison had to "wait in line" while less-qualified players were inducted.

[46] Invariably, he would request that his face be in the shadows, hidden by trees.

pre-Manning season and the rough year that followed but always played hard and kept things exciting with huge hits. Eventually, Belser was present for the lightning-fast turnaround in 1999 when the Colts rose to national prominence.

An excellent open-field tackler, he punished running backs in the flat. Upon his departure for Kansas City after the 2000 season, Belser garnered a "Thanks for the Memories!" band on his giant photo that greeted visitors to the RCA Dome. Until Bob Sanders came along, the Colts missed his physical presence in the secondary. The season after he left the team, the Colts allowed the most points in the NFL.

Ted Marchibroda: Head Coach 1992-1995

Ted Marchibroda was a Colts' icon, a true bridge between the Indianapolis and Baltimore Colts. He led the Baltimore Colts to the playoffs in each of his first three years as head coach, and was tabbed by the Irsays to help straighten out the mess developing in Indy after Jeff George was drafted. He accomplished this by running George clean out of Indianapolis.

Coach Marchibroda brought not only an unparalleled offensive mind to the Colts, but a strong sense of conviction. It was his ballsy decision to dump the high-priced Craig Erickson in favor of the aging Jim Harbaugh that transformed the Colts into a Cinderella that Hoosiers would never forget.

Marchibroda unfairly never got a chance to follow up the dream of 1995, and his contract was not renewed despite three seasons at .500 or better in four campaigns. That ratio of respectable seasons was unmatched in Indianapolis before Tony Dungy arrived in 2002. He later returned to Indianapolis and was in the announcers' booth as the color announcer alongside Bob Lamey when Indy finally took home a Super Bowl trophy in 2006. Indy fans count him as one of their own, and his name is featured in the Ring of Honor.

Marchibroda passed away in January 2016 at the age of 84.

The Second Quarter

After fourteen years, the Colts were finally a legitimate part of the Indianapolis landscape. The success of the middle 90s earned them a place in the hearts of Hoosiers, but basketball still wore the crown. The Colts competed with the Pacers and Reggie Miller for the heart of the city, while amateur basketball was more popular than ever. Each March, the Indiana State High School Boys Basketball Finals invaded the Dome. Tens of thousands of patrons witnessed hardwood legends play for the high school championship. In 1997, more people came to watch 18-year-old boys play basketball than came to watch the Colts play the New England Patriots.[47] At the time, basketball's grip on the state was secure.

Indiana had always had a one-class tournament[48] for high school basketball. It was the crown jewel of the state sporting culture. The David and Goliath story, as depicted in the movie *Hoosiers,* rarely played out in reality, but the importance of the myth to the people of Indiana cannot be overstated. In a stunning and unpopular move, the IHSAA[49] elected to dispense with the traditional format for the tournament and begin a four-class tournament that would crown four separate state champions based on school size. Hoosiers were furious. A part of our unique identity as a state was sacrificed on the altar of progress. Everything was about to change.

The implications continue to unfold years later, but the most immediate consequence came in March, 1998. The first multi-class championship was held at the RCA Dome, and attendance was dismal. There was an instant drop of almost 50 percent, as fewer than 30,000 fans came to see the four champions crowned. Despite averaging more than 56,000 fans a year for the eight years before the change, attendance would never again top 35,000 in any year. Hoosiers were

---

[47] The 1997 State Finals total attendance was 55,125. The Colts and Patriots drew just 53,632 fans. In all, there were three games in the 1997 season with smaller attendance than the IHSAA basketball finals.

[48] This means all schools, regardless of size, played for a single post-season championship.

[49] The Indiana High School Athletic Association is the governing body for Indiana high school sports.

angry and disillusioned at the state of high school basketball. The betrayal of the IHSAA created a hole in the heart of the Indiana fan.

At the time, the other occupant of the RCA Dome seemed unlikely to fill the void. Despite the steps forward during the Harbaugh Era, the Colts were coming off a 3-13 season and once again had the first pick of the NFL draft. Just four weeks after the first four-class championship, the Indianapolis Colts announced to the world that they would select a fresh-faced quarterback out of the University of Tennessee to be the new symbol of the franchise.

Everything we knew about sports in Indiana had just changed, and we didn't even know it yet.

Chapter Five
1998-2001
So Good, So Soon

Record: 26-26

Highest Finish: 1st (1999, AFC East)

Head Coach: Jim Mora

Leading Passer: Peyton Manning

Leading Rusher: Edgerrin James

Leading Receiver: Marvin Harrison

The disappointing 1997 season led to one of the first and most important decisions Jim Irsay faced as the new owner and CEO of the Indianapolis Colts. While Bill Tobin had moved the Colts into the realm of respectability, the gains were not holding. The day after the '97 season ended, Irsay took drastic action. He acquired Bill Polian from the Carolina Panthers. Polian was already a four-time Executive of the Year award winner and the architect of the Buffalo Bills teams that appeared in four-consecutive Super Bowls. Irsay handed the keys of the franchise to Polian and trusted him to make one of the toughest decisions any draft manager had faced in years.

Polian had to choose between two highly-touted college quarterbacks. One was considered a "safe" choice with limited upside. The other was riskier, but scouts loved his cannon arm. The Colts kept everyone in suspense for weeks, but finally announced that they would select Peyton Manning of Tennessee to be their quarterback. Polian followed up the first pick by selecting two wide receivers and an offensive lineman with his next three picks.[50] A new age of offense was dawning in Indy.

---

[50] Jerome Pathon, wide receiver, was the 32nd-pick (second round). EG Green, WR, was the 71st (third round), and Steve McKinney, C, was the 93rd (fourth round). All played meaningful years with the Colts.

Though there were signs that Manning would eventually become a good pro, his first season was difficult. After all, he had inherited a weak football team. New head coach, Jim Mora, did a good job instilling discipline in the young team, but the growing pains were evident to all. Manning threw 14 interceptions in his first six games, including three picks in three separate games. Manning went on to set the rookie record with 28 interceptions for the season.

Despite just three wins, 1998 wasn't all bad. Manning found his footing after a rough start and closed the year with 20 touchdowns and 14 picks in his final ten games, also setting the rookie record for touchdown passes. The Colts got a huge year from Marshall Faulk who posted one of the great seasons in NFL history with 2,227 total yards. Perhaps the best sign for the future was that the Colts offensive line gelled, and Manning only absorbed 22 sacks on the year, a vast improvement over the beating Harbaugh and others took the season before.

The 3-13 season gave the fans enough reason to be hopeful, but the off season proved tumultuous. Faulk wanted a new contract and was expected to hold out. Polian was never one to tolerate hold outs, so he made it clear Faulk would be moved. On the eve of the 1999 draft, Polian swung a trade with the Rams for Faulk. He then used the fourth-overall pick on a relatively unknown running back out of Miami named Edgerrin James.

The 1999 Colts shocked the football world with one of the greatest turnaround seasons in history. Led by the dynamic running of James, who posted more than 1,500 yards rushing and nearly 600 yards catching the ball, the Colts ripped off an 11-game win streak in the middle of the season. In just one year, they had gone from also-ran to Super Bowl contender.

While the arrival of James and his physical running style was the catalyst for the turnaround, the credit largely belonged to the second-year quarterback of the Colts. Overnight, Manning transformed himself into an All-Pro. In his second season, Manning raised his completion percentage and his yards-per-pass, and he cut his

72

interceptions. He posted a passer rating of 90.7 while throwing for more than 4,000 yards.

Most importantly, he helped the team win ball games. Manning was unflappable at the end of games, leading the Colts to six come-from-behind wins in the fourth quarter. The Indy offense scored the third-most points in the NFL that season, a far cry from the anemic attack Colts fans had grown accustomed to. As the cover of *Sports Illustrated* put it, Manning had become, "so good, so soon." The Colts won the AFC East and claimed the second-overall seed in the conference. Most importantly, Indianapolis was going to host a playoff game for the first time.

Unfortunately, the Colts met with defeat in the '99 playoffs. The Titans' defense clamped down on the Colts, and the team lost receiver E.G. Green to a broken leg in the first half. Manning led a nice comeback effort, but the Colts fell 19-16.

The most disturbing development was that more than 10,000 Tennessee fans came up from the Nashville area. A large block secured tickets in one end zone and made enough noise to disrupt the Colts' offense. It was clearly that despite growing in popularity, but the Colts still had a long way to go to fully win the support of the region.

The sudden success of 1999 elevated expectations for the 2000 season. The offense continued to grow and develop as "the Triplets" of Manning, Harrison, and James all produced excellent seasons. The Colts offense was elite, but there were obvious defensive shortcomings.

In the middle of the 2000 season, the Colts lost five of six games, all in heartbreaking fashion. The team rallied to win their final three games, however, and once again secured a playoff spot. A second-consecutive playoff appearance was an accomplishment, but it resulted in disappointment as the Colts blew a comfortable lead, losing in overtime to the Miami Dolphins after kicker Mike Vanderjagt badly missed an attempt that would have won the game and sent the Colts to the second round.

The Colts were a top-heavy team. James and Harrison were formidable weapons, but despite the Colts' ability to score, the offense was incomplete. Manning had an incredible year, topping 4,400 yards and posting 33 touchdown passes to go with a passer rating of 94.7. He was improving every season, but the Colts were limited because neither Jerome Pathon nor E.G. Green developed into a reliable second receiver. Teams knew that if they shut down Harrison (102 catches for 1,413 yards and 14 TDs), they could put the clamps on the Colts. Defensively, the Colts did not have an abundance of dynamic players and were mediocre against the run and the pass. The Colts were talented, but flawed.

The problem with teams that rely too much on a few players is that if one of them gets hurt, an entire season can unravel. Such was the Colts' fate in 2001. The offense started the season strong, posting back-to-back 40-point games, but the defense fell apart. The 2001 Colts finished last in the NFL in the important category of points allowed, surrendering more than 30 points a game.

For a few weeks, Manning's offense simply outscored teams, but when Edge James blew out his knee in Kansas City during the sixth game, the offensive load was heavier than even the great quarterback could handle by himself. Halfway through the season, the Colts staggered along with a record of 4-4. As the games wore on, the offense continued to produce points but could not match the rate that the defense allowed them. Ten of the Colts' 16 opponents scored at least 27 points. The Horse lost five consecutive games, culminating in a humiliating 41-6 loss to the Dolphins on Monday Night Football.

The team finished 6-10 on the year as Manning pressed down the stretch. He finished with 23 interceptions and failed to make the Pro Bowl.[51] Harrison maintained his dominance, but without the full effect of the Triplets to carry them, the Colts regressed. Polian took decisive action to set the team back on the right course, demanding Mora fire defensive coordinator Vic Fangio. Mora refused to pass the blame for the worst defense in the NFL and was fired.

A promising chapter in Colts history was closed. Despite the early success, the Colts were faced with uncertainty. The Edge still had

---

[51] It was the last healthy season that he didn't make the Pro Bowl until his 2015 campaign in Denver—his last as an NFL player.

to recover from a catastrophic knee injury. The team had limited offensive options, the worst defense in the league, and no head coach. There were rumblings in the media about the Hoosier Dome being inadequate and whispers of a potential move to Los Angeles were in the air. The Colts began the Manning Era with a .500 record after four seasons. The franchise needed a strong hand to guide them through a tumultuous time.

The question was: where could they find an accomplished winner to coach the team? After all, top-shelf NFL head coaches are rarely out of work for long.

Understanding 1998-2001

The Second Age of Jim Irsay

The FedEx envelope arrived at the house.

Two end zone seats to the game and $200 in cash, Mr. Irsay's gift to me, just one of his tens of thousands of loyal Twitter followers.

All because I happened to know the name of a Jets placekicker from the 80s.

It is not fair to say that he simply got out of the way.

The glory associated with the early 2000s Colts teams always falls at the feet of Peyton Manning. The genius behind it all, Bill Polian, gets his due. Everyone is quick to shower Tony Dungy with affection. But just as important as their prodigious contributions was the steadying hand of a man who knew the football business from the ground up.

After the death of his father, Irsay immediately went to work finding an architect who could build the Colts into a perennial contender, something he had never managed to do himself. He identified Polian from the Carolina Panthers and traded for him.

75

Polian had worked with Jim on the Dickerson trade and was renowned as the best personnel man in the business.

To his credit, he did allow Polian unprecedented control of the team, but he was not a disinterested party to events. As owner, Irsay functioned as guiding influence and the emotional center of the franchise. He was closely involved in the process of drafting Peyton Manning and urgently sought to bring Tony Dungy on board as head coach of the Colts.

Irsay broke with his father's habit of alienating public officials. As the RCA Dome became an increasingly obsolete home for an NFL franchise, Irsay never once threatened to move the Colts out of Indianapolis. Rumors swirled in the background that Los Angeles was interested in bringing the Colts out west, but Irsay was careful to maintain his commitment to the city. His greatest accomplishment was the construction of Lucas Oil Stadium. The public-private collaboration cost him $100 million, but ensured that the Colts would stay in Indianapolis long enough that memories of the Midnight Move from Baltimore would fade into the past.

The Second Age of Irsay was marked by his efforts to make the Colts an elite franchise that felt as if it belonged to the people of Indiana. His success as an owner was indisputable. Under his watch, the Colts have posted 19 winning seasons and a Super Bowl victory. All over the state of Indiana, Hoosiers bleed blue and white. Whenever there was a check to be written or a player to be had, Irsay never flinched. The Colts kept their stars and built a dynasty.

Irsay promoted a vision for a special kind of NFL franchise. Dungy recalled his conversations with Irsay about the identity of the Colts as a driving factor in his decision to come to Indianapolis.

"We talked about the Colts' family, about values, about community. He said he wanted to win, but he wanted to win the right way. And if we ever did win the Super Bowl, he wanted Indiana to feel a personal connection, for it to be *their* team and *their* trophy."[52]

The Colts were simultaneously compelling and boring. They were dynamic and fun to watch, but also tight-lipped and conventional. Against that backdrop, Irsay's own flair for the dramatic shined through.

Whether it was dressing up like Willy Wonka, or giving away thousands of dollars in Twitter contests, Irsay craved and received copious amounts of attention. He was an accessible owner who readily contrasted with his curmudgeonly general manager and straight-laced head coach.

To the public, Irsay was a man who had slayed his demons, both personal and familial. He was generous-a social benefactor who spent large sums of money on historic guitars and manuscripts, but put them on display for the public to appreciate. He was a clown prince who spouted incomprehensible song lyrics and riddles on social media.

For a brief moment in time, Jim Irsay had it all.

A ring.

A stadium.

Respect.

The son of the one of the worst owners in team sports had become one of the best.

---

[52] Tony Dungy, *Quiet Strength* (Carol Stream, IL: Tyndale Press, 2007), 203.

Bill Polian

For years, the Pro Football Hall of Fame in Canton, Ohio, had only two pure general managers enshrined as Hall of Famers.[53]

By the time Bill Polian came to the Indianapolis Colts, he had already built himself a legacy worthy of consideration for Canton. His first master-stroke was establishing the Buffalo Bills as a power in the AFC in the late 80s and early 90s. The Bills teams he built went to four-consecutive Super Bowls,[54] and for his efforts Polian was named Executive of the Year in the NFL in both 1988 and 1991. He then moved on to Carolina where he built the expansion Panthers into an NFC Championship Game participant in just their second season in existence. He won two more Executive of the Year awards in 1995 and 1996 for his work with the Panthers.

It is little wonder how a man with such an attractive resume caught the eye of Jim Irsay. The owner knew Polian well, having worked with him on the trade to bring Eric Dickerson to Indianapolis, and offered him not just the role of General Manager, but Team President as well. Though some flinched at giving the oft-acerbic Polian the keys to the franchise, Irsay jumped at the opportunity to hire the best personnel man in football to run the Colts. It cost the Colts a third-round draft pick as compensation to the Panthers, but the owner felt it was worth the risk and the price.

Polian took over the team at a moment when the rules of a salary cap in the NFL were changing the way teams were constructed. It was no longer possible to stockpile talent. The NFL dynasty was supposed to go the way of the dinosaur. For an NFL team to accomplish year-after-year success, it would take an unblemished streak of excellent draft picks. It was no longer enough to merely draft a good player and plan to pencil him in at a key position for a decade.

---

[53] Jim Finks and Tex Schramm were the only non-owner "team builders" in the Hall of Fame.

[54] Polian was GM of the team for the first three and was dismissed just before the Bills played in their fourth.

Now, the smart GM would have to prioritize which positions mattered most. He would have to identify new talent to keep a team competitive. It was a near impossible task.

Polian's first order of business in Indy was to find a coach who could guide his young team to maturity. He tabbed Jim Mora to fill that role, knowing that Mora's track record of success in New Orleans was exactly what the Colts needed to return to respectability. His second task was more important. He had to decide who the Colts were going to select in the 1998 draft. He passed the test with ease, selecting a future Hall of Famer, Peyton Manning.

Polian's skill as a talent evaluator and manager of the franchise became increasingly evident over the course of the next several seasons. Every difficult personnel decision turned into gold. He traded the disgruntled Marshall Faulk only to select Edgerrin James. He ripped off an unbroken string of excellent first-round picks, selecting key players like Reggie Wayne, Dwight Freeney, and Dallas Clark. His scouts helped to mine talent in the later rounds like fourth-rounder Ryan Diem, fifth-round pick Robert Mathis, or sixth-round picks Cato June and Antoine Bethea. In total, 11 different Colts drafted by Polian would go on to play in Pro Bowls.[55]

Polian's knack for uncovering talent in unlikely places was not limited to the draft. The Colts became adept at finding undrafted players who would go on to become stars. Classic Colts like Jeff Saturday, Gary Brackett, Dominic Rhodes, and Raheem Brock were among the many players undrafted or tossed aside by other clubs who went on to become major contributors in Indianapolis.

Polian worked the new system to his advantage by not taking the bait on expensive free agent players. He signed a few when it was absolutely necessary, bringing in Chad Bratzke to shore up the defensive line, and replacing Mike Vanderjagt with Adam Vinatieri, but for the most part, he understood that success had to be built from the ground up. The Colts were going to have to draft to win and bring up players to play "Colts football."

---

[55] Two others, Tim Jennings and Marcus Washington, went to Pro Bowls with other teams after being drafted by Polian.

Polian helped to establish a tone of excellence and meritocracy in the organization. The best players played. The coaches had freedom to give undrafted players a fair shot to make the team. Polian never demanded that one of his high draft picks be given a starting job over a harder working, more talented player. Under his direction, the Colts were a franchise dedicated to winning and winning the right way.

Despite an often-uneasy relationship with the media, Polian developed a good relationship with the owner and his head coaches. He proved to be fiercely protective of his coaches and players in the press, constantly deflecting credit and praise away from himself and onto the rest of the organization. As president of the Colts, Polian supervised all aspects of the franchise, helping to build the Colts into a model NFL organization.

Of course, all the smart moves and great picks in the world are meaningless without victories. Under Polian, the Colts won consistently. Aside from two Super Bowls, the Colts appeared in the playoffs in 11 of Polian's 14 seasons with the team. They won a staggering eight division titles, set a record for the most wins in a decade, and overall won 143 games for a winning percentage of .638. Polian was honored again as Executive of the Year, for his work with the Colts in both 1999 and 2009, giving him a record-breaking six such honors for his career.

Nothing lasts forever, however, and when Manning's neck went, Polian's control went with it. As the Colts lost week after week, the dark cloud around Polian grew increasingly tempestuous. After years of giving his general manager free rein, Jim Irsay stepped in to take back his team. Polian was fired after his first losing season in a decade.

While media members danced like banshees around the funeral pyre that was the end of the Polian era, fans dredged up imaginary grievances about how badly Polian had performed. The truth was that Polian had essentially fired himself. Years of acerbic rule left him with too few friends in the building or the press to save his job when things soured.

Polian got the last laugh on everyone when he joined the media himself and was inducted into the Hall of Fame in 2015. In the end, the "boy genius" hired to replace him became just as reviled in the media and talk radio as Polian was.

Every good thing that happened to the Indianapolis Colts over the next decade can be traced back to Jim Irsay's decision to hire Polian to run the franchise.

There is now another true general manager in the Hall of Fame. There was no argument as to his worthiness. There is no doubt as to his worth.

The Decision: Manning or Leaf?

Manning. Leaf. Leaf. Manning. It was all we heard for months. Each new report or feature on either player made me angry. I was still loyal to Jim Harbaugh. I kept hoping the Colts would trade the first pick and select Brian Griese in the second round.[56] I figured that the odds were against either man becoming a Hall of Fame quarterback.

Like a lot of fans, I liked Manning more than Leaf, but honestly, I didn't really want either of them.

The bedrock upon which any modern NFL franchise is built is the quarterback. Unfortunately for NFL general managers, they are hard to come by. Not every draft has an NFL-ready passer sitting at the top of the draft. It's possible that Bill Polian considered himself lucky to have two sure-fire prospects to choose from.

---

[56] This strategy was also endorsed by Bill Walsh, who felt that Griese had the makings of a great pro quarterback. I may have been wrong, but at least I was in good company.

On one hand, Peyton Manning had the perfect pedigree. The son of a legendary quarterback,[57] he was a four-year starter at the University of Tennessee and played in the demanding South Eastern Conference (SEC). He would have been the first pick in 1997 but chose to stay in school just because he loved college so much. He was the runner up for the Heisman Trophy and led the Volunteers to the National Championship game. He was a living legend in Tennessee and was one of the smartest college quarterbacks in history. Manning was confident but humble, knew all the right answers, and was polished with the media. In short, he was the safest pick in the draft. He was a sure thing.

Oh, but the other hand was loaded as well. Ryan Leaf from Washington State had a cannon arm. Just a junior, he rocketed to stardom, leading the Cougars to the Rose Bowl, finishing third in the Heisman voting in the process. He was everything Manning wasn't. He had a gun for an arm. He was brash. He was arrogant. Many considered him more "real" than Manning with a bravado that would translate well in the NFL. His magic word was "upside." Choosing Leaf would be more of a gamble, but many felt the payoff would be enormous. Everyone projected Leaf as a future Pro Bowl quarterback. He was a sure thing.

The rivalry dominated media coverage of the '98 draft, and the Colts were at the center of the discussion. Teams were desperate to trade into the top two spots to get their hands on one of the two prize quarterbacks. Meanwhile, the Colts went to work, diligently researching every aspect of the lives and skills of the two young men. The Colts hired some of the greatest minds of the game to study game film of the passers. Hall of Famer Bill Walsh, perhaps the greatest mind in football history, said of Manning,

"The great ones have spontaneity, intuitiveness, inventiveness. They're intelligent. They know they need to know everything.

---

[57] Archie Manning, Peyton's father, is a member of the College Football Hall of Fame and was a Pro Bowl quarterback for the New Orleans Saints.

Peyton Manning could be that player. He's further along than any college quarterback I've seen in years. Maybe ever."[58]

The decision came down to the final days. Polian later claimed that the Colts' staff was leaning toward Leaf. There were arguments made for both quarterbacks, but Manning said that he did everything he could to take control of the situation:

> "'I asked if I could see Bill Polian before I left the building,' Manning recalled. 'So I went into his office, and Bill and coach [Jim] Mora were in there. Those are two of the most intimidating people I have ever known, and here I was, wanting to know what they were going to do. To be honest, I felt they were kind of stringing me along. So I said, 'I'd really like to come here if you want me. But if you don't, I promise you I'll come back and kick your ass for the next 15 years.'"[59]

Ultimately, the choice between Manning and Leaf was about more than just arm strength, five-step drops, and out routes. It was about who would represent the franchise. The Colts needed an identity, a face. They needed someone who would become a symbol not only of the team, but of the city as well. Whoever they picked, they needed to be able to trust him. There were rumors that Leaf was a party boy. He did not appear to take his workouts or conditioning as seriously as Manning, showing up 20 pounds overweight to the scouting combine. Manning, on the other hand, was always prepared, asked insightful questions, and had plenty of experience with life in the NFL fishbowl, having been a high-profile quarterback since he was in high school.

Whatever coin it was that Polian and the Colts flipped that allowed them to choose Peyton with the first pick in the 1998 draft, it

---

[58] Peter King, "The Toughest Job in Sports," *Sports Illustrated*, August 17, 1998, 48.
[59] Peter King, "The Lessons of '98," *Sports Illustrated*, April 28, 2008, 48.

was a magic one. The Colts settled on Manning, and the San Diego Chargers traded up one spot to select Leaf.[60] Just as everyone had foretold, the two were drafted 1-2.

It didn't take long for everyone to realize that the Colts had made the right selection. Just months into their NFL careers, the media had already dubbed them "Goofus and Gallant"[61] because of how well Manning was handling the pressure of being the face of the franchise and how petulant and immature Leaf was.

By the end of their first season in the NFL, Manning had already won over doubters. Leaf battled injuries, failed to complete 50 percent of his passes, and had a passer rating of just 39.0 thanks to two touchdowns and 15 interceptions. The Colts had made the right choice in the short run.

The long-run ramifications unfolded in spectacular and unexpected ways. Leaf continued to struggle with his health and was a disaster in the locker room and the community. His play was so poor and his presence so toxic that the Chargers had to cut him after only two seasons. Indianapolis became a playoff team just a year later, but the Chargers wouldn't see the postseason again for half a decade.

To this day, Leaf is considered the single worst pick in the history of the NFL draft. He had the physical tools to become a star, but was ill-prepared for the pressures. After washing out in San Diego, he spent just part of one more season in the NFL. Eventually, his life would completely unravel, and he would later face criminal charges for burglary and drug offenses. His life has become a cautionary tale for high draft picks and front-office gurus alike.

When it comes to the NFL draft, there are never any sure things.

Well, almost never.

---

[60] The trade to move up one spot cost them two first-round picks.
[61] Austin Murphy, "Advantage, Manning. Bad as he's been, Peyton has edge on Leaf," *Sports Illustrated*, October 12, 1998, 61.

The Edge–Edgerrin James

I was already in a bad mood. I wasn't happy about the Colts dealing away my favorite player, Marshall Faulk. When it came time for the Colts to announce the fourth pick in the 1999 draft, I sat in my dorm with my friends, preparing to hear the name Ricky Williams.

When the announcement came that the Colts had selected Edgerrin James, my buddies all laughed. I just started to throw things.

How could Bill Polian be so stupid?

Colts fans have been spoiled when it comes to watching great running backs. We had the privilege of watching a Hall of Fame runner in his prime when Eric Dickerson was in town. Then for four years, we weekly enjoyed the jaw-dropping exploits of Marshall Faulk. As far as the Colts are concerned, however, the man who followed those two was the best back in franchise history.

The decision to draft Edgerrin James, a junior out of Miami, was controversial. The most renowned back going into the draft was Ricky Williams out of Texas. He had set the NCAA record for most career rushing yards and was the Heisman Trophy winner. Moreover, the New Orleans Saints had let it be known that they were willing to trade their entire draft for the rights to select Williams. It's true that with the departure of Faulk, the Colts needed a new running back, but they had just finished 3-13. They needed a new everything!

Bill Polian was never a man to be fooled by meaningless accolades, and was not about to draft Williams based on the trinkets in his trophy case. As the Colts did their due diligence on James, they saw a dynamic player in the passing game who ran with ferocity but did not have nearly the number of carries in college as the more highly-regarded Williams.

The decision was not popular in town. Edgerrin "Edge" James was not the kind of player season ticket holders were comfortable with. He had a weird, unspellable first name. He was from Miami.[62] He had dreadlocks and gold teeth. Despite being an intelligent man, he was not well-spoken and clean-cut like Faulk or Dickerson, who would both later go on to careers in television after retirement. Edge James was not interested in impressing anyone with his outward appearance. On top of everything, he held out for three weeks of training camp. The doubters lined up for a chance to rip the newest Colt and the reckless GM who passed on a sure thing to take him.

Whatever animosity James inspired did not last long. He was too hard a worker, too magnetic a personality, and too incredible a player. Edge rushed for over 100 yards in his first game as a Colt, and the fans warmed to him quickly. His rookie season was astounding as he dazzled the league with a variety of runs that combined the feet of a ballet dancer with the blunt-force trauma of a battering ram. James fancied himself "an every-down back," a complete player who could run, catch, and block like no other in the league.

His rookie year was a total triumph for Edge, Polian, and the Colts. James won the 1999 Offensive Rookie of the Year award after posting an impressive season of 1,553 yards rushing, 62 catches for another 586 yards, and 17 total touchdowns. His counterpart in New Orleans was a massive disappointment. Ricky Williams failed to hit the 1,000-yard barrier and scored only two touchdowns on the year as he battled injuries. Bill Polian's faith was rewarded, and fans began to wonder if he was prescient.

The Edge continued to improve. He participated in legendary off-season workouts with Manning and Harrison, as the triplets who were the heart and soul of the Colts worked tirelessly to improve their overall game. The results paid off on the field in James's second

---

[62] Miami's rivalry with Notre Dame made it an unpopular school in Indiana.

season. He posted even bigger numbers than before, rushing for a club-record 1,709 yards,[63] 594 yards receiving, and 18 touchdowns.

Disaster struck in 2001, however. James suffered a torn ACL in Kansas City, and many feared he would not recover. Despite only playing six games, James had already posted more than 850 yards from scrimmage with five games over 100 yards rushing. Edge worked too hard not to return to the game, but the dominant, spectacular James was gone forever.

The Edgerrin James that replaced him was still an excellent runner, but lacked the home-run spark that he had before his injury. Over the next four seasons, James would rebound to have strong rushing totals, twice topping 1,500 yards, even surpassing 2,000 yards from scrimmage in 2004. One thing that changed was his elusiveness in the passing game. James caught nine touchdown passes in his first two seasons, but only two the rest of his years with the Colts. His yards-per-reception dropped as well.

James' contract was up after the 2004 season, but the Colts applied the franchise tag to keep him in town.[64] After the disappointing playoff loss in 2005, the Colts declined to re-sign James, who then became a free agent. It was a bitter moment for James and Colts fans, but Polian knew that it made little sense to pay a running back whose best days were behind him. Again, the ghost of Dickerson decided the fate of a Colts back. Like Faulk before him, James was moved in favor of a younger player. James signed a lucrative deal with the Arizona Cardinals, and the Colts went on to win the Super Bowl without him. James posted two workman-like seasons with a terrible Cardinals squad before helping to lead them to their first Super Bowl in 2008.

---

[63] Four of the five greatest rushing seasons in Colts history belong to James.

[64] Under the collective bargaining agreement, teams can designate one player a "franchise player" to keep that player from becoming a free agent. The player played for a one-year contract but had to be negotiated with (or tagged again for more money) the next year.

The affection that everyone in Indianapolis felt for The Edge was unwavering. He was so highly thought of by Jim Irsay that the owner sent James a Super Bowl ring after the Colts won in 2006. He wanted to honor the role that James played in helping to build the right kind of character and ethic in the franchise. James would later return to Indianapolis as a member of the Seahawks, and he received a standing ovation from the fans. He was the Colts' honorary captain before the AFC Championship game in January 2010 and presented the Lamar Hunt Trophy to the Colts.

There are two qualities that James possessed that must never be forgotten or taken for granted. The first was that no one worked harder. Despite a fun-loving personality, James was all business when it came to football and was considered an exemplary member of the Colts locker room. Archie Manning said of him, "Peyton tells me all the time that in the 19 to 20 years he's been playing football, Edgerrin James is the best teammate he's ever had...The one regret they all have is that they couldn't have won while (James) was still there."[65]

The second quality that James embodied was toughness. He was the best pass blocker of his day, repeatedly putting himself in harm's way to protect his quarterback by delivering bone-shattering blows to blitzing linebackers. He worked relentlessly to return from his knee injury. He never wanted to come out of a game to rest. He gave everything he had to the Colts. No one could have asked for more.

He is the greatest running back in Colts history, holding the record for most rushing yards in a career, most rushing yards in a season, and most rushing yards in a game. He has more receptions than any Indianapolis Colts running back. He has the most rushing touchdowns in a career with the Colts. The Edge accomplished more than any ball carrier in franchise history.

James was not on the roster when the Colts finally claimed a championship, but he was, and always will be, in the hearts of everyone who bleeds blue.

---

[65] Dan Bickley, *Arizona Republic*, December 15, 2007.

Classic Colts

Tarik Glenn: Left Tackle 1997-2006

The foundation to a winning team is the quarterback, and no one is more important to protecting the quarterback than the left tackle. The Colts selected Tarik Glenn out of the University of California in the first round in 1997. At the time no one knew it, but Glenn would soon become responsible for protecting one of the best quarterbacks in history.

Glenn was a massive man but was commonly regarded as one of the nicest and most thoughtful men to play for the Colts. He anchored an offensive line that routinely protected the quarterback better than any in football.[66] With Glenn protecting Manning's blind side, the Colts led the NFL in adjusted sack rate four times and finished second four other times.

Fans loved to poke fun at Glenn's propensity for false starts. A local radio station coined a little jingle that went, "Oh Tarik Glenn, oh, Tarik Glenn. Please don't false start again!" Offensive line coach Howard Mudd often defended him claiming that Glenn was just so fast off the ball the officials got confused.

Toward the end of his career, Glenn began to get the recognition he deserved and was named to the Pro Bowl in 2004, 2005, and 2006. After winning a Super Bowl in 2006, Glenn decided to retire on top, walking away from the game at the relatively young age of 30. He has since dedicated himself to community service, seeking to improve the quality of life for Central Indiana students.

---

[66] According to the Football Outsiders (www.footballoutsiders.com), the Colts' offensive line ranked first or second in adjusted sack rate every year that Glenn played left tackle with the exception of 2001, when they were seventh.

Ken Dilger: Tight End 1995-2001

Fans always love tight ends because they break tackles and run over smaller safeties and corners. Ken Dilger was no exception during his days in Indianapolis. A native of Mariah Hills, IN, Dilger was a true Hoosier, and the fans loved him for it. He broke into the league in 1995 as a second-round pick with a stellar rookie season, posting 42 catches for 635 yards and 4 touchdowns. He spent seven seasons as a Colt and ranks ninth in Indianapolis history in both receiving yards and receptions.

He had good speed and a penchant for breaking tackles. A quarterback in high school, he even threw a touchdown pass to Marvin Harrison in the 2001 season. He finally made the Pro Bowl following the 2001 season but was released by the Colts soon afterward.

Teaming up with Marcus Pollard, Dilger gave a young Peyton Manning an excellent target during his early years in Indy. Whenever Dilger would pick up a first down or make a big catch, the PA announcer would give an extra growl at the end of his "Ken Dilgerrrrrrr." True fans will never forget him leaping over defenders and garnering a DILGERRRRRRR from the fans at RCA.

Marcus Pollard: Tight End 1995-2004

In 1995, the Colts took a chance on a raw talent out of Bradley University who didn't play college football but rather basketball. Little did they know that Marcus Pollard would wind up as a Colt for a decade. He was a major contributor for the Colts, peaking in 2001 with 739 yards and eight scores. Pollard was a deep threat and once scored an 86-yard touchdown on a catch-and-run hook up from Peyton Manning.

Pollard was a fan favorite for his touchdown celebration of dunking the ball over the goal posts.[67] He is perhaps best remembered

---

[67] An homage to his basketball-playing days in college.

for getting unforgivably mugged on consecutive plays at the end of the 2004 AFC Championship game, including the deciding fourth down play where he was dragged to the ground with no call. Pollard scored a respectable 40 touchdowns in his career with several teams.

He ranks eighth in Indianapolis history in receptions, seventh in yards, and fourth in touchdown catches.

The Third Quarter

Once upon a time, if you asked a Hoosier to describe the ultimate coach: his manner, his strategies, and his successes, he would probably have described someone a lot like Robert Montgomery Knight. Oh, Bob Knight was far from universally loved in Indiana, but he was universally relevant. The General was the kind of loud, in-your-face presence that could not be ignored.

No matter what anyone thought of his style or his methodologies, he had to be dealt with. He won too often for anyone to ignore him. At Indiana University, he piled up scores of wins, 11 Big Ten Championships, and three giant red NCAA banners in the rafters of Assembly Hall in Bloomington. Knight was a legend, an icon of Indiana Basketball. He was known for his temper, his profanity, his harsh treatment of players, and his results.

Perhaps it was inevitable that Knight's tenure at Indiana would come to an unhappy end. In many ways, Knight was trapped in the past, and the world was moving on. His antics grew less heroic over the years as his methods no longer seemed to fit the changing mores on how best to lead, motivate, and discipline young people. In the spring of 2000, Knight was notified by Miles Brand, president of Indiana University, that there would be "zero tolerance" by the school toward any future missteps. We all knew it was only a matter of time before he would be fired.

Predictably, the grace extended to Knight did not last long. The end came as something of an anti-climax as Knight was released for a minor incident involving a mouthy student. Many were outraged that so great a man could be toppled by so small an infraction, but most of us accepted the fact that Knight had dug his own grave at IU. More than because of his behavior, Knight lost control of his destiny when he committed the cardinal sin of coaching: he stopped winning.

Just like that, Indiana had lost a legend. The largest symbol of basketball greatness in the state was gone. Indiana University had fired Knight. Hoops fans were stunned. It meant more than just trying days for the Hoosiers' fans and alumni. It signaled to the state that change was coming. The old ways of coaching had no place in the modern world. Screaming, cursing, and belittling players were no longer acceptable.

Hoosiers needed a new role model with a new approach.

Indiana needed a new icon to define the ultimate coach. He would have to have a new manner and new strategies, and he would have to have unprecedented success.

That coach was coming, but not to basketball.

Chapter Six
2002-2005
Dungy Ball

Record: 48-16

Highest finish: 1st in AFC South (2003, 2004, 2005)

Head Coaches: Tony Dungy

Leading Passer: Peyton Manning

Leading Rusher: Edgerrin James

Leading Receiver: Marvin Harrison

The Mora Years ended with frustration and uncertainty. The Colts needed a new coach and new methodology. Before the 2002 season even started, it was clear that serious changes were coming to Indianapolis. The franchise was in need of a new coach who could take the team to the next level. Miraculously, one of the most well-respected coaches in football just happened to come available.

Tony Dungy turned around the Tampa Bay Buccaneers franchise. He had posted four playoff seasons in six years with the Bucs, a franchise that had enjoyed only two winning years in its entire history before Dungy. He was known as a defensive guru, an innovator who created a unique style of defense called "The Tampa 2."[68] Under Dungy, the Bucs had fielded a top-ten scoring defense every year. Colts' owner, Jim Irsay, wasted no time in calling Dungy personally, famously leaving a long voicemail in which he said,

---

[68] The Tampa 2 was a zone defense that asked a speedy middle linebacker to drop into coverage. It emphasized sound tackling, limiting big plays, and generating pressure from the defensive line.

"You're the only person I want for this job…Don't worry about your salary, and don't let your agent mess this up. I'll pay you whatever you want. We just need to talk man-to-man."[69]

The addition of Dungy showed up in the next draft. The Colts used their first pick on a speedy, undersized defensive end out of Syracuse. Dwight Freeney became the first end taken by the Colts in either of the first two rounds since Steve Emtman[70] in 1992. The choice to take Freeney was widely criticized by draft experts who considered him too small to play end in the NFL. The Colts took defensive players with six out of seven picks that year in an effort to give Dungy the kind of players he needed to fix what ailed the Colts.

Aside from a new coach and a new commitment to defense, another important change happened before the 2002 season. The Colts got a new division. After years of competing in the AFC East, the Colts were placed by the NFL into a brand-new division: The AFC South. While it would have made more sense for Indy to be paired with Cincinnati, Cleveland, and Pittsburgh, the NFL protected some traditional rivalries and slotted the Colts with the Tennessee Titans, Jacksonville Jaguars, and expansion Houston Texans. Snow trips to New England, Buffalo, and New Jersey were about to be replaced with sunshine and domes. It played right into the Colts' hands.

The 2002 season opened with a 4-1 start, but it was clear from the go that the Colts were still an incomplete football team. The defense was a work in progress, and the offense was alarmingly top-heavy. Edgerrin James was not fully recovered from his ACL injury, and second-year wideout Reggie Wayne struggled to acclimate to the offense. Freeney was limited to part-time duty as a situational rusher, and there were grumblings that both young players might turn out to be busts.

---

[69] Tony Dungy, *Quiet Strength* (Carol Stream, IL: Tyndale Press, 2000) 203.
[70] Emtman played tackle in college, but lined up mostly as an end for the Colts.

Without a healthy Edge or a viable second wideout, Manning leaned heavily on Marvin Harrison, who almost single-handedly carried the Colts to the playoffs. Harrison put together a mind-blowing season, shattering the league record for catches in a season with 143, besting the previous record by 20 receptions. Harrison's 1,722 yards receiving are the seventh-most in a single season for a receiver. Without any other reliable targets, however, Manning once again threw too many interceptions, firing 19 times to the wrong team.

Dungy's work on the defense was strong, and as the season progressed, Freeney worked his way into the starting lineup and managed to post 13 sacks by year's end. The defense improved overall, giving up 170 fewer points than in the 2001 season. The team was still adapting to Dungy's scheme, however, and the progress vanished come playoff time.

The Colts managed to win 10 games and qualify for the postseason as a wild card team. Once again, the playoffs proved to be a horror show for the Horse as the Jets stifled the limited Indy offense while shredding the Indy defense. The final score was 41-0, and the questions began to flow from the media and the locker room.

The Colts were 0-3 in playoff games in the past four years, and the blame fell at Manning's feet. Media types began to question if Manning had what it took to "win a big game." Meanwhile, Mike Vanderjagt gave an interview on Canadian television questioning both Dungy and Manning. The commonly-held opinion was that the Colts were too soft mentally and too much of a finesse team to seriously contend for a Super Bowl.

The franchise was at a crossroads. Dungy had stabilized the defense, but the offense was still unbalanced. Polian surprised all the experts at the 2003 draft by taking another offensive weapon, tight end Dallas Clark out of Iowa. It was time to diversify the offense and give Manning more weapons in the passing game than just Harrison.

The arrival of Clark, a unique hybrid tight end/pass receiver, and the maturation of Wayne gave the Colts the balance they needed. Dungy had stern words for Manning, imploring him to cut down on his interceptions.[71] The Colts were going to have to be more efficient on offense if they wanted to make the jump to the next level.

Manning responded by silencing his critics in 2003. He led the Colts to 12 wins, and Indy won the AFC South in part thanks to two bruising victories over the Titans. Manning and Steve McNair of Tennessee dueled all season for the division crown, and as a result, both men shared the Most Valuable Player award. The Colts proved that they were not soft, and Manning had elevated his game thanks in part to Wayne chipping in with 838 yards and seven scores. The old bugaboo still loomed for the Colts. For the season to be considered a success, they had to perform in the playoffs.

By virtue of their division title, the Colts had earned their second playoff home game. This time they were facing the Denver Broncos, a team that had beaten them at the RCA Dome just weeks before. Manning quieted his critics with a virtuoso performance as the Colts crushed Denver 41-10. Manning threw more touchdowns (five) than incompletions (four) and posted a perfect passer rating of 158.3. The next week, he followed his brilliance by leading the Colts to an upset win at Kansas City. The Colts never punted, winning a shootout 38-31. In consecutive playoff wins, Manning had thrown for 681 yards and seven touchdowns and completed 78.6 percent of his passes.

The Colts ascended to the AFC Championship Game, and one of the greatest rivalries in NFL history was born. They traveled to New England to play the Patriots. On a cold and windy day, the Patriots prevailed thanks in part to a horrendous passing day by Manning who threw four interceptions. The Colts stayed close, but their final drive ended as Marcus Pollard was tackled by Patriots' defenders before getting the opportunity to catch a fourth-down pass from Manning. The New England defensive backs abused the Colts' receivers all day, repeatedly grabbing and bumping (or "chucking") them on downfield routes.

The season ended in disappointment, but the fateful loss in New England would reverberate throughout the league. In the off-

---

[71] Manning had 41 total interceptions from 2001-2002.

season meetings, the NFL competition committee, on which both Polian and Dungy had seats, decided to create a "point of emphasis" that would direct NFL officials to enforce long-standing rules against illegal contact with receivers. Since 1978, the NFL had a rule preventing defensive backs from chucking receivers more than five yards past the line of scrimmage. Many officials had become lax, allowing an overly-physical style of play that was expressly forbidden by the rule book. As a response, the league directed them to call games according to the written rule that had been on the books for 25 years.

Fresh off his first MVP award, Manning was signed by the Colts to a mammoth new contract. The deal was worth an astonishing $99.2 million with Manning receiving $34.5 million guaranteed as a signing bonus. The deal was so lucrative that Jim Irsay had to pay money out of his own pocket to cover it. All the pressure was back on Manning's shoulders. He had to go out and earn his money.

He responded by turning in perhaps the finest display of passing the league has ever seen. The 2004 team struggled defensively, like many teams that year, but Manning took advantage of a stable of excellent receivers. He assaulted the record books, throwing 49 touchdown passes and posting a league-record passer rating of 121.1, shattering the old marks by Hall of Fame quarterbacks Dan Marino and Steve Young. Once again, he won the MVP award of the league and led the Colts to another first round trouncing of the Denver Broncos in the playoffs.

The 2004 season, for all its glory, ended the same way the 2003 season did with a loss to the eventual champion New England Patriots. The Colts had to play in the snow and wind, and the elements are not conducive to the kind of high flying precision offense the Colts ran. The Patriots defense harassed the Colts into three fumbles and three points as they rolled over Indy with long plodding drives. The final score of 20-3 reflected the kind of team the Colts would need to become if they were going to take the leap.

The 2005 draft brought more tough defenders into Indianapolis. The Colts had selected a sledge hammer of a safety in Bob Sanders in 2004, but he spent most of the year out with injuries. A year later, they added six defenders and two linemen with their first eight picks, throwing excellent tacklers like Marlin Jackson and Kelvin Hayden in the mix. The Colts were building a physical, sure-tackling secondary in an attempt to shore up a defense that was 19th in the NFL in points allowed in 2004.

Dungy had now been with the team for three full seasons and had had some success, but in 2005, he helped the defense find a new gear. Freeney led a group of fast, aggressive players as the Colts shaved nearly a touchdown a game off of their points allowed from the previous season. Freeney had a wonderful season, posting his second-consecutive All Pro campaign. He would be joined in the Pro Bowl by Cato June and Bob Sanders.

On offense, teams were determined not to let Peyton Manning throw 49 touchdowns again. Manning had matured past the point where he could be goaded into poor throws, however. He became Captain Checkdown, patiently throwing underneath for shorter gains. The result was the same for the opposition; the Colts scored the second-most points in football.

A dominant offense and a dominant defense. The Colts had finally become a complete team. They, in turn, dominated the 2005 season, opening the year with 13-consecutive victories before losing a tough game at home to the San Diego Chargers. The Colts had already wrapped up home-field advantage throughout the playoffs, an Indianapolis first, when tragedy struck. Just days before the 14th game of the year, Dungy's eldest son committed suicide.

The news devastated the team and the community. James Dungy was a bright and well-loved young man, whom all the players knew well. Sorrow engulfed the team. Coach Jim Caldwell took over temporarily for Dungy as the coach mourned. The Colts' starters played sparingly over the final two games. The team finished the year 14-2, still tied for the best regular season in franchise history, but much of the joy was drained from the journey.

The Colts took on the Pittsburgh Steelers in the first round of the playoffs. The offense struggled to find its rhythm against the Steelers' blitz early on, and despite a strong comeback effort led by

Manning, the Steelers prevailed 21-18 as Mike Vanderjagt missed a game-tying field goal in the final seconds.

Four years of Dungy ball had brought the Colts to new heights, but 2005 closed with more questions. Many doubted Dungy would return to the team after the season. Manning received criticism in increasing measure as he unfairly bore the entire weight of the Colts' playoff failures. Around Indianapolis, people openly wondered if the Colts had what it took to become champions.

The verdict was still out on Dungy Ball.

Understanding 2002-2005

Tony Dungy

He did not yell or scream or curse. He did not grab attention for himself. He never called out players through the media. He didn't put bounties on players or make bold guarantees. All he did was win.

Tony Dungy already had a reputation around football before joining the Colts. He was known as an excellent defensive tactician and the kind of man who could build a franchise. He had completely turned around the Tampa Bay Buccaneers, one of the worst franchises in NFL history. He was a different kind of head coach from the NFL stereotype, and perhaps because of that, it took a long time for him to get hired. He was African-American, and in the early and mid-90s, that was an obstacle to landing the top job with an NFL team. He was also mild-mannered and soft-spoken, and many questioned if a man who was so nice and so principled could coach in the violent, aggressive NFL.

The instant Dungy became available, excitement surged. He was the logical choice to be the next head coach of the Colts. After all, the 2001 team was horrid defensively, and Dungy was just the man to fix it. We were excited over the possibility of bringing a Tampa-style defense to Indianapolis. Fortunately, Jim Irsay was every bit as enthusiastic, pulling out all the stops to lure Dungy to the Colts.

From the beginning, Dungy worked to change the culture of the Colts. His emphasis was on smart, disciplined play. He made it a point that his teams would be among the least-penalized in the NFL each and every year. He preached forcing turnovers on defense and avoiding them on offense. In 2001, the Colts had 38 turnovers. In 2002, Dungy's first season, they had 32. By 2003, the number was slashed to 20. Over the next five seasons under Dungy, Indianapolis would post fewer than 20 turnovers every year.

Dungy was the perfect complement to Bill Polian. The most important feature of the Colts' front office was the trust and working relationship the men established. Dungy saw his job as that of coach, and while he had tremendous input into the formation of the roster, there was no bickering or petty power plays between the GM and the coach. They publicly supported each other. Whereas Polian was gruff and truculent with the media, Dungy was warm and cordial. Together they formed a kind of good cop/bad cop that produced a steady string of winning seasons.

Dungy's teams never got too high or too low. Because of that, the concept of a trap game[72] was completely eliminated. In Dungy's seven seasons with the Colts, they lost a total of six games to teams that finished the season with losing records.[73] He became a master of keeping his team calm in tight situations, and the Colts responded with some of the most memorable come-from-behind performances of all time. Under Tony's guidance, the Colts posted 28 come-from-behind wins in the fourth quarter of games. Dungy's leadership ensured that opponents had to beat the Colts; the Colts rarely beat themselves. Subsequently, they won 10 games every season he coached them, never missing the playoffs.

---

[72] A "trap game" is a game against a losing team sandwiched between two more "important" games. They are called trap games because often NFL teams overlook the lesser team and suffer an unnecessary loss.
[73] Two of those games came early in the 2008 season while Manning was still suffering from the effects of off-season knee surgery.

His tenure was not without difficulties. The Colts experienced some troubling losses in the playoffs, but Dungy's response was never to panic. He kept his faith in the core principles the team was built around and never overreacted to a defeat. This was best illustrated after the crushing loss to the Steelers in the 2005 playoffs. Many openly questioned Dungy, his style, his strategies, and the Colts in general. After the Indianapolis run defense fell apart late in 2006, there were pundits who suggested that Dungy might never win a Super Bowl.

Dungy stayed the course, however, choosing to tweak and teach rather than to overhaul and tear down. His faith in his team and his principles was rewarded as the Colts won the Super Bowl in 2006. The pivotal moment came in the AFC Championship Game against New England. With his team trailing 21-3, Dungy exhorted his team that it was "still our time."[74] Players later credited his sense of calm with helping them to overcome the deficit and storm back to beat the Patriots 38-34.

Dungy is still an influential figure in Indiana. His evangelical Christian faith plays well in the Bible Belt. His respectful, thoughtful demeanor was a welcome change to the bluster and brutality of Bob Knight. He offered an alternative to the "old school" kind of coach, while at the same time affirming traditional values of respect for authority, faith, and good citizenship.

There were still small pockets of the state that were slow to embrace African-American coaches. Tyrone Willingham, Isiah Thomas, and Mike Davis all met with considerable resistance while leading high-profile teams in Indiana.[75] Ultimately, Dungy succeeded where they failed simply by winning. The man who couldn't get a job interview became the first African-American coach to win a Super Bowl.

---

[74] Dungy was echoing a speak Jeff Saturday delivered the night before the game.
[75] Willingham coached Notre Dame football, Davis the Indiana Hoosiers basketball team, and Isiah Thomas the NBA Pacers.

He saved his finest coaching job for last. The 2008 Colts were battered by injuries and did not get off to their best start. He kept the team collected and managed to squeeze 12 wins out of a suspect roster. His last season as head coach would be his 11th winning season in 13 years of coaching and a record sixth consecutive season of at least 12 wins. He walked away from coaching to spend more time with his family and to focus on ministries involving young men.

When he finally departed the Colts, he left behind a strong team with a solid foundation. He had mentored Jim Caldwell to replace him. Caldwell was given the title of Assistant Head Coach in 2008, and Dungy prepared him to lead the team after he was gone. He retired with dignity and fanfare, and had done his job so well that no one felt he was abandoning the franchise.

In 2016, he received recognition for a race well-run with his enshrinement as the first African-American Head Coach in the Hall of Fame.

He was quite simply the finest coach any of us will ever see in Indianapolis. He changed the culture of the team and meshed perfectly with the culture of the state. Neither the Colts, nor Indiana, will ever be the same.

49

My father-in-law is a big Chargers fan, so I took him to the game the day after Christmas. As the Chargers dominated, he happily cheered them on throughout the afternoon.

As Manning led the Colts downfield to tie the game, his gloating grew quieter.

As the 49th touchdown pass left Manning's hand and streaked toward the wide-open arms of Brandon Stokley, I leapt to my feet.

It was my turn to cheer.

Isn't that the point of sports?

After the 2003 season, Peyton Manning signed the then-richest contract in NFL history. Some people wondered how he would handle the pressure.

Manning handled it by having the greatest single quarterbacking season in the history of the NFL.

The 2004 season got off to a rocky start as the Colts dropped the opener to New England. Manning had an effective game and threw a couple of touchdown passes, but there was nothing to indicate what the year had in store.

The first clue that Manning was about to unload a torrent of touchdowns came in the third game against the Packers. Green Bay foolishly decided to try and blitz Manning. The result was a devastating aerial attack. Locked in an historic duel with Brett Favre, Manning threw five touchdowns in the first half and 393 yards for the game as the two legends combined for 753 yards, nine touchdowns and no interceptions. The Colts won 45-31, and Manning had nine touchdowns for the year.

His frenetic pace mounted as he tossed another eight scores in his next three games. Passing was up all over football, thanks in part to a renewed enforcement of longstanding rules preventing defenses from mugging receivers. The beneficiaries of Manning's largess were the Colts' receivers. Marvin Harrison was on his way to his typical 1,100 yards and 15 scores, but Reggie Wayne and Brandon Stokley each also passed 1,000 yards and 10 touchdowns. The 2004 Colts would become the first team in history to field three receivers with at least 1,000 yards and 10 touchdowns apiece.

Ironically, it was the defense that lit the fire under the Colts to pass so much. The Colts' seventh game against the Chiefs was a replay of the 2003 playoffs. Manning threw five touchdowns to give him 22 for the year, but the Colts still lost 45-35. It was clear that the Colts would have to outscore teams to win. For the first time, people began to murmur about 48.

In 1984, a young Dan Marino had the greatest passing season in history to that point. He was a touchdown machine, throwing for 5,084 yards and 48 touchdowns. The touchdown record stood for twenty years without serious challenge. Other than Marino himself, only Kurt Warner had ever reached 40 in a season. As 2004 wore on, it was clear Manning would challenge the record.

The Kansas City game sparked a remarkable run wherein Manning threw 24 touchdown passes in just five games. He threw for four in a tense Monday night affair against the Vikings. Then he pitched five more against the lowly Texans. Finally, he threw an insane ten touchdowns in four days as the Colts throttled the Bears and then the Lions on Thanksgiving. Against the NFC North division alone, Manning threw 19 touchdowns and just one interception. The season still had five games left, and Manning already had 41 touchdowns.

Teams pulled out all the stops to prevent Manning from leading the Colts to points. Jeff Fisher's Titans team attempted three onside kicks in the first quarter against the Colts. Peyton still threw three touchdown passes, and the Colts piled up 51 points. After two more scores against the Texans, Manning had three games to post the final three touchdowns.

The first game came against the Baltimore Ravens. The Colts controlled the action, but the Ravens held Indy to a pair of first half field goals. Manning broke through in the third quarter, hitting Harrison off a beautiful play-action fake. His 47th score of the year gave the Colts a ten-point lead. Late in the game, an interception gave the Colts the ball at the four yard line with less than a minute to play. Manning had a chance to tie the record at home on national television. Instead, sporting a 10-point lead, the Colts knelt on the ball. A garbage-time score was no way to break a hallowed mark.

With just two games remaining, Manning took the field the day after Christmas, 2004. He threw two second-half touchdowns including a clutch 21-yard pass to Stokley to tie the game against the San Diego Chargers. It was his 49th touchdown of the season, a new NFL record. Manning played just a single series in the final game at Denver as the Colts rested starters before a rematch with the Broncos.

Just as significantly, Manning shattered the NFL record for highest passer rating in a season. His mark of 121.4 was nearly nine points higher than Steve Young's old record. Manning won his second consecutive MVP award, collecting 49 of 50 votes, capping one of the greatest quarterbacking seasons in NFL history.

Manning's record was broken just three years later by Tom Brady, who threw 89 more passes than Manning did in 2004. The door to huge passing totals had been broken down and a record that went without serious challenge for two decades fell repeatedly over the next few years. In 2013, Manning returned the favor and broke Brady's record with an unthinkable 55-touchdown season.[76]

No one questioned his huge contract again. Manning was worth every penny. Over the life of that $99 million deal, Manning would win three MVP awards and take the Colts to two Super Bowls.

Apparently, he could handle the pressure.

---

[76] These are generally accepted to be the five greatest passing seasons in history. Manning's 2004 had the highest YPA and second-highest passer rating.

	Year	Comp	Att	Comp %	Yards	TD	INT	YPA	Rating
Dan Marino	1984	362	564	64.2	5,084	48	17	9.0	108.9
Peyton Manning	2004	336	497	67.6	4,557	49	10	9.2	121.4
Tom Brady	2007	398	578	68.9	4,806	50	8	8.3	117.2
Aaron Rodgers	2011	343	502	68.3	4,643	45	6	9.0	122.5
Peyton Manning	2013	450	659	68.3	5,477	55	10	8.3	115.1

"Vandershank"

I couldn't watch. The entire game had been an uphill struggle. I had seen enough Vanderjagt kicks to know what was going to happen.

I closed my eyes. I listened for the roar.

The groan told me everything I needed to know.

He had missed another big kick.

A part of me died.

It is not fair to blame everything wrong that happened on Mike Vanderjagt. Not every important loss was his fault. It just felt that way.

Vanderjagt was brought in by Bill Polian to replace stalwart place kicker Carey Blanchard. Blanchard had been an excellent kicker for the Colts, hitting countless game winners and making a Pro Bowl in 1996. Still, new coach Jim Mora felt it was time for a change, and the Colts brought in a free agent from the Canadian Football League. Mike Vanderjagt had been a championship kicker under the harsh conditions in Canada, and won the job away from Blanchard.

Vanderjagt's career with the Colts got off to an excellent start. He hit 89.6 percent of his field goals in his first three seasons with the Colts, including a hearty 7-of-11 from beyond 50 yards. He also hit several clutch kicks to win games. Eventually, he became the most accurate kicker in the history of the NFL, making 87.5 percent of his kicks during his career with the Colts. In 2003, he hit all 37 field goals he attempted. On the surface, Vanderjagt was a star.

110

Looks can be deceiving, however. Vanderjagt was always a little off, a little weird. He had a big mouth and loved to give quotes to the media. Marcus Pollard said of him, "he carries himself different on the field. He's different in the locker room. Nobody dresses like him. He's just 'Mike.'"[77] Vanderjagt was brash, even cocky, which was unusual for an NFL kicker. Ultimately, whatever idiosyncrasies he had were easily overlooked as long he kept banging the ball through the uprights.[78]

The problem was that Vanderjagt didn't always hit the big kicks. The first sign of trouble came in the 2000 playoffs. With a chance to win the game for the Colts in overtime, Vanderjagt missed a 49-yard field goal, well within his normal range. Any kicker can miss a kick, but what was shocking was how badly he missed it. He did not just push the ball slightly askew. Instead, he violently yanked the kick wide to the right. It was never on line and never had a chance. It was a miss that was shocking both in its execution and in its consequence. The Colts never saw the ball again and lost minutes later.

In the 2002 playoff loss, Vanderjagt missed an early field goal with the Colts trailing 7-0. The next time Indianapolis saw the ball, they were already trailing 17-0. While his missed kick certainly was not the difference in a 41-0 game, it did not help the situation. Even more alarming were the bizarre and indefensible comments he would later make on Canadian television.

In an interview in the off-season, Vanderjagt went after Peyton Manning and Tony Dungy. He said of Manning, "Some guys have it and some guys don't." He then went on to savage Dungy, remarking,

> "He doesn't get too excited; he doesn't get too down, and I don't think that works either. I think you need a motivator. I think you need a guy that is going to get in somebody's face when they're not performing well enough. Peyton and Tony

---

[77] Mike Chappell and Phil Richards, Tales from the Indianapolis Colts Sideline, (New York: Sports Publishing, 2004). 109.
[78] In many respects, he was similar to Pat McAfee who was also vocal with the media.

are basically the same guy. They work hard; they mark their Xs and Os and go out and execute. If it doesn't happen, there's nothing we can do about it. I'm not a big Colts' fan right now. I just don't see us getting better."[79]

The words reverberated around the league, causing major embarrassment for the Colts. Manning struck back with a vengeance during a nationally-televised Pro Bowl interview calling Vanderjagt "our idiot kicker" and joking that he "got liquored up and ran his mouth off." Though both men would later apologize, fans would never view Vanderjagt the same way. Dungy considered cutting the kicker for the offense. Failing to do so might have been the biggest mistake of his career.

"Vanderjerk," as he came to be known around Indianapolis, rebounded the best way any kicker can. He came out and drilled every kick in the 2003 season. That record came with a bit of an asterisk because he actually missed a potential game winning kick against the Buccaneers, but got a second chance after a penalty call.[80] After a perfect season, he had a chance to win the Pro Bowl with a last-second field goal, but he missed the kick badly. It was his only missed kick of 2003.

He had another solid year in 2004, but his string of 42-consecutive made field goals[81] came to a screeching halt in the first game of the year. With the Colts trailing New England by just three points with seconds to play, Vanderjagt missed the 48-yard try. The loss would eventually mean the Colts had to play in New England in the playoffs once again. Before the rematch, Vanderjagt went out of his way to provoke the Patriots, declaring them to be ripe for an upset. His mouth was not an asset as a motivated Pats team rolled the Colts 20-3.

---

[79] Chappell and Richards, 112-113.
[80] His game-winning kick was an ugly duck that slammed off the right upright and bounced through.
[81] An NFL record, later broken by Adam Vinatieri.

None of his "sins" would haunt the Colts nearly as much as what happened against the Steelers following the 2005 season. After staging a near-miraculous comeback, the Colts needed a field goal to force overtime in the Divisional playoff game. Trailing 21-18, they sent Vanderjagt out to attempt a game-tying kick. In our hearts, we all knew what was coming.

It was 2000 all over again. Vanderjagt shanked the kick wide to right. It was never on line. It never had a chance. The most accurate kicker in history had missed yet another clutch playoff field goal. To make matters worse, Vanderjagt appeared on David Letterman's *Tonight Show* just days later and made an identical 46-yard field goal with ease. The display was bitter for Colts fans and management alike. His contract was up, and the Colts did not re-sign him, instead signing Adam Vinatieri, known as the most clutch kicker in history, away from the New England Patriots. Vinatieri hit five field goals against Baltimore in the 2006 Playoffs, and the Colts won their first Super Bowl.

Vanderjagt was briefly signed by the Cowboys, but lasted only a handful of games. Despite being the most accurate kicker in history, he was radioactive. No team in the league would trust him. He never got another NFL job after being let go by Dallas.

There will never be a less popular, more despised player to wear an Indianapolis uniform than Mike Vanderjagt, aka Vanderjerk, aka Vandershank.

Classic Colts

Justin Snow: Long Snapper 2000-2009

Justin Snow signed as an undrafted rookie free agent in 2000 and has played his entire career in blue and white. During his career, he excelled at being the long snapper on special teams for punts, field goals, and point after touchdowns. Snow, Mike Vanderjagt, and Hunter Smith (holder) became the NFL's first trio to go an entire season, including the playoffs, without missing a field goal or point after touchdown in 2003.

Hailing from the same high school as Dominic Rhodes, Snow had one of his finest moments in 2002 when he talked head coach Tony Dungy into allowing Vanderjagt to attempt a 51-yard field goal to win the game in overtime. Snow's job was one that leaves him anonymous to all but the most die-hard fans, but he was a key part of every big kick the Colts have made for a decade.

Rob Morris: Linebacker 2000-2007

Rob Morris was a first-round pick in the 2000 draft out of BYU, but in his early years he took abuse from fans and never produced according to expectation. When Dungy arrived and changed defenses, Morris was ill-suited for the new style. Still, he never complained, worked hard, and even re-signed with the team despite little hope to regain his starting spot.

He selflessly played on special teams, becoming an excellent gunner on kicks. His finest moment occurred late in 2006. With the defense floundering because of the terrible play of linebacker Gilbert Gardner, the coaches turned to the veteran Morris to take over. Morris's play was marked by discipline and an understanding of his role. His return to the starting lineup was a major factor in the improvement of the defense in the playoffs.

Morris's career ended after a knee injury the following season. In some ways, he didn't achieve all the accolades of other top picks by the Colts in the decade, but his character, determination, and hard work helped him achieve Super Bowl glory and a spot among the most well-loved Colts of all time.

Hunter Smith: Punter 1999-2008

Hunter the Punter was the most popular Colt that fans hated to see on the field. Indianapolis's punter for ten seasons was always well-liked in part because he was a Notre Dame graduate. A man of impeccable character, Smith was also an excellent athlete, able to run and throw as well as kick. One of his smartest moves was to develop a rugby-style punt that died easily inside the 10-yard line. Knowing that the Colts had a top offense, it was more important that he pin teams deep with a short field rather than to try to boom long punts. Despite a fraction of the attempts of other punters, Smith managed to land at least 20 balls inside the 20-yard line in six different seasons.

His two greatest claims to fame include an excellent hold on a key field goal in the playoffs against the Baltimore Ravens when he took a bad snap and managed to get the hold down in time for Adam Vinatieri to make an important kick. He also famously tackled Deion Sanders on a punt return. Sanders had bragged that he knew he would score if he saw a punter trying to tackle him. The next day, Smith dragged Sanders down short of the goal line, showing what great speed he possessed.

Upon retirement, he started the appropriately named Hunter Smith Band and wrote an excellent book chronicling the spiritual struggles of life in the NFL entitled *The Jersey Effect*.

The Fourth Quarter

Basketball in Indiana was not dead, but it was sick. The one thing that still kept fans' spirits up was the Pacers. Reggie Miller loomed over the state as the most iconic athlete to play in Indiana in the past 30 years. The Pacers were perennial contenders and, in 2004, clearly had the best team in the NBA. The Colts were popular, but they still could not match the Pacers' track record of constant success. Peyton Manning was a star, but he was no Miller.

The death of basketball as Indiana's first love was not November 19, 2004, but it might as well have been. Early in the season, the Pacers were rolling toward the best record in the league, and on a Friday night in Detroit, they dominated the defending champions on their home court. Thanks to the highly irresponsible actions of Ben Wallace and the woefully lax security in the Palace of Auburn Hills, a savage brawl broke out late in the game as Pacer Ron Artest charged into the stands and began swinging wildly at fans.

The game was nationally televised, and Commissioner David Stern felt compelled to act. He came down hard on Artest and other Pacers, essentially giving the death penalty to Indiana's 2004 season. Despite the fact that the entire incident was provoked and perpetuated by the thuggery of Ben Wallace and the Detroit fans, the Pacers took the bullet for the league.

Miller admirably carried the Pacers down the stretch and into the playoffs, even advancing the team to the second round. Ultimately, he was not enough. Miller had lugged the Pacers as far as they could go. He had already announced that it would be his final season in blue and gold. The greatest Pacer of all walked away from the game, taking the hearts of Hoosiers with him.

In the subsequent seasons, the Pacers suffered on and off the court. They regressed the following season, but still made the playoffs. The cast of characters that they assembled was a far cry from the beloved Pacers teams of the 90s, however. Ron Artest's antics made him anathema in Indianapolis, eventually forcing the Pacers to trade him. Jamaal Tinsley and Stephen Jackson also had incidents around town involving firearms in the 2006 and 2007 seasons.

The Pacers became an impossible team to root for. There were too many bad seeds, too many police reports, and too few wins. The buzz that had dominated Pacer games for almost 20 years dissipated with the departure of Miller. The love affair between the city and its basketball team had grown cold.

The Colts offered the perfect replacement. The Super Bowl win in 2006 sealed the transformation. The Colts accomplished what the Pacers never had: a championship.

Miller was gone. Manning had the city all to himself.

More importantly, the Colts built a reputation of being a "moral" team. After winning the Super Bowl, Tony Dungy declared that they had done things "the Lord's way." Colts rarely showed up in the police blotters. The public image of the Indianapolis Colts was clean and upright, but the Pacers were criminals who jumped in the stands to beat up "innocent fans". The assessments of the two teams were neither completely accurate nor fair, but they stuck. The Colts had taken the moral high ground and replaced the Pacers as the city's most beloved team.

The Colts had surpassed basketball at every level in Indiana. From high school to the NBA, the sport that once defined the word "Hoosier" had withered.

The king was dead.

The Colts were king.

Chapter Seven
2006-2008
Blue Reign

Record: 37-11

Highest finish: 1st in AFC South (2006, 2007)

Head Coach: Tony Dungy

Leading Passer: Peyton Manning

Leading Rusher: Joseph Addai

Leading Receiver: Reggie Wayne

The loss to the Steelers to close the 2005 season left everyone reeling. This defeat was unquestionably the darkest moment for most Colts fans.

On top of everything else, the loss was the final game by Edgerrin James in Colts' blue. James played the 2005 season under the franchise tag, and the Colts let him walk away as a free agent. To replace him, they drafted a back out of LSU named Joseph Addai. Many experts declared that the Colts' window had closed.

Even if it had, Peyton Manning flung it open again. Despite severe problems on defense, Manning deftly carried the team to nine-consecutive wins to open the 2006 season. Once again, the Colts were at the top of the AFC. Eventually, however, the team's inability to stop the run grew to be too much to overcome. Indianapolis dropped four out of six games coming down the stretch, and fans prepared for another disappointing postseason. Bill Polian did what he could to bolster the defense with a midseason trade for tackle Anthony "Booger" McFarland, but the new defender was slow to acclimate.

Ironically, the tide began to turn during one of the worst losses in Colts history. In the 13th game, the Jaguars slaughtered the Colts 44-17. The Jags rushed for 375 yards, embarrassing the defense by gashing them with a series of long gains. There was a silver lining, however. All season, the run defense had been plagued by a lack of "gap control."[82] Young linebacker Gilbert Gardner had a particularly difficult time understanding his responsibilities and routinely found himself out of position. During the Jacksonville game, he was replaced by veteran Rob Morris. No one knew it at the time, but it would be one of the two critical changes that would save the season.

2006 postseason was a series of exorcisms for the franchise and the fans. The Colts limped in at 12-4, but were the third seed. The first-round opponent was the Kansas City Chiefs and their superstar running back Larry Johnson. It was a matchup nightmare. The Chiefs planned to run the ball all day and grind the Colts into the RCA Dome turf.

Fortunately, that plan failed. The Colts limited the Chiefs to 44 yards rushing thanks to inspired play from McFarland and star safety, Bob Sanders. Sanders had spent most of the season battling injuries, but once he returned to the lineup, he transformed the defense. His physical style and play-making ability clamped down the Chiefs' running game, and the Colts cruised into the second round. The ghost of Jacksonville had been vanquished.

The second-round game was played at Baltimore. It was the first time the Colts returned to Baltimore for a playoff game.[83] The Ravens had a ferocious defense and a rabid crowd seeking revenge for the Midnight Move more than 20 years earlier. Indianapolis prevailed in a bruising game, conquering their past.

The win set up a rematch with the New England Patriots. This time the game would be played in Indianapolis. It was a watershed moment. The old foe that had denied them so many times before had to come to the Dome to play the biggest game of the decade. The Colts fell behind 21-3 early but rallied back.

---

[82] In the Colts' defense, linebackers were responsible to maintain their position to fill gaps in the line created by the defenders in front of them. If a linebacker over-pursues the ball carrier, he will leave his spot open, and big gains can result on simple cutbacks by the runner.

[83] The Colts had already played several regular-season games in Baltimore.

With less than two minutes to play, Addai blew through the heart of the Patriots' line for a 38-34 lead. Moments later, Marlin Jackson dropped to the turf after intercepting a Tom Brady pass, and the Colts were finally on their way to the Super Bowl. The specter of the Patriots was no more.

Indy took advantage of the long-awaited trip to the Super Bowl by defeating the Chicago Bears in a driving Miami rain storm. Despite an early deficit, the Indy defense and run game augmented a strong game from Manning, and the Colts were finally crowned champions.

Thousands filled the RCA Dome to welcome the team back to Indianapolis. The team celebrated the accomplishment by sending the Lombardi trophy on parade throughout the state. By beating the Bears, the constant rival they rarely played, the Colts had claimed Hoosierland as their own. It took more than two decades, but the Colts were triumphant on the grandest stage of all.

Many teams would have suffered a letdown after such a magical run through the playoffs, but the Colts came back in 2007 ready for action. They opened the 2007 campaign by drubbing the New Orleans Saints at home and proceeded to win their next seven games.

The victories came at a price. Injuries piled up. Morris was lost for the season and never played for the Colts again. McFarland went down in training camp. Marvin Harrison suffered a knee injury early in the year and missed more than half the regular season. By the time the Colts took on the equally undefeated Patriots, the lineup was hardly recognizable. The Patriots took the game, leaving the Colts as the pursuers once again.

That loss was nothing compared with the heartbreak still waiting. The next week, the Colts dropped a disappointing game with the Chargers, but the real devastation came in the form of a season-ending injury to Dwight Freeney. While Robert Mathis and Raheem Brock played well down the stretch, they both suffered injuries as well.

The Colts got a rematch with the San Diego Chargers in the playoffs and managed to get a number of players back for the game, but most were noticeably unprepared. Marvin Harrison made it back on the field but played the worst game of his career. His fumble deep in Chargers' territory kept San Diego in the game. Without Freeney, the Colts managed no pass rush at all. A vintage performance by Manning was not enough to overcome a bevy of mistakes by the rest of the team. It was the last game ever played in the RCA Dome, and Indianapolis suffered a crushing 28-24 defeat.

The loss left a bad taste in everyone's mouth, but the Colts were still an elite team. The 2007 season may have been derailed by injuries, but it was plain to see that when healthy, the Horse was a force. The 2007 Colts might well have been the best Colts' team of all but finished the year with nothing to show for their greatness.

The wave of injuries continued through training camp in 2008, and to make matters worse, Manning found his way on to the injury report. Thanks to a bursa sac issue,[84] he was still recovering from surgery when camp opened. Though he missed the entire preseason, he made it back to the starting lineup in time for the season opener. It was a momentous occasion because it marked the grand opening of Lucas Oil Stadium, the new home of the Colts.

Manning's play early in 2008 was ragged. Other injuries began to mount, too. Addai, Saturday, and Clark all missed significant time. Halfway through the season, it appeared that the Colts' string of postseason appearances was over. A crushing loss to the Titans on Monday Night Football left the Colts with only a wild card spot as a realistic hope.

The injury report continued to swell. Both starting corners and middle linebacker, Gary Brackett, went down. Fortunately, Manning's knee improved, and he caught fire. Bolstered by the incomparable play of Manning and brilliant seasons from Mathis and Freeney, Tony Dungy turned in the finest coaching performance of his career.

Manning willed the Colts to nine-consecutive wins to end the year, clinching both an improbable 12-4 record and a seventh-straight

---

[84] The bursa sac helps to lubricate joints. Manning had an infected bursa sac in his knee that needed to be removed.

trip to the playoffs. For his herculean efforts, Manning was voted the NFL's Most Valuable Player for a record-tying third time.

The Colts' reward for refusing to quit was a playoff date at San Diego. All season long, the Colts struggled to run the football behind a patchwork line. It finally came back to bite them as they could not run out the clock to put away a win. They lost a heartbreaking and controversial game in overtime.

Following the gut-wrenching defeat, Colts fans received more bad news. Dungy, the man who had brought so much success to the team, was stepping down as head coach. He had life ambitions beyond football and decided that it was time to walk away. He was replaced by coach-in-waiting Jim Caldwell.

Despite their best efforts to maintain continuity in the organization, the departure of Dungy marked the end of an era. The Colts had more questions than answers heading into 2009, and fans had to hope that Caldwell could be the man to take the Colts back to the top of the NFL.

Understanding 2006-2008

38-34

At halftime, my brother called me from the Dome. He was distraught. "Should I stay? I can't watch them lose this game."

"Stay. You have to stay for at least the first drive of the second half," I told him.

*He called me after the game. I couldn't hear a word he said. The roar
from the crowd was too loud. It didn't matter anyway. I knew what he wanted to
say...*

We did it.

The Patriots and Colts defined the first decade of this century.
Unfortunately for Colts fans, the Patriots did most of the defining, at
first. New England knocked the Colts out of the playoffs in both 2003
and 2004, and at one point the Patriots had won six-consecutive games
in the series, including the playoffs.

Patriots' quarterback Tom Brady and Peyton Manning framed
the debate, not only over who was the best quarterback in football, but
over what a quarterback should be and do for his team. The Colts and
Patriots represented a culture clash, a war of world views, and for the
first half of the 00's, the Boston view had all the bragging rights.

Colts' fans were optimistic heading into the 2006 AFC
Championship game, however. The Colts had won the last two
matchups and by virtue of a big win in Foxboro in November had the
right to host the Pats for the playoff rematch. It was now or never for
the Indianapolis Colts. If they failed to make it to the Super Bowl this
time, many feared they never would.

The crowd filled the RCA Dome early that January night. By
the time the game started, the Dome was hot, and the crowd was
already in a surly mood. Nothing went right for the Colts early in the
game. The Patriots drove downfield with their second possession,
converting a fourth-and-1 for 35 yards down to the Colts' 13-yard line.
On third-and-1 from the 4, Brady fumbled the snap from center.
Several Colts fell on the ball, but it squirted out and into the end zone
where Patriots' lineman Logan Mankins recovered it for a touchdown.

The Colts answered with a field goal, but the Pats again ripped
down the field for a 14-3 lead. The Colts needed a big drive to answer
the momentum but instead, Asante Samuel stepped in front of a pass
intended for Marvin Harrison. He cruised home for a touchdown,

putting the Colts in an almost insurmountable hole. It was a complete disaster.

After another Indianapolis punt, the Patriots drove for the kill shot. Facing a third-and-6 inside the Colts' 30, Brady hit tight end Ben Watson for a key first down. Fortunately, the play was overturned on an offensive pass interference penalty. Another Pats' penalty knocked them further out of field-goal range before Dwight Freeney finally ended the Patriots' possession with a sack of Brady. Still, the Patriots had to feel confident leading by 18 with only three minutes to play in the half.

The greatest comeback in championship game history started slowly. The Colts mounted a spirited final drive of the half and reached the New England 6-yard line but had to settle for a field goal that cut the deficit to 21-6. At half time, Tony Dungy's calm demeanor paid off. He echoed Jeff Saturday's message from the night before the game. He told the team, "This is still our time!"

The Colts exited the locker room a changed club. They opened with a 14-play drive for a touchdown, and the energy level in the building rose. Fans could sense a comeback was in the making.

The game turned in an instant. After a New England punt, the Colts marched 76 yards in eight plays. Manning threw a touchdown pass to Dan Klecko and tied the game with a two-point conversion throw to Harrison.

The Patriots were far from done, however. Over the next quarter-plus, they managed to stay one step ahead of the Colts. If they needed a touchdown, they got it. If they needed a field goal, they converted it. No matter what the Colts did, they could not get the lead. With 3:22 to play in the game, the Patriots held a 34-31 lead and the ball. They needed just one first down to end the Colts' season.

The Colts responded with an excellent stand on defense, and Bob Sanders broke up a third-down pass from Brady to Troy Brown. After a New England punt, the Colts took over on their own 20-yard line. Manning had just 2:17 and one timeout. The Colts needed 80 yards.

The tension was unbearable as Manning went to work. He hit Reggie Wayne for 11 yards. He found Brian Fletcher for 32. Just before the two-minute warning, he dialed Wayne's number again. As Wayne bounded toward the 20-yard line, the ball was poked loose from his control. For an agonizing moment, the ball hung in the air before he pulled it back into his body.

A dubious roughing-the-passer penalty[85] on the Patriots moved the ball to the 11. The Colts had driven the first 69 yards in just 17 seconds. Instead of hurrying up, they had to try and drain the clock. Two runs moved the ball eight yards. The Colts huddled on third-and-2 from the 3. The Patriots were exhausted.

The building was hot and loud. Harrison spoke up in the huddle and said, "Let's run it." If even Marvin Harrison wanted a run play, no one was going to argue with him.

Manning handed the ball to Joseph Addai. The Patriots' defenders fell like chaff as Saturday pancaked defensive tackle Vince Wilfork. Addai shot through the hole untouched and emerged on the other side of the goal line and on the other side of history. Tens of thousands in the Dome and millions more in their homes yelled, screamed, and went "horse". The Colts led 38-34 and were just 1:02 away from the Super Bowl.

The Patriots tried to mount a final drive, but they were fresh out of miracles. Brady released his final pass of the 2006 season with less than 30 seconds left. It nestled safely into the arms of Marlin Jackson who triumphantly slid to the turf, slaying the dragon that had conquered the Colts so many times before.

While it is true that the win would have been meaningless without a Super Bowl victory to follow it up, there has never been a celebration like that one in Indianapolis. Confetti streamed from the rafters and the whole building became a canyon of heroes. All of the nonsense about Manning and Dungy not having the right "stuff" to be champions washed away. All of the pain of 2005, the missed opportunities and empty-handed winters, were gone.

---

[85] Perhaps a makeup call for an earlier missed hit on Manning.

128

38-34. It was everything.

It was the game of the decade. It was the greatest comeback in championship game history. It was tangible proof that good could triumph over evil. It was the greatest moment Colts Nation could imagine.

Dwight Freeney

He was too small.

He was drafted too high.

He was a tweener.[86]

The experts had all kinds of reasons for panning the Colts' decision to take a young defensive end out of Syracuse named Dwight Freeney. Seven Pro Bowls, 122.5 sacks, and 46 forced fumbles later, no one questions Dwight Freeney any more.

He was the first pick of the Dungy era, and immediately the decision was questioned by the football intelligentsia, who asserted that Indianapolis reached for the under-sized lineman. During his rookie year of 2002, the Colts brought him along slowly. Despite four sacks early in the year, there were whispers in the local press that Freeney might prove to be a bust. None of the plays he had made were significant, and he was not in the starting lineup.

The Colts finally let him open a game in Philadelphia in Week 10, and Freeney rewarded the coaches' faith by making life miserable for Donovan McNabb, sacking him once and forcing three total fumbles. Freeney was a monster the rest of his rookie year, posting 13 sacks and a stunning nine forced fumbles. The draftniks were humiliated by Freeney's incredible skills and production.

---

[86] A tweener is a college prospect whose size and weight falls between the norms for two positions on the football field. Freeney was considered too big to play linebacker and too small to play end.

Freeney became one of the best pure pass rushers in the league and one of the greatest Colts in history. His blinding speed, coupled with a whirling spin move, complemented his deceptive strength and unstoppable bull rush. Freeney was the key to the Colts' version of Tony Dungy's Tampa-2 defense. The entire scheme was predicated on getting to the quarterback without blitzing extra men. In each of his first four seasons in the league, Freeney posted double-digit quarterback sacks. Only three players have forced more fumbles in a career than Freeney.[87] Despite constant double teams, Freeney consistently demonstrated remarkable big play ability.

Dwight's play always rose to the occasion in big games. In 17 postseason games with the Colts, Freeney accumulated nine sacks. Even in some of the Colts' most heart-breaking losses, Freeney was getting after the opposing quarterback, doing his best to keep the Colts in the game. His finest play came in the 2006 AFC Championship when he ended a key Patriots' drive with a sack of Tom Brady. With just seconds to go in the game, it was Freeney who hit Brady in the chest, forcing him to throw right to Marlin Jackson for the game-ending interception.

Freeney was granted a new contract by the Colts after the Super Bowl victory in 2006, but again there were those who questioned his impact on the defense. Unfortunately, Colts fans learned all too well just how important Freeney was to the team in 2007.

Freeney endured the first serious injury of his career against the San Diego Chargers in the ninth game. He suffered a lisfranc fracture to his foot, ending his season. The defense never recovered, and the subsequent loss to the Chargers in the playoffs showed just how much they missed his ability to generate pressure.

Freeney returned from the injury in 2008 to post one of the most heroic campaigns any Colt has ever had. Not only did he

---

[87] Robert Mathis is the all-time leader with 51, followed by Julius Peppers and John Abraham with 48 and 47 respectively.

recapture Pro Bowl form with 10.5 sacks[88] and four forced fumbles, but he chose critical moments to make his best plays. Two of his forced fumbles were returned for touchdowns by teammates in the fourth quarter of close games and directly lead to Colts victories.

Even in the tough loss to the Chargers to end the season, Freeney had two sacks to keep his team in the game. During this season, Freeney made the jump from great player to one of the greatest Colts ever.

His play elevated to another level in the 2009 campaign. The 13.5 sacks and All Pro honors do not encapsulate everything that he meant to the team. During the AFC Championship game against the Jets, Freeney landed awkwardly on his ankle as he tried to avoid hitting Jets' quarterback Mark Sanchez. The gasp from Colts fans as he limped off the field told everything about Freeney's importance to the team.

He did manage to play in the Super Bowl two weeks later, and he even recorded a crucial sack of Drew Brees in the first half. Unfortunately, he missed the first drive of the second half while the team re-taped his ankle. When he did return, he did not have the same push as before. The Colts' pass rush disappeared without him. The defense surrendered 18 points in just three drives in the second half.

Freeney finished out that big contract playing every year he was signed for and racking up 51 sacks and four Pro Bowl appearances in his final six seasons in Indianapolis. One of the few Colts to survive The Purge after the release of Peyton Manning, he continued to make his impact felt until the end.

Freeney currently ranks 18th in NFL history in sacks. As he wraps up his career, Indy fans continue to root for him to have productive seasons even though his time with the team is long over.

---

[88] Half-sacks are awarded when multiple players sack a quarterback at the same time.

Freeney most likely needs another five to ten sacks to be considered a strong contender for the Hall of Fame.[89]

What made Freeney special is more than the stats and the honors. He was the Peyton Manning of the defense. He was the one player that the other team always accounted for and schemed against. He altered games even when he failed to show up on the stat sheet.

The man who was too short and too light to make an impact in the NFL became the central defensive player on a team that won more games in a decade than any team in history.

Bob Sanders-The Zombie

I've owned jerseys from four Colts players in my life.

Jim Harbaugh.

Peyton Manning.

Andrew Luck.

Bob Sanders.

There are endless jokes about Bob Sanders.

They call him "Bobzilla."

"Bob Sanders doesn't do push ups. He pushes the earth down."

"70 percent of the earth is covered by water. Bob Sanders covers the rest."

"They call the Colts' defense Cover-2 because everyone covers just two players. Bob Sanders covers the rest by himself."

---

[89] At the time of printing, Freeney was a free agent and had not declared his intent to retire.

Few players in Colts history inspired more awe and more "ooohs" than Demond "Bob" Sanders. The hard-hitting safety out of Iowa owns a special place in the hearts of all Colts' fans.

You see, he won us a Super Bowl.

Fine. It's not exactly fair to say that Bob Sanders won the Super Bowl by himself, but looking back at the 2006 season, it's easy to see why so many people see it that way. Before the 2006 postseason, Bob Sanders was already a popular Colt. The second-round pick out of Iowa was known for his penchant for big hits from the secondary. Whenever Sanders was on the field, the run defense improved thanks to his explosive speed and raw hitting ability.

Unfortunately, Sanders has had a difficult time staying healthy. He is not a large man. Standing just 5'8" and playing at 200 pounds, Sanders hit opposing ball carriers with an authority impossible for a man of his stature. Even before the Colts drafted him, he struggled with injuries. He played in only six games during his rookie campaign before making the Pro Bowl in his second season.

In 2006, he was an on-again off-again proposition. Despite playing in the season opener, Sanders played in just four regular season games, and the Colts missed him. He made his first valiant return from injury just in time to play against the New England Patriots in Foxboro. Sanders led the team in tackles and had an interception in the critical victory that would later give the Colts home-field advantage for the AFC Championship game. Bob returned to the inactive list the next game as the defense imploded down the stretch.

The run defense was not only the worst in the league, allowing an average of 173 yards a game, but also allowed 5.3 yards a carry, a number so bad that it was nearly a half-yard worse than the next worst team. In fact, the 2006 Colts fielded one of the worst run defenses in history. While Sanders was not the only reason the Colts won the Super Bowl,[90] his presence altered the face of the Colts' run-stopping ability.

---

[90] Rob Morris's return to the starting lineup and Booger McFarland's contributions were also important.

In the playoffs, the Colts allowed only 82.8 yards a game and only 4.1 yards-per-carry. Sanders had innumerable big hits and also forced three turnovers. His forced fumble and interception in the Super Bowl made him a prime candidate for MVP honors.

As the years pass, some may come to doubt the impact that Sanders had that postseason. After all, fans have a tendency to remember special players in a way that is vastly outsized compared to their actual impact. With Sanders, however, his effect was more real than it was mythical.

Sanders was far from finished thrilling Colts fans. He came back healthy in 2007 and elevated his play. He played in 15 games and helped to hold the Colts together after Dwight Freeney was lost to injury. He did a little bit of everything, racking up 2.5 sacks, a couple of picks, 71 tackles, and the NFL Defensive Player of the Year award.

Over his final three seasons with the Colts, Sanders appeared in nine total games. The severity of his collisions took their toll, leaving fans to wonder "what if?" Sanders may well have hit too hard for his own good, and the team ultimately had to part ways with him after the 2010 season. He appeared in just two games for the Chargers before ultimately retiring from football.

Bob Sanders played in just 48 games in a Colts' uniform, but he will forever be a legend in Indianapolis.

After all, he won us a Super Bowl.

Jeff Saturday

Center is not typically a glory position in the NFL. In most cities, the team's starting center would be virtually anonymous to the average fan.

Not so for more than a decade in Indianapolis.

The heavily bearded face of Jeff Saturday was one of the most recognizable on the Colts' roster. Everyone expects the star quarterback to get the attention, but the Colts' center graced the cover of national publications as well. The story of how a cast-off lineman became a star is almost as incredible as his play on the field.

Coming out of the University of North Carolina in 1998, no one wanted Jeff Saturday. The 1998 draft saw such luminaries as Cam Quayle, Jason Chorak, and Jomo Cousins selected, but no team wanted to take a chance on an Academic All American who happened also to be an All-ACC member of a 12-1 team. The Baltimore Ravens signed Saturday as an undrafted free agent, but waived him two months later. Saturday sat unclaimed until January. He got a normal job back in Raleigh, NC but kept lifting weights, just in case an NFL team changed its mind.

Saturday was considered too small by many to play line in the NFL. He was not tall. He was not heavy. Fortunately, the Colts' system demanded slightly smaller, more agile linemen, and after nearly a year without an NFL job, Saturday got a call from the Colts. He made the team in 1999, spending most of the year as a backup guard. By 2000, he was the starting center and was in the middle of the Colts' most successful run ever.

Saturday was neither a prototypical star nor player, but he exceled in the unique demands made on him because of the Colts' offensive system. The Colts rarely huddled, and even when they did, almost all plays were subject to change. Just as Peyton Manning deciphered the defense to put the offense in prime position to capitalize with the right play call, Saturday also analyzed the rushers to call out the complementary blocking scheme to execute the play. Like Manning, Saturday's greatest weapon was his mind. Together, the two outwitted opposing defensive coordinators week after week. Saturday often joked that they are like an old married couple continually arguing and fighting, but able to read one another's minds as well.

Saturday's influence impacted the Colts for years, but everything came to a head in 2006. Few centers have ever had the kind of remarkable game that Saturday did in the Colts thrilling 38-34 win over the Patriots. The night before the game, it was Saturday who challenged his teammates, saying, "This is our time!" a cry echoed by Dungy in the team's darkest moments the following night.

During the game, Saturday made two of the Colts' biggest plays. Not only did he recover a Dominic Rhodes' fumble in the end zone for a key touchdown that tied the score, but he also delivered the signature block that freed Joe Addai to run for the game-winning touchdown.

Saturday was recognized by popular NFL writer Gregg Easterbrook as the "Tuesday Morning Quarterback Non-QB Non-RB NFL MVP" after the '06 season.

Saturday was active off the field during his time in Indianapolis. Because of his recognizable face, he became a popular pitchman for a variety of products and companies.

He was the NFL Players Association representative for the Colts and was a member of the influential executive committee. He played a pivotal role in ending the 2011 lockout, forming a bond of trust with New England Patriots owner Robert Kraft.

In the end, his play spoke louder than even he did. Saturday made six Pro Bowl squads (five with the Colts) and was a two-time All Pro. One of the most difficult decisions ever to face the Colts was whether or not to re-sign the captain of the line after the 2008 season. Saturday was set to become a free agent, and despite his importance to the team, the Colts were against the salary cap. All indications were that they would have to let the popular leader test the market. Fortuitously, a last-minute increase to the salary cap gave the Colts just enough money to sign Saturday to a deal that kept him in Indy almost to the very end of his career.

The signing not only kept the Saturday/Manning rapport together, but also served to anchor an offensive line in flux. While the 2009 Colts played better up front than the 2008 Colts, the line still suffered from numerous changes, including some during the season. Through it all, Saturday played spectacularly and managed to keep the confusion to a minimum. Had the Colts not re-signed Saturday, they likely would have experienced little of the success they ultimately had in 2009.

Like so many great players, Saturday was a victim of the Great Purge that saw many veterans cut or leave via free agency. He played one season in Green Bay, and made the Pro Bowl. Despite the fact that Manning was playing for the AFC side, the game was halted, and Saturday was allowed to deliver one last snap from his friend, though neither wore horseshoes on their helmets.

In most NFL towns, no one knows the center. In Indianapolis, everyone knows Jeff Saturday's name and face. On top of that, his name graces the Ring of Honor. To this day, hundreds of fans still wear Saturday on Sundays.

The Football Barn

There was an ice-skating rink underneath the field.

There were figure skaters performing on it.

We were deep in the bowels of Lucas Oil Stadium at a Super Bowl pre-party, surrounded by Hall-of-Famers, free food, and a band, and all I could think was, "Why is there an ice rink here?"

More than the zip line down Capitol Avenue, more than the concerts or the attention for my home town, and even more than seeing Flava Flav in the souvenir line, I think the coolest thing I saw Super Bowl week was that ice rink.

Well, that or Tom Brady taking a safety on an intentional-grounding call in the Super Bowl. That was pretty great too.

When Hoosiers build a football palace, they can't help but make it look like a basketball barn.

It became clear early in the 2000s that the RCA Dome was not a long-term solution for the Colts. It was the smallest venue in the NFL, and there was considerable controversy over what to do with the structure. Once the Convention Center attached to it had become too small to stay competitive with top-shelf centers in other cities, Indianapolis had to act. The city depends on convention traffic for continued economic development. The only way to expand the Convention Center was to take down the Dome.

Whatever lingering doubts remained about a new stadium were lifted when the NCAA committed to including Indianapolis on a permanent rotation as a Final Four host site for both men's and women's basketball. With a marquee event guaranteed to help anchor the stadium, the city and the Colts entered into an agreement to design and construct a new building. The roughly $700 million dollars that it would cost was to be paid mostly by the city and state while Jim Irsay and Colts contributed $100 million to the effort.

The result of the public/private partnership was a unique and beautiful structure. If the RCA Dome was an alien craft that landed in Indy from another time and place, Lucas Oil Stadium[91] captured the essence of the area and immediately belonged to the people of Indiana. The building was built to resemble classic basketball halls like Hinkle Fieldhouse and the immaculate Banker's Life Fieldhouse, home of the Pacers.

It was a sign that football had finally come of age in Indiana. The Colts were no longer foreign; they were native. By building "the Luke," the state had ensured that the Colts would never pack up in the night and fly off to some other city, but rather would stay and grow and thrive in Indianapolis. The new building was pure Hoosier in a way the Dome never was.

In the nine years that the team has occupied The Luke, the Colts have gone 48-24 (4-1 in the playoffs) at home. The stadium has a retractable roof, allowing the Colts to play outdoor home games when the weather permits. It took some time to get used to Peyton Manning throwing to Marvin Harrison in the Sunday-afternoon sunshine, and the open roof has allowed for sunny games as late in the year as November.

Citizens expressed concern over the considerable tax increases necessary to build Lucas Oil Stadium, and many wondered why the extra $100 million-dollar retractable roof was necessary at all. Cost overruns in the regular maintenance of the building also threatened to wreak havoc on the local budget. At one point, the IHSAA said that

---

[91] Lucas Oil, an Indiana-born company, secured the naming rights for $120 million.

138

they could not afford to hold the state football championships at the building because it was too expensive, though the Colts stepped in as corporate sponsor to ensure that they remained.

Despite the challenges and economic pressures, Lucas Oil Stadium, like the RCA Dome before it, signaled to the rest of the country that Indianapolis is a major player on a national level. As a result of building the new stadium, the 2012 Super Bowl was awarded to the city. The culmination of a dream first imagined more than 30 years ago was sweet.

Indianapolis threw a party to remember, and while football fans won't forget watching Eli Manning's Giants break the hearts of Tom Brady's Patriots (again), the rest of the country remembered Indianapolis as a fantastic host. Unseasonably warm weather and massive local crowds turned downtown Indy into a week-long party.

While the city technically "lost" a little more than a million dollars, the massive amount of goodwill and publicity the event generated more than offset the expense. The swell of civic pride and the bump in national reputation was exactly what the city leaders dreamed of all those years ago. Like the Hoosier Dome before it, Lucas Oil Stadium further established the city as a national player.

Yes, football is finally at home in Indiana. It even has its own barn.

Classic Colts

Dominic Rhodes: Running Back 2001-2006, 2008, 2010

Dom Rhodes was the epitome of a Classic Colt. He joined the team in 2001 as an undrafted rookie free agent. After the horrific knee injury suffered by Edgerrin James, Rhodes stepped in and posted 1,104 yards rushing. He was the first undrafted running back to run for 1,000 yards in his rookie season. Dom spent the next several years as a jack-of-all-trades for the Colts. He was the backup running back, a kick

139

returner, and a special-teams player. Whatever he was asked to do, he did. His kickoff return for a touchdown against the Chargers in 2004 was a key play in one of the most exciting Colts wins of the decade.

After the departure of James, Rhodes became the starting running back, filling that role in all 16 regular season games in 2006. Once the playoffs arrived, Dom became the closer, picking up most of his carries later in games. Throughout the Colts' 2006 run, Rhodes picked up key first downs late in games.

The culmination of his career in blue and white was the Super Bowl. Rhodes rushed for 113 yards and a touchdown to lift the Colts to victory. He earned the privilege of filming the iconic "I'm going to Disney World!" commercial after the game.

After a year in Oakland, Dom returned to the Colts for the 2008 season where he helped the Colts back to the playoffs as the backup running back. He had another cup of coffee with the team at the end of the 2010, season as well.

Dallas Clark: Tight End 2003-2011

Drafted out of Iowa in the first round in 2003, Dallas Clark was going to be hard-pressed to be as admired by fans as Ken Dilger was during his time with the Colts. Surprisingly, it did not take him long to become even more beloved.

From the start, Clark showed unique abilities that made him one of the most dangerous pass catchers in football. Clark's hybrid skills created matchup nightmares for defenses. Too big to be covered by corners and too fast for linebackers, Clark allowed Peyton Manning to switch freely from a two-tight-end alignment to a three-wideout alignment, all while keeping the same players on the field.

While Clark was an important but secondary weapon during his early years with the team, his true value showed during the 2006 playoffs. After suffering what was first called a season-ending knee injury in November, Clark fought to stay off injured reserve. During the four-game run to the Super Bowl, Clark was a force. He had 103

140

yards receiving against the Chiefs, followed it up with a clutch first down against the Ravens, and then pulled in a team-high 137 yards receiving in the 38-34 win over the Patriots.

Clark posted a breakout season in 2009 with 100 catches, 10 touchdowns, and 1,106 yards receiving. His play earned him both Pro Bowl and All Pro honors. Clark holds all Indianapolis Colts records for tight ends, passing Hall of Famer John Mackey in most categories.

Another victim of The Purge, Clark was well known for being a hard worker and excellent teammate and ranks among the most popular Colts of all time. He finished his career with the Bucs and Ravens before retiring in 2013 with 53 career touchdown catches.

Gary Brackett: Linebacker 2003-2011

Gary Brackett's story is as inspirational as it is incredible. An undrafted free agent out of Rutgers University, Brackett made the roster and stuck, despite enduring the death of both parents within a 16-month stretch. Brackett triumphed over the pain and adversity in his life to become the Colts' starting middle linebacker and team captain.

A great leader and one of the finest citizens to play in Indianapolis,[92] Brackett also showed a penchant for making big plays. His biggest moment was forcing a Jerome Bettis fumble in the 2005 playoffs. Brackett was the only Colts linebacker in the '00s to gain a second contract with the club as a starter. As the middle linebacker, his responsibilities include covering the middle of the field on passing downs. His injury late in the 2008 season directly led to the Colts' loss in the playoffs that year.

---

[92] Gary Brackett's IMPACT Foundation seeks to "promote health, to advance education, and to relieve the poor, distressed, and underprivileged by providing resources and opportunities to children including children who are mentally challenged, physically challenged, socially disadvantaged, or economically disadvantaged."

After the 2009 off-season, he was re-signed to a five-year contract. He played out just two of those seasons before succumbing to The Purge. He ultimately retired as an Indianapolis Colt. He is seventh all time in tackles in franchise history.

Brackett remains active in the Indianapolis community and owns multiple businesses.

Tom Moore: Offensive Coordinator 1998-2010

For nearly half a century, Tom Moore has been working the sidelines and booths of football fields around the United States. By the time he arrived in Indianapolis, he had already spent decades in coaching. He joined the Colts' staff in 1998 and took on the enviable task of helping to mold a young Peyton Manning. After Mora was fired, Tony Dungy kept Moore as Offensive Coordinator. Often a new coach will replace the former assistants, but Dungy knew Moore well. Moore was his head coach at the University of Minnesota in the 1970s. Moore helped get Dungy into the NFL as an assistant with the Pittsburgh Steelers, and later the two coached together under Chuck Knoll.

The close relationship between coach, coordinator, and quarterback proved the perfect mix. Moore's time in Indianapolis was egoless. He never sought a promotion or gunned for a head coaching job. There were never any battles over Manning audibling out of his plays. Instead, he patiently game-planned and worked with Manning to put the Colts in the best position possible on every down.

Under Moore's guidance, the Colts offense had unprecedented success thanks in part to his excellent preparation and the freedom he gave his quarterback. Perhaps the best testament to Moore was the frustration shown by Manning during Moore's brief retirement before the 2009 season.[93] Manning's public comments let everyone know just how important Moore was to him.

Despite his humble nature, Tom Moore is one of the giants in Indianapolis Colts' history. He was honored with a half-time ceremony celebrating his contributions during the 2011 season.

He still coaches as an assistant with the Arizona Cardinals.

---

[93] Tom Moore and Howard Mudd "retired" from the NFL due to a dispute with the league's pension program for assistant coaches. Both were subsequently brought back to the team as "consultants" for the 2009 season, though they retained their former responsibilities.

Chapter Eight
2009-2011
Pain in the Neck

Record: 26-22

Highest finish: 1st in AFC South (2009, 2010)

Head Coach: Jim Caldwell

Leading Passer: Peyton Manning

Leading Rusher: Joseph Addai

Leading Receiver: Reggie Wayne

The Colts were at a crossroads following the 2008 season. Tony Dungy retired, leaving the untested Jim Caldwell in charge. Marvin Harrison was released by the team after 13 incredible seasons. The club had to make a tough decision about re-signing Jeff Saturday. Coaches Howard Mudd and Tom Moore flirted with retirement after a dispute about a league policy involving pensions. Peyton Manning openly questioned the chain of communication in the organization. Many outside the Colts family wondered whether the decade of dominance was over for the club. The team had more questions than answers.

From the start of training camp, it was clear that not everything had changed. The coaches continued their policy of only playing and keeping the best players. Starting left tackle Tony Ugoh was demoted to make way for the hard-working Charlie Johnson. Young linebacker Phillip Wheeler was replaced by unheralded veteran Tyjuan Hagler. On the practice field, it was clear that the Colts were going to be an improved team. But questions still lingered. Could Caldwell guide the club as effectively as Dungy had?

Within a few weeks, it was clear the answer was yes. Indy opened with six consecutive wins. But as had happened so many times in recent seasons, injuries popped up all over the roster. Stalwarts like

Adam Vinatieri, Marlin Jackson, and Bob Sanders all suffered what turned out to be season-ending injuries.

True to form, the Colts shrugged off the bumps and bruises and just kept winning. Young players like Pierre Garçon stepped in admirably as the season wore along, but the true story of the 2009 season was Manning and his remarkable ability to lead the team to victory in the closing moments of games. Aided by Pro Bowl seasons from Dallas Clark and Reggie Wayne, Manning set an NFL record with seven fourth-quarter come-from-behind drives.

The wins came in bunches, and fans began to wonder if a perfect season might be in the making. The Colts managed to clinch home-field advantage throughout the playoffs by the end of the 13th game of the season.

After a thrilling victory over the Jaguars secured the record for most victories in a decade by a franchise, the Colts elected to rest players. Two days after Christmas, the 14-0 Colts held a slim 15-10 lead at home over the Jets. Caldwell, who up until that moment had had a flawless rookie year as head coach, benched Manning and the rest of the starters in the third quarter. The Colts' lead lasted mere minutes. By the end of the day, the perfect season was over, and controversy ruled in Indianapolis.

Many fans were outraged. They felt the Colts had betrayed them and were sure to lose in the playoffs. But as they had so many times before, Indy answered every question thrown at them. They came out and dominated their first playoff game against Baltimore, hammering the Ravens 20-3, thanks in part to an incredible play by Garçon who chased Ed Reed down the field, forcing him to fumble the football after a Manning interception.

The second-guessers were not done yet, however. To make the Super Bowl, the Colts still had to topple the Jets. The Jets only made the playoffs because of the Colts' largess. Once again, the Colts proved that the choice to rest players was the wise one. Behind perhaps the greatest performance of Manning's career, the Colts rode the right arm of their now four-time MVP to a 30-17 victory and a spot in Super Bowl XLIV.

146

Indianapolis came into the Super Bowl as a heavy favorite against the New Orleans Saints, but there was one major worry for the Colts. An injury to Dwight Freeney late in the AFC Championship game kept him from playing at full strength. The Colts jumped out to an early lead, but a series of bad plays, bad luck, and bad decisions ultimately doomed the team. Despite holding a one-point lead in the fourth quarter, the Colts lost a game they were trying to win for the first time all season. What promised to be the greatest season in Colts history ended in disappointment, 31-17.[94]

Without a second Lombardi trophy to validate years of hard work, the front office was forced to reload on the fly. Picking at, or near, the bottom of the draft year after year had thinned the roster. As the 2010 season rolled around, the cracks in the foundation began to show. Age and injuries mounted, and for the first time Peyton Manning's play led to losses rather than wins.

The Colts endured injuries at nearly every offensive position, with only Wayne, Manning, and Ryan Diem suiting up for all 16 games. At one point, Manning was throwing passes to the likes of Blair White. A devastating mid-season slump saw the Colts drop four out of five games, with three losses by a combined eight points. Manning threw seven touchdowns to 12 interceptions.

Still, as they always managed to do in the Manning Era, the Colts finished strong. With the season on the line, they ripped off wins

---

[94] *The original ending of this section read:*

There is not much that can console a fan when the team comes so close to winning it all, only to see it slip away. If ever there was a fan base that could take heart after such a loss, Colts fans can. Long forgotten are the disastrous three win seasons and yearly irrelevance. The Colts will enter the 2010 season among the favorites for a title. They still have one of the youngest squads in football and have none of the question marks that loomed over 2009. Despite the tough loss, these are the salad days for Colts fans.

The decade is done. The dominance is not.

in their final four games to snake the AFC South championship away from the Jacksonville Jaguars. Their postseason stay was short lived, however. They lost on a last-second field goal to the Jets on Wild Card weekend.

Manning never threw another pass for the Colts.

Labor strife followed fast on the heels of the 2010 season. The NFL owners locked out the Players Association as the two sides hit an impasse in negotiations. Amid the uncertainty over the collective bargaining agreement, news that Manning was having neck surgery was an afterthought. He had had surgeries before. He would be fine. He was always fine.

The collective bargaining problems eventually passed and football returned on schedule, but Manning didn't return with it. At first, news trickled out that he would miss the entire preseason and there were whispers that his arm strength hadn't returned.

The situation was worse than anyone knew. Exactly one week before the opener, rumors swirled: Manning wouldn't be coming back. Not in time for Week 1. Probably not in time for Week 17. Maybe not ever.

The Colts signed veteran backup, Kerry Collins, to steady the helm while they waited for yet another Manning surgery. Collins didn't make it three games before giving way to Curtis Painter. As losses mounted, Painter found himself benched in favor of Dan Orlovsky. Nothing helped. The Colts just kept losing football games.

They eventually broke through a couple of times, scoring victories against the Titans and Texans at home, but when the dust cleared, the wreckage of a once-proud team was all that was left.

2-14. The worst record in the league.

Without Peyton Manning to cover up the flaws, the Colts were exposed as old, injured, and generally lacking talent. Bill Polian and Jim Caldwell were held accountable and replaced with a new GM/Coach combination.

As for Manning, no one knew if he had anything left. Jim Irsay faced one of the toughest decisions in NFL history.

He released Manning and ended one of the great eras of NFL history.

Understanding 2009-2011

Jim Caldwell

His was never going to be an easy task.

There is no manual on how to replace a legend, but Jim Caldwell is qualified to write a chapter or two. The quiet, thoughtful man from Beloit, Wisconsin, coached football for more than 30 years before ascending to head coach of an NFL team. Caldwell joined the Colts, along with Dungy, in 2002 and served as Peyton Manning's quarterbacks coach before being named assistant head coach after the 2007 season.

It was that promotion that caught everyone's attention. Caldwell, an African American, interviewed for several head coaching jobs with teams trying to comply with the Rooney Rule.[95] Caldwell was impressive in his interviews and was highly regarded as a potential head-coaching candidate. Dungy had already given notice that he did not plan on coaching forever, and the Colts decided to promise the top job with the Colts to Caldwell whenever Dungy left.

Caldwell spent a year apprenticing as Dungy's top assistant, and when Dungy stepped down, the keys to the franchise were passed to him. It was Caldwell's first head coaching job, but it would be inaccurate to call Caldwell a rookie. His resume was extensive. He coached in college football for many years, notably as a member of legendary coach Joe Paterno's staff at Penn State. His only job as head

---

[95] The Rooney Rule states that teams must interview qualified minority candidates before hiring a new head coach from outside the organization.

coach came at Wake Forrest where he took an historically moribund program to a bowl-game win for just the third time in school history.

Caldwell had a near-flawless first season as coach of the Colts. For a year at least, it seemed as if nothing had changed with the departure of Dungy. The Colts avoided the kinds of mistakes that often plague teams with substandard coaching. There were no wasted timeouts, botched two-minute drives, or late game swoons. Under Caldwell, the 2009 Colts were consistently the best team down the stretch of games, content to let their opponents panic and make critical mistakes.

Even under heavy criticism from the fans and media for his decision to bench players against the Jets, Caldwell maintained his cool and stood by his decision. All season long, the only negative thing that could be said of Caldwell was that he tended to be too conservative in certain game situations.

In the end, this proved to be the only blemish on his first year. After the Colts jumped out to an early lead in the Super Bowl, Caldwell managed the game too conservatively. He made critical tactical errors. The first was his desire to run the ball three times with the Colts backed up on the Saints' goal line. Three runs and a punt gave the Saints the ball in position for a field goal, which cut the Colts lead 10-6 at the half.

Later in the fourth quarter with the Colts leading by just a point, he inexplicably sent Matt Stover out to attempt a 51-yard field goal. It had been three full seasons since the 41-year-old kicker had hit a kick of more than 48 yards. Stover's kick died at the end, leaving the

Saints with excellent field position. Within minutes, the Saints had scored what proved to be the game-winning touchdown.[96]

Though Caldwell escaped most of the blame for the Super Bowl loss, it didn't take long for heat to find him. He was wrongly criticized for calling a timeout late in the 2010 playoff loss to the Jets. With the Jets already in makeable field goal range, Caldwell gambled that a sack could save the season. When the Jets completed a pass to turn a long, but makeable field goal into a chip shot, Caldwell was ridiculed. In reality, the game was likely already lost, and the decision to attempt to force Mark Sanchez into a mistake made perfect sense.

None of the dings to his resume were as severe as what happened in 2011. With Manning gone, every weakness the Colts had was on full display week after week. Caldwell made a series of baffling in-game decisions, never fully wrapped his head around what was happening to the offense, and ultimately lost his job over the 2-14 record.

For all their flaws, however, the 2011 Colts continued to play hard and stay positive. They never checked out or quit on their coach. Most people forget that they were in one-score games in the fourth quarter 11 times that season. For as much as fans and the media characterized Caldwell as dispassionate to a fault, his teams played liked they cared.

---

[96] *The original ending of this section read:*

It is obviously unfair to judge a coach for the mistakes he made in one game, especially when there were other plays that helped determine the outcome that he had no control over. Still, as Peyton Manning continues to influence and alter the face of strategy in the NFL, Caldwell must grow in his understanding that the "old rules" no longer apply in today's pass-heavy, score-quick league.

These are ultimately minor quibbles with a man who answered the question 'How do you replace a legend?' in the best way possible: by winning.

Bill Polian was fired after the season, but Irsay debated bringing Caldwell back. While he ultimately decided to move on to a new era, Caldwell had established enough of a track record to get a second chance in the league, this time with the Detroit Lions. He has had a solid tenure there, but one which further underscores his strengths and weaknesses as a coach and a leader.[97]

He is a good man and knows how to motivate players. Unfortunately for the Colts, his over-conservative nature and failure to grasp the nuances of in-game strategy probably cost them a Super Bowl title.

Imperfect Rest

I could see it all unfolding before it happened. From the moment Curtis Painter came in, there was only one way it was going to end.

Painter dropped back to pass. Calvin Pace hit him. The ball tumbled loose, bouncing toward the end zone. The Jets fell on it.

Touchdown.

I sat in stunned disgust. I agreed with the decision to rest players, but there was something ugly about the way it all unfolded.

For the first time in history, a 14-0 football team was soundly booed by their home fans.

The Colts had created exactly the kind of problem that most teams would love to have. They had a perfect record and already controlled home-field throughout the AFC playoffs with two games still left to play. "Will they, or won't they?" became the guessing game de jour in Indianapolis. Despite hints from Jim Caldwell and Bill

---

[97] In three seasons with the Lions, Caldwell is 27-21, with two playoff appearances, but no post-season victories. He was 26-22 in his three years with the Colts.

Polian that the team would rest players, many were convinced that the Colts were duty bound to pursue a perfect season.

What happened was a perfect storm for fan outrage. Two days after Christmas, the Colts played their final home game of the season. The city was fully invested in the Colts' perfect season, and fans expected one more quality game from the team.

The first half of the game favored Indy, but was frustrating. Despite stifling defense from the Horse, the Colts were unable to capitalize on several prime scoring opportunities, even missing an extra point, and only led 9-3 at the half. After the Jets took the opening kickoff back for a touchdown, Peyton Manning led the starters on a quick scoring drive to reestablish the Colts in front by a score of 15-10. It was his final drive of the game.

After the starting defense held the Jets out of the end zone, rookie backup quarterback Curtis Painter entered the game. The result was disastrous. Painter was woefully unprepared for the moment and fumbled on his second possession. The Colts only managed one first down the rest of the game as the Jets waltzed to an easy 29-15 win.

Colts Nation was irate. The players were angry as well. It was shocking to see the Colts lay down on their home field. Management tried to explain their logic, but every explanation made the hard feelings worse. Caldwell assured fans that the Colts did not lose the game on purpose. Polian inexplicably tried to argue that 16-0 was not a significant accomplishment. Meanwhile, the fury of the fans continued to swell as the Colts only played their starters for a quarter in a blizzard in Buffalo, which lead to another trouncing.

Several factors led to the extreme reaction. First was the timing of the game. The Jets debacle was just two days after Christmas; many fans were attending the game as a gift. By not informing the fans before the game what the strategy would be, the team risked angering and disappointing thousands of parents and children who gave and received tickets for the holiday.

Second, many people were under the false assumption that the strategy of resting players in other years had led to playoff defeats. Though there was no evidence at all that resting starters hurt the team, some in the media touted the idea repeatedly. Some fans believed that the Colts were doomed to an early exit because of the decision.

Fans felt strongly about the chase for 16-0 because the hated New England Patriots had accomplished a perfect regular season only two years earlier. Some in the media felt that if the Colts could go 19-0, they would be called the greatest team of all time and would be the team of the decade. Fans wanted their team to hold those honors.

Finally, the way the game was managed did not make sense. Caldwell coached the first half conservatively. If the Colts had been honestly trying to win the game, it only made sense to maximize the number of possessions the starting offense would see. By punting twice in Jets' territory, it sent the message that the Colts wanted to lose.

From the team's perspective, they had already had two consecutive postseasons destroyed by injuries to key players. The Colts felt that a fully healthy team was more important than ancillary records. The only goal remaining was the Super Bowl, and they would allow nothing to derail that effort. They had even said so publically, though never expressly stating their specific plans.

Ultimately, though the team handled the decision to rest players in a sloppy manner, the wisdom of the decision was proved over time. While there was no excuse to disappoint people by being coy, the Colts were a banged-up football team. Several starters were not going to be available to the team regardless of whether the Colts wanted to rest players. The chase for a perfect season would have ended in the Buffalo blizzard the following week anyway. When New England star wideout Wes Welker blew out his knee in the final game of the regular season, many realized what a risk it is to play star players in meaningless games.

Moreover, when the playoffs finally arrived, the Colts were anything but rusty. Whereas the Baltimore Ravens had played a physical game in New England the week before, the Colts were at full strength. They easily handled the Ravens and the Jets and made the Super Bowl. All the foolish talk about rust or momentum proved to be nonsense that had no bearing on what happened on the field.

Ironically, the Colts' fear of injuries proved well founded as Dwight Freeney's turned ankle in the AFC Championship game possibly made the difference between winning and losing the Super Bowl.

The entire controversy was a remarkable study in just how far the franchise had come in Indianapolis. Fans are now so passionate about the team that even a 14-2 season felt strangely disappointing. Animosity over the incident was so high that it was widely cited as one the significant reasons why many celebrated the end of the Polian Regime.

Super Bowl XLIV

The Super Bowl is an all-or-nothing affair. Players and coaches prepare all season, every season for the chance to be crowned a champion. For Colts fans, the forty-fourth Super Bowl was supposed to be a coronation. In the span of a few minutes, the dreams of many evaporated in the Miami night.

The Colts were moderate favorites over the New Orleans Saints, but much of the enthusiasm was tempered with uncertainty over the status of Dwight Freeney. For the two weeks before the game, the only story line of consequence was his health. Though no one doubted he would give his best effort, there were serious questions as to how long he could be effective.

The game itself could not have started better for the Colts. The defense looked good early, and the Saints were jittery. The Colts stormed out to a 10-0 lead after Peyton Manning hooked up with Pierre Garçon on a 19-yard strike for a touchdown. The Saints tried to answer, but could only muster a field goal thanks to an unbelievable one-handed sack by Freeney of Drew Brees. Just 20 minutes into the game, everything was breaking the Colts' way.

In any close loss, there are ultimately dozens of plays that decide the outcome. For the Colts, the first and one of the most damning came after the first Saints' score. Facing a third-and-4 from the Indy 28 half-way through the second quarter, Manning hit Garçon in stride near midfield. With plenty of room to run, it looked as if Garçon could set the Colts up for another successful drive.

Unfortunately, the ball slipped right through his hands. He had struggled with dropped passes during stretches of the regular season, and he dropped one more at the worst possible time. Manning, who started the game on fire, would not get to throw another pass for the next 12 minutes of game clock.

The Saints drove the ball, but came up short of the end zone with 1:55 to play. The Saints went for the touchdown from the Colts' 1-yard line. Gary Brackett and Clint Session sniffed out the play, but the Colts were trapped against their own goal line.

Faced with the prospect of giving the ball back to the Saints, Jim Caldwell made his first strategic error of the game. Instead of allowing the offense to operate normally, he called for three run plays. The final attempt came on third-and-1 from the 10. Mike Hart was swarmed immediately, and the Saints got the ball back with plenty of time to get a second field goal to cut the lead to 10-6.

Saints coach Sean Payton knew he had to try and steal a possession from the Colts. On the opening kickoff of the second half, he attempted the first non-fourth quarter onside kick in Super Bowl history. Little-used Hank Baskett fell in front of the ball, allowing it careen off his facemask. A vicious scrum followed, and though the Colts appeared to have fallen on the ball first, the Saints were awarded the football.[98] With Freeney still on the bench having his ankle taped, the Saints sliced through the defense for a quick touchdown and the lead.

Manning responded with an impressive drive to put the Colts back in front, but there were signs that the game was going to go the wrong way. The defense was overmatched in the second half as

---

[98] Baskett claimed he had recovered the kick, but tried to stand up after hearing an official announce, "Blue ball!" Instead of staying safely on the ground, Baskett had the ball popped out of his grasp as he took to his feet.

Freeney became increasingly ineffective as his ankle worsened. The defense forced only one third down the entire second half.

After a Saints' field goal cut the Colts' lead to 17-16, the Colts took the ball for the critical drive of the game crossing into the fourth quarter. After a clutch fourth-down conversion to Reggie Wayne at midfield, the Colts drove to the Saints' 31. On third-and-11, Manning saw the matchup he wanted. Receiver Austin Collie drew coverage from linebacker Jonathan Vilma. Normally, a linebacker could never cover Collie downfield, but Vilma made an incredible play to stay with Collie. Manning threw the ball deep across the middle, but Collie stopped and tried to draw contact. There was none, and the ball fell incomplete, leaving the Colts with a difficult decision.

Fourth-and-11 is certainly not an easy down to convert, and punting was not an attractive option from the 33-yard line. Under normal circumstances, a 51-yard field goal attempt would not be an unusual decision by a head coach.

Unfortunately for the Colts, Adam Vinatieri was hurt and had not played in weeks. Caldwell called upon 41-year-old kicker Matt Stover to attempt the field goal. Stover had not hit a field goal longer than 48 yards in an NFL game in any of the previous three seasons. The choice was disastrous. Stover's kick fell short, and the Saints took over at their own 41-yard line.

The Saints responded again with another quick touchdown and two-point conversion. With 5:45 to play, the Colts suddenly trailed by seven points. Worse yet, the Saints still had three timeouts. Even if the Colts managed to tie the game, New Orleans was going to get the ball last.

The Colts got as deep as the Saints' 31, but on third-and-5, Reggie Wayne stumbled out of his break on a short pass. Tracy Porter of the Saints stepped in front of the pass and ran it back 74 yards for a touchdown that sealed the Colts' fate. Indy tried to mount a desperate final drive, but it ended at the Saints' 5-yard line as Wayne dropped a touchdown pass on fourth-and-goal.

Manning took the blame, but replay indicated that it was Wayne's stumble that caused the interception. He had tweaked his ankle in a walk through the day before, and on the key play, he never fully came out of his break to catch the pass. He was the third option on the play, but both Collie and Clark were covered. The players solemnly chalked it up to a miscommunication and refused to cast blame on anyone.

The defeat stung. A remarkable season came up agonizingly short. The whys and what ifs were numerous. What if Garçon had caught that third down? What if Caldwell had not been so conservative? What if Freeney had been healthy? What if Baskett had used his hands and not his face to recover the ball?

What if?[99]

The Choice

It was early evening when the emails came through.

More than one.

Different people with the club.

Same story.

Manning was seriously hurt.

After talking to a source in the building, I knew it was time. I called the team for comment. I expected a polite "we don't comment on rumors." Instead, the answer was muddled and confused. The ever-so-short conversation did eventually find its way to "no comment," but I knew I had the truth.

Peyton wasn't playing that Sunday. Or maybe any Sunday.

---

[99] *The following was the original ending to this section:*

The sting of defeat should not overpower the glory of a tremendous season and an unparalleled decade of excellence by the team. Still, no matter how proud I am of the team I root for, I can't help but wish this book had a happier ending.

An NFL quarterback takes dozens, even hundreds, of big hits during his career, and Peyton Manning was no exception. There's no telling for sure which savage blow lead to his career-threatening neck issues, but the problems seem to stem from an illegal hit he suffered in 2006.[100]

As Peyton aged, it was easy to see his effectiveness on deep passes wane. It was noticeable from the 2007 season on. He had knee issues. Defenses were playing him differently. There were a multitude of explanations, including just the natural wear-and-tear of a brutal league, but there was no question that physically at least, Manning was on the decline.

His neck and back issues necessitated long and painful therapies, and Manning spent many hours getting adjustments and in traction. He even had surgery for a pinched nerve before the 2010 season. Still, despite the pain, Manning kept throwing touchdowns; he kept winning games.

But then during the 2011 lockout, chronic turned into crisis. Manning had surgery on a herniated disc that alleviated much of the pain he had been living with, but there was a price. His right arm atrophied and just wouldn't bounce back. He lost feeling, even a sense of control over it. Forget throwing a football, Manning had concerns he would be able to do anything useful with his right arm.

Once the lockout lifted and the Colts returned to training camp, the team was eager to evaluate Manning's rehab progress, and the staff was horrified by what they saw. Far from being able to complete deep balls, Manning could scarcely throw the ball ten yards.

---

[100] Two Washington Redskins sandwiched Manning and ripped his helmet back awkwardly. Manning called timeout after the play. He finished the game with a masterful second half and no one gave it another thought. Years later, the then Redskins' defensive coordinator, Gregg Williams, was to be punished by the NFL for encouraging his players to target quarterbacks for injury.

Tom Moore was once asked by Jon Gruden why the Colts didn't let backup quarterbacks take more snaps. His response, "If '18' goes down, we're fucked. We don't practice fucked."[101]

18 had gone down. And, as for the rest of Moore's quote, yes, they very much were. The coaching staff had no Plan B because there was no plan to make. The Colts were hardwired on both sides of the ball to perfectly fit Manning's skills. There was no other quarterback that could have come in and made that offense function correctly. Even the defense was built around the conceit that Manning would be scoring points early and often.

With Manning flying all over the world seeking alternative treatments for his dead arm, stunned disbelief gave way to irrational denial among the coaches and front office. Kerry Collins was signed just before the final preseason game to be a stop-gap solution, and even though it was increasingly obvious that Manning not only wouldn't be ready on time and was possibly in need of another surgery, there was still no internal adjustment. The once tight-lipped building sprang leaks left and right as the reality of a season without Manning set in.

Manning had his third neck surgery in early September while the team on the field trudged through a series of losses without him. Collins quickly gave way to Curtis Painter whose play ranged from bad to embarrassing. Meanwhile, the whispers grew louder every week that Manning may never recover.

It was clear that without their star, the Colts were the worst team in football, but in fairness, the quarterback problem made a bad situation impossible. Painter was truly terrible, but too often he was not put in a position to succeed. Against the Saints on the road, the coaches opted to let him run a Manning-style no-huddle attack that resulted in one of the most humiliating defeats in franchise history.

---

[101] Ron Jaworski, *The Games that Changed the Game* (New York: Random House, Inc. 2010), 273.

As fans saw the team's record careen toward oblivion, they turned their eyes toward Stanford senior Andrew Luck, the presumptive first-pick in the 2012 draft. "Suck for Luck" became the battle-cry outside of the West 56th Street headquarters, while inside, turmoil took hold.

By December, the Colts were the front-runners for the top pick, and there was every reason to believe that they would be serious players for Luck. Knowing that his future was elsewhere, Manning conjured up a bold play to get back on the field.

Even though he could barely throw ten yards, he organized an on-field workout to illustrate that he could run an offense inside the 20-yard line. His thinking was that he could come back for the final couple of games, and play a sort of short-field quarterback. This would let the league know where he was in his recovery and be a statement that he was serious about a comeback. He wanted a showcase. He knew he was out.

The results were disastrous. Bill Polian caught wind of the unauthorized workout and put a stop to it, but not before Manning had embarrassed himself with his lack of arm strength. The mere concept was crazy enough to begin with, but the once-great passer simply couldn't throw any more. Worse yet, he had shown the organization that he very well might be done for good.

The season ended with the Colts in possession of the rights to draft Luck. Irsay took bold action in dismissing both Bill and his son Chris Polian.[102] The new regime he brought in made it clear that they had no say in Manning's role in the future of the team. Ryan Grigson and Chuck Pagano practically refused to say his name out loud in the introductory press conferences. Irsay and Manning began dueling PR campaigns using the national media to create alternate versions of reality.

Manning began conducting private workouts, working in earnest to get his arm functional. The Colts had just seen him throw and believed any comeback would have to be miraculous. People

[102] Chris Polian had been promoted to General Manager in 2009.

around the complex were so worried about his future health that when the following training camp rolled around, they spoke of Manning's comeback with sincere concern and muted fear. Everyone loved him. No one wanted to see him diminished or even seriously hurt.

The end was as painful as it was inevitable. No last-minute cell-phone videos of deep balls could change the tide that was already rolling in. Manning and Irsay had a heart-to-heart and parted ways. Manning cried as he left Indianapolis, thanking the fans for the privilege of playing for them.

Irsay made his choice.

Peyton Manning would become a horse of a different color.

The Great Purge

They just couldn't wait for it to happen. After years of being treated poorly by Bill Polian, the minute the Colts started losing, the media rose up en masse to celebrate his demise.

The end of the golden age of football in Indianapolis was never going to be pleasant. As soon as word spread that Manning was likely going to miss the 2011 season, criticism of Polian took hold. His drafts were bad. The Colts didn't have an adequate backup quarterback. He was too controlling. He promoted his own sons to important positions in the franchise. He was a big ol' dumb meany.[103]

Despite an unbroken run of success that spanned more than a decade, the local media, and as a result, the local fan base, began clamoring for Polian's head just weeks into the 2011 season. First fans

---

[103] That's not a direct quote, but it feels like it could have been.

162

complained that the Colts were too slow to play Curtis Painter. Then they complained that they stuck with Painter too long.[104]

Within the walls of the Colts complex, Polian wasn't doing himself any favors. His demeanor had metastasized from prickly to toxic thanks to the strain of the losses. When Manning took the field for his ill-conceived workout in December, Polian was furious. He marched in and put a stop to the entire proceeding.

After Manning's self-called audible, Polian's paranoia grew. One insider likened his demeanor to that of Captain Bligh.[105] He was impossible to be around, and his inability to behave in a civil manner was something Jim Irsay could no longer overlook. It wasn't bad drafts or nepotism that did Polian in. Simply put, he was a first-class pain-in-the-ass, and the owner couldn't take it anymore.

The dismissal of both Polians was the first domino to fall from the greatest run in Colts' history. Key roster components leaked away little by little culminating in the once unthinkable release of Peyton Manning himself.

Fans scarcely had time to dry their tears when later that week the team announced more staples of the Manning Era were being cut loose. Gary Brackett, Dallas Clark, Joseph Addai, and Melvin Bullitt were all released in the same afternoon. Throw in the fact that Jeff Saturday's contract had expired and he would not be re-signed, and suddenly the team was unrecognizable. Pierre Garçon left as a free

---

[104] A narrative sprang up that, had Dan Orlovsky been named the starter earlier in the year, the Colts would have won more games. Nothing could be more ridiculous. Orlovsky played horribly as a starter but had a habit of posting great numbers in the fourth quarter of blowout games. For example, he lead a late cosmetic rally in the closing minutes of a 31-3 debacle in New England. When the Colts finally won a game, it was only because Orlovsky was forbidden from throwing passes for the final 23 minutes of the game. Orlovsky was every bit as terrible as Painter. Whereas Painter would start strong and finish poorly, Orlovsky would start poorly and finish strong. Either way, both players were terrible, and far too much was made of it all.

[105] Bligh was the infamous captain depicted in *Mutiny on the Bounty*. "All he needed was a set of ball bearings," said one source.

agent as well, and Dwight Freeney was actively being shopped on the trade market.[106]

Reggie Wayne and Robert Mathis were re-signed in moves that helped solidify and stabilize the identity of the franchise, but the message was sent. Polian was gone. Manning was gone. Most every player associated with them was gone.

Something new was being built. They said it was a monster.

Classic Colts

Raheem Brock: Defensive Line 2002-2009

Raheem Brock was one of the rare Colts of the '00s who wasn't drafted by Bill Polian, but you can forgive fans for not remembering that fact. Brock was picked up by the Colts after the team that drafted him (the Eagles) did not sign him. Brock made the team in training camp and spent the next seven years as a fixture on the defensive line.

Brock was a player who did everything the team asked of him. He was frequently required to change positions. A natural end, he helped to solidify the Colts at defensive tackle as well. Brock was a hard-working hustle player who always put himself in good position to make plays. Brock could regularly be found hustling downfield to hit ball carriers. He combined with Dwight Freeney to force a key fumble of Sage Rosenfels in the great comeback in Houston in 2008.

Brock's final playoffs with the Colts produced one of his finest moments. With the Ravens trailing 20-3, Baltimore back Ray Rice ripped off a 20-yard run. Fortunately for the Colts, Brock never gave up on the play. From the other side of the field, Brock came over and punched the ball free inside the Colts' 30-yard line. The fumble sealed

---

[106] Freeney was never moved or released, meaning the Colts had to pay him more in 2012 than they would have paid to keep Manning.

the victory and served as a punctuation mark for Brock's seven years with the Colts.

Joseph Addai: Running Back 2006-2011

Joseph Addai's only flaw is that he had the misfortune of following three Hall-of-Fame-caliber running backs in Indianapolis. The Colts' 2006 first-round pick started his career with a bang. His rookie season, he became the first back to run for 1,000 yards in a season despite not starting a game.

He was a huge factor in the playoffs, scoring the game-winning touchdown against the Patriots and combining for 150 yards rushing and receiving in the Super Bowl. He followed up his stellar rookie year with a strong season in 2007. He again rushed for over 1,000 yards, scored 15 touchdowns, and was selected to the Pro Bowl for the first time.

Unfortunately for Addai, the Colts began to suffer injuries and retirements on the offensive line. The instability up front hurt his production, and a lackluster 2008 had fans wondering if Addai was destined for the bench. The Colts drafted Donald Brown in the first round in 2009 to help take the load off Addai, who struggled with injuries of his own. Addai handled the situation with grace, openly mentoring Brown and refusing to take his selection as a slight.

The result was a gritty, fan-winning performance in 2009. Addai was one of the stories of the year. His rushing numbers were far from spectacular, but it became apparent to everyone that the problem was not with the running back. Addai ran hard all year, posting 13 total touchdowns, 828 yards rushing, and 51 catches. Most importantly, Addai was a savage blocker for Peyton Manning in the passing game. His ability to pick up blitzers and give Manning time to throw opened the eyes of even his harshest critics.

Addai's signature moment came against the San Francisco 49ers. Trailing in the fourth quarter, the Colts shocked the world by running a halfback pass play. Addai, a left-handed quarterback in high school, sprinted to his left and threw to a wide open Reggie Wayne in the end zone. Wayne made an incredible diving catch for a 22-yard touchdown to give the Colts the lead for good.

Injuries took a toll on Addai through the 2011 season, and he was eventually released as part of The Purge. Whether running, receiving, blocking, or even passing, Addai did everything asked of him and deserves the honor of being a Classic Colt.

Howard Mudd: Offensive Line Coach 1998-2009

Howard Mudd was once a stellar lineman in his own right,[107] but Colts fans will remember him for the 12 years he spent coaching the men who protected Peyton Manning and opened running lanes. During Mudd's tenure as line coach, the Colts never spent a first-round pick on an offensive lineman,[108] but still managed to assemble units that consistently kept their quarterback safe. Mudd trained a group of players heavily comprised of undrafted and late-round picks and produced offensive lines that always finished among the best in football.

Mudd was gruff and demanding of his players, but well-loved as well. With Mudd coaching the line, Colts running backs three times led the league in yards from scrimmage, and the Colts finished first or second in fewest sacks per passing attempt 11 times in 12 years.

Adam Vinatieri: Place Kicker 2006-Present

By the time he came to the Colts, Adam Vinatieri was already one of the most celebrated kickers in the game. The owner of three

---

[107] Mudd was selected to the NFL's All Decade Team of the 1960s for his work as an offensive lineman.
[108] Tarik Glenn was a first-round pick before Mudd arrived. Tony Ugoh was a second-round pick, but was acquired by trading the 2008 first-round pick for the right to select him.

championship rings from his time with the New England Patriots, Vinatieri built his reputation through a series of clutch kicks, including two different kicks to win Super Bowls at the final gun.

After the debacle that was Mike Vanderjagt's last kick in a Colts' uniform, Indy fans were ready for a reliable leg again. For a long time after signing with the Colts as a free agent, Vinatieri was still regarded as a visiting Patriot, but years of drilling kicks helped fans come to accept him enthusiastically.

During his 11-plus years in Indianapolis, Vinatieri has hit numerous game-winning kicks and has rarely showed his age. In fact, at 42-years old, he led the league in field-goal percentage and was named an All Pro for the third time. At 43, he set an NFL record for most consecutive field goals made. He is the all-time leading scorer in Colts history, and will likely be inducted into the Hall of Fame.

Antoine Bethea: Safety 2006-2013

Antoine Bethea was not the most famous safety on the Colts, but he was by far the most reliable and durable. Originally a sixth-round pick out of Howard in the 2006 draft, Bethea wasted no time in grabbing a starting job and spent the next eight seasons anchoring the secondary. The team made the playoffs seven times in that span.

In contrast to the oft-injured Bob Sanders, Bethea missed only five games as a Colt, and played in 16 games a year in each of his final six seasons. Bethea's presence was a calming influence in a secondary that suffered from frequent turnover.

In multiple playoff games, Bethea forced potentially game-winning fumbles that bounced right back to the receivers in question.[109] Though the Colts ultimately lost both contests, Bethea was in the thick of the action.

---

[109] He forced Antonio Gates to fumble in overtime in San Diego in 2008 and Braylon Edwards of the Jets to fumble on the Jets' final drive in 2010.

He made the Pro Bowl in both 2007 and 2009 and ranks fifth in Indianapolis history in interceptions with 14. After leaving the Colts, he went onto a third Pro Bowl with the 49ers.

Overtime
(The Third Age of
Irsay)

The Colts ruled Indiana, but for how long?

Jim Irsay had to feel the weight of it.

The cultural dominance of the Colts was not to be taken for granted. Peyton Manning was the lynch pin holding the team and city together. The Colts had finally found their quarterback. He had all the physical skills and top draft status of Jeff George. By the end of his second year in the league he already had more come-from-behind wins than Captain Comeback did during his entire career in blue.

We all knew that neither the once-in-a-lifetime player nor the once-in-a-lifetime success he created could last forever. No one knew it better than Irsay.

In the winter of 2012, Irsay faced the toughest decision of his professional life and didn't blink. He chose the future over the past. He fired Bill Polian. He released Peyton Manning.

Irsay forcibly took back the keys to his franchise.

He arranged the flight. He set up the press conference. He brought back a legend just long enough for everyone to get a good cry in. Then he took back his football team.

The tears were scarcely dry before he green-lit a Friday-afternoon roster purge that sent 400 combined wins out the door.

The owner had learned from his first two lives in football. He had shaped the team from within as general manager. He had shaped the team from without, exercising restraint in letting Polian have a free hand. Now in his third act, Irsay was determined that the Colts be his team, run by his people, led by his quarterback.

For the Colts to continue as kings of Indiana, they would need new blood, a new direction. They needed a new hero. The one thing they didn't need was a new boss.

They already had one. Same as the old boss. The fate of the franchise was in his hands now. Things would be done his way.

Chapter Nine
2012-2016
The Lucky Break

Record: 49-31

Highest finish: 1st in AFC South (2013, 2014)

Head Coach: Chuck Pagano

Leading Passer: Andrew Luck

Leading Rusher: Frank Gore

Leading Receiver: T.Y. Hilton

It was a new dawn of harmony and good feelings.

Liberated from the "tyrannical" rule of Bill Polian, the franchise welcomed in a new general manager and a new head coach united in their efforts to erase the stain of a decade of unprecedented and uninterrupted success.[110] Together, Chuck Pagano and Ryan Grigson would rewrite the future of the Indianapolis Colts, but first they had to finish killing off its past.

The first task was to jettison the team's most recognizable player. Jim Irsay took that job on personally, sparing his new duo the shame of ushering a legend out of town. Of course, the release of Peyton Manning also created a cultural void in the building. The out-sized influence of Manning and Polian had dominated the Colts Complex for so long that it was difficult for anyone to remember what life was like before they came to town.

The Great Purge left the Colts with significant roster holes and limited cap space with which to fill them. As for the leadership vacuum, they leaned on the few remaining veterans to supply what was lost. Reggie Wayne and Robert Mathis were re-signed, allowing a small modicum of continuity with the old days.

---

[110] Yes. I'm being sarcastic. So very sarcastic.

The 2012 draft brought with it a new generation of potential stars to replace the classic Colts that had departed. Grigson loaded up on offense in the first two days of the draft, adding the long-awaited Andrew Luck, as well as tight ends, Coby Fleener and Dwayne Allen, and a new receiver in T.Y. Hilton. All indications were that the Colts were building around the quarterback once again.

Not all the changes were on the field. The sidelines would be different as well. Whereas Tony Dungy and Jim Caldwell had been low-key, quiet presences to balance the emotional energy radiated by the fiery Polian, the Colts' new coach was cut from a different cloth.

Pagano filled the complex with enthusiasm and energy. Throughout training camp, players were seen wearing t-shirts that poked fun at football experts who picked the Colts to finish with the worst record in football for a second-straight year. He challenged his team to defy expectations and to live in a vision of success. In just a few months he managed to bond with his team in a meaningful way.

No one could have ever imagined how important that vision would soon become. Just three weeks into his head-coaching career, Pagano was diagnosed with leukemia and was forced to take a leave of absence. Through the darkest of times, Pagano clung to a vision of life. His players clung right along with him.

On the sidelines, Bruce Arians, the newly-arrived offensive coordinator and a long-time Pagano friend, took over the team and performed miracles. Led by Luck's stunning come-from-behind performances, the Colts finished the season on a 9-2 streak, and by the time Pagano returned for the final game of the season, his team had already locked up a Wild Card berth. Arians won Coach of the Year for his performance.

Despite having their fundamental underlying weaknesses exposed in a playoff loss to the eventual Super Bowl champion, the Baltimore Ravens, Luck's rookie year was a success. The Colts went from the worst team in the league to being a fringe contender in just one season.

Having cleared the salary-cap rubble from the release of so many high-priced veterans the year before, Grigson followed up on his

NFL Executive of the Year Award by spending heavily in free agency in the offseason. The Colts' roster was still talent-depleted, but Grigson hoped an influx of new veteran signings would rejuvenate both sides of the ball. Aside from signing LaRon Landry, Eric Walden, and others, he also was quick to trade away draft picks, adding cornerback Vontae Davis and running back Trent Richardson in the process.

Everyone felt the team was on the verge of contention. As Pagano often put it, they were "building a monster."

The 2013 team took significant strides forward. They once again won 11 games and came up with strong showings against both eventual Super Bowl teams that year.[111] Because of the across-the-board improvement to the roster, the AFC South title returned to the Circle City.

Their incremental success on the field translated to the postseason as well. Despite falling behind the Kansas City Chiefs 38-10 in the third quarter of the first-round game, a furious Luck-fueled comeback delivered the first post-Manning victory in the playoffs. Any hopes for a deeper run were squelched, however, as another brutal January trip to Foxboro, Mass, ended in disaster at the hands of the Patriots.

Ascendency was the theme of the newly-minted Andrew Luck Era, and with an eye on the Lombardi Trophy, the Colts again doubled-down on free agency to fix an aging roster. More veterans like Mike Adams, D'Qwell Jackson, and Arthur Jones were brought in to toughen up the defense, but there was no clear strategy to address a stagnant pass rush.

There were signs at the time that success would be fleeting. Grigson's lust to "win now" had left the cupboard bare come draft day. The team had no first-round pick in 2014 thanks to the recent mid-season trade for Richardson.

Philosophically, that deal signaled the Colts' long-stated intent to become a run-first team, and though Richardson played poorly

---

[111] The Seattle Seahawks and Denver Broncos both lost in Indianapolis.

throughout the 2013 campaign, the coaching staff was determined to feed him the ball in 2014.

Practically, it didn't work out at all. The plan lasted all of two weeks, as the Colts dropped a pair of close games to open the season. Richardson was slow and overweight. Rumors swirled about his off-field habits, and it became obvious to everyone that the trade to acquire him had been a disastrous miscalculation.

To compensate for the lackluster play of their star runner, the coaching staff turned to Luck to bail out the offense. From Week 3 on, Luck threw the football early and often. His right arm set the Colts off on a six-game winning streak and made him an MVP contender. The team was winning despite the best-laid plans of the coach and general manager.

Now in his third season, the young quarterback blossomed. His heroics included 40 touchdown passes and a passer rating of 96.5, and the team charged to another 11-win season.

A favorable playoff draw inched the team forward toward a championship. The Colts dumped a flailing Cincinnati team and vanquished a hobbled Peyton Manning in Denver to advance to the AFC championship game.

A trip to the Super Bowl was almost palpable.

Unfortunately for the Colts, the boulder that is the New England Patriots rolled right back down on top of them. Again, they faltered in Foxboro, failing to even keep the game close.[112]

Despite another January setback, the mountaintop was in sight now. Sensing his team was on the cusp of greatness, Grigson again spent the winter months dialing up free agents to supply what the team was lacking. In theory, the Colts were one player away, so Grigson

---

[112] Trent Richardson was left off the roster for the game for missing the team flight. By this time, he had already been demoted to gunner on special teams. He was, without question, the worst player to ever wear a Colts' uniform, and the trade to acquire him was the most ill-fated transaction in franchise history. As a wise man once said, "I cannot describe the contempt I have for this trade."

signed three. He inked aging stars Andre Johnson, Frank Gore, and Trent Cole.

The 2015 season was supposed to be a dream-come-true for fans of the Horse, but it unfolded like a nightmare.

For three years, Luck had lugged around the rotting husk of a defense and a patchwork offensive line, fooling everyone into believing that 11-win seasons were his birthright. He had pulled off so many miracles in three years that fans believed him to be the physician that could heal himself.

As it happened, all the hits and abuse from years of extending plays and doing the impossible caught up with him. Luck battled injuries throughout 2015. He started only seven games and struggled even when he did play. After Luck was finally KO'd for the season with a kidney injury, veteran Matt Hasselbeck filled in. He led the Colts to five wins on his own, but he too succumbed to injuries before the year was out.

Without a consistent offense to bail them out, the Colts languished, slipping back to 8-8. While the .500 season was hardly an embarrassment, rumors from inside the complex grew louder. Tensions ran high all season between Pagano and Grigson, and with Pagano's contract due to expire at the end of the season, most felt the lost 2015 season would trigger a regime change.

Talk radio and Twitter feeds lit up with opinions and theories as to who Irsay would tap to redirect the franchise. To everyone's surprise, he not only declined to part ways with Pagano, he took a step further and extended both the coach and the general manager for four more seasons. For good or for bad, this was Chuck's team now.

Perhaps chastened by his apparent loss of power within the structure of the front office, Grigson's offseason priorities changed. Luck was signed to a long-term contract, but for the first time in several years, the Colts sat out the bidding war for top-tier free agents. When draft day rolled around, they invested a first-round pick in an offensive lineman, center Ryan Kelly.

The newfound emphasis on grit over flash did little to improve the fortunes of the team on the field. The Colts endured a rocky 2016 season marked by late-game collapses and inconsistent play. Despite a rebound campaign by Luck, the defense continued to languish and the team failed to capitalize on winnable home games. Another 8-8 season meant that there would be no post-season trip for the second-consecutive year.[113]

This time there were no reprieves, at least not for Grigson. A lack of quality coaching candidates perhaps saved Pagano's job, but the mountain of irreconcilable tensions between coach and general manager proved intolerable to Irsay.

The time for good feelings was over.

Grigson was fired a year after receiving a contract extension. At least for the time being, Pagano won his war of attrition. A new general manager was hired. It was now Chris Ballard's job to return the Colts to their once lofty perch as perennial contenders in the AFC.

Understanding 2012-2016

#chuckstrong

Chuck Pagano was not content just to fire up the players. He wanted to fire up everyone.

Even with a gaggle of media members shoving microphones in his face, Pagano radiated passion. "This is a great experience for all of us," he said. "This is a great time for all of us. The energy, enthusiasm, excitement." He looked each of us in the eyes, a true believer with nothing to hide. He had his dream job and was committed to enjoying every moment of it.

Charisma dripped off him the way sweat dripped off the rest of us. Pagano entered his first training camp as head coach of the Indianapolis Colts so secure in

---

[113] The Colts had not missed the playoffs in consecutive seasons since 1997 and 1998.

who he was that he even invited Tony Dungy to come and address the team, as if he was completely unconcerned whose shoes it was he had to fill. He was uninterested in being anyone but himself.

None of it felt like an act. Ron Meyer had been the consummate used-car salesman and Dungy the family pastor, but Pagano was the quintessential motivational speaker. He was genuine, sincere, and laser-focused on helping everyone around him be their best. He felt more like a life coach or a personal trainer than a football coach.

From the first day of the first practice, one thing was clear:

Chuck believed in Chuck, and he wanted everyone else to believe in him, too.

It is not possible to separate Chuck Pagano's journey to becoming an NFL head coach from his performance as an NFL head coach. His primary tool for extracting success on the field is the force of his own personality. As Ryan Grigson noted in Pagano's first interview with the Colts, "Players will run through a brick wall for this guy."[114]

He had a different kind of resume, but, after all, Pagano was hired to be a different type of coach than Jim Caldwell. Jim Irsay and Ryan Grigson found his ability to cast vision and lead via inspiration compelling. Though he had only served one year as a defensive coordinator at the NFL level and had never been a head coach at any level, what he lacked in specific experience, he more than made up for in longevity.

Pagano is both the son of a coach and the brother of a coach. He broke into the family business as a graduate assistant at USC in 1984, and by the time Irsay dialed his number, he had spent nearly 30 years coaching at the college and professional levels.

His pedigree was deeply connected with the defensive side of the ball, and given the number of times the defense had failed Peyton

---

[114] Chuck Pagano, *Sidelined: Overcoming Odds through Unity, Passion and Perseverance* (Grand Rapids, MI: Zondervan, 2014), 34.

Manning through the years,[115] Irsay's fixation with that side of the ball made sense. The hiring of Pagano represented a sea change in the way that the Colts thought about their identity as a franchise.

Pagano made it clear to everyone inside and outside of the Colts Complex that being an NFL head coach was his dream job. Though there were signs early in his tenure that he was not a master of in-game tactics, every indication was that he was destined to be successful at cultivating a new attitude in the franchise.

It took less than one season for Pagano to be confronted with a radical adjustment to his worldview and priorities. After just three games, his coaching career was put on hold. Fatigue and bruising had forced him to see his doctor over the bye week. The diagnosis he received pushed the limits of his faith. Acute promyelocytic leukemia. Cancer.

The news rocked the team and the city. Pagano immediately began chemotherapy and turned control of the team over to Bruce Arians. Over the next few brutal months, Pagano became a symbol of hope to thousands and an icon for his team to rally around.

Just weeks after his diagnosis, he visited his team in the locker room after a thrilling 23-20 victory over the Miami Dolphins. As his players huddled around their still-recovering leader, he spoke to them.

> "I mentioned before the game that you guys were living in a vision and you weren't living in circumstances. Because you know where they had us in the beginning. Every last one of them. But you refused to live in circumstances and you decided consciously, as a team, and as a family, to live in a vision. And that's why you bring things home like you brought home today. That's why you're already champions, and well on your way. I got circumstances. You guys understand it. I

---

[115] Manning's teams were on the losing end of five playoff games in which they had the lead in the fourth quarter. On three occasions, the Colts led the game with less than a minute remaining, only to lose (2000, 2008, 2010).

180

understand it. It's already beat. It's already beat. My vision that I'm living, see two more daughters getting married, dancing at their weddings, and then hoisting that Lombardi several times and watch that confetti fall on this fucking group right here. Several times, we're going to hoist that baby. I'm dancing at two more weddings. And we're hoisting that trophy together, man. Congratulations."[116]

In his darkest moment, Pagano became a bright light. He credited his faith in God, his family's strength, and the support of an entire city for aiding in his eventual victory over cancer. The Twitter hashtag #chuckstrong became a rallying cry throughout the season as his afterthought team rallied for victory after improbable victory.

By the time Pagano returned to the sideline in time for a Week 17 victory over the division champion Houston Texans, he was no longer coaching the supposed worst team in football. His Colts had already wrapped up a playoff berth.

A head coach has to be good at many things to be successful. Not everything would break Pagano's way over the next few years, and not all of his vision has come to pass. Throughout his tenure in Indianapolis Pagano has had many weaknesses.

But one thing he has never been is weak.

[116] "Chuck Pagano Speech: Colts Coach Speaks To Team After Win Over Dolphins." Huffington Post. November 4, 2012, http://www.huffingtonpost.com/2012/11/04/chuck-pagano-speech-colts_n_2073778.html.

Andrew Luck

It was hot that summer. The only shade to be found came from the long shadow of a man who wasn't even there.

It was my first training camp as a national columnist. It was Andrew Luck's first camp as a professional quarterback. The similarities ended there.

I stumbled about, constantly worried that I was parking in the wrong place, standing in the wrong place, doing the wrong thing.

Luck was eminently confident and upbeat. Everyone's attention was fixed on his every move. The comparisons between the quarterback gone and the quarterback now come hung like a muggy vapor over camp.

"He has easy heat," George Bremmer[117] said to me. It was apt. His arm was a cannon, and his delivery was effortless.

Luck's skill was overwhelming, his physical gifts obvious. Over the course of the next two weeks, whispers about Manning dried up. The new kid was almost too perfect. If Archie and Olivia Manning had ever had a fourth son, he would have been Andrew Luck.

By the time camp broke, everyone was too busy staring into the sun of a bright future to worry about the past. Luck was just so good, so soon.

Andrew Luck is the Harrison Bergeron of the NFL. Despite the ankle weights imposed on him by Chuck Pagano, Handicapper General, his natural brilliance made him soar above the stage that is the NFL, as he succumbs to a hail fire of pass rushers.

The son of a quarterback and a standout collegian at Stanford, Luck entered the league with as much acclaim as any passer since Peyton Manning. He was universally accepted as the best pro prospect in fifteen years. And, as fate would have it, he fulfilled his destiny from his rookie year on.

He took over a 2-14 roster and, on the strength of seven fourth-quarter game-winning drives, including four come-from-behind

---

[117] Reporter for the *Anderson Herald-Bulletin.*

victories, willed his team to an 11-win season. Luck showed tremendous poise in the pocket, an ability to escape from impossible situations, and an unflappability that belied his age.

Stories of Luck's bookishness and awkward nature became endearing footnotes. His ever-ballooning sack rate was blamed on the general manager. His bouts of inaccuracy were troubling, but in the face of near-constant record setting and a second season that saw him pull off one of the great come-from-behind victories in NFL history, criticism of Luck slid off his back like grease off Teflon.

The whispers started early, and before long they became full-throated yells: Andrew Luck was better than Peyton Manning! By the time he led the Colts to the AFC Championship Game in just his third season in the league after throwing 40 touchdowns in the regular season, it was all but a confirmed fact that Luck would go down in history as the best quarterback to play in Indianapolis.

In some ways, it's easy to understand how so many people were mistaken. The offensive environment of the NFL had changed drastically since Manning entered the league, and many of Luck's raw totals eclipsed those of Manning. Just look at how both quarterbacks stand against each other using many traditional metrics through their first five seasons.

	Yards	TD	INT	YPA	Rating	Sacks
Andrew Luck	19,078	132	68	7.2	87.3	156
Peyton Manning	20,618	138	100	7.3	85.9	108

The average observer would be hard-pressed to see much of a difference, and it wouldn't be a stretch to give Luck an edge. Lurking beneath those numbers, however, was the uncomfortable truth that Luck's inconsistency and propensity to take sacks was holding him back. What many couldn't see was that more sophisticated metrics[118] showed a chasm between young Manning and young Luck.

By the start of his fourth season, the cracks in Luck's foundation began to show. After a brutal first-game hit late in a loss to Buffalo, Luck struggled. He could scarcely finish the third game in the season due to an aggravated shoulder. The constant beating he absorbed throughout his career had taken a toll.

On the whole, the 2015 season was one Luck would like to forget. He was largely ineffective when he did play, and he eventually missed more than half the season with a variety of injuries, including internal organ damage. His numbers dropped off, and the Colts missed the playoffs for the first time in his career.

Despite the injuries, Luck signed the largest contract in NFL history in the 2016 offseason. After all, one injury-plagued campaign wasn't enough to dissuade anyone from the idea that Luck was the safest bet in the NFL.

In many ways, Luck rebounded for a strong 2016 season. His numbers were back up near his career-best 2014 season. He even led the team on a few miraculous drives to win games, but as the Colts

---

[118] The Football Outsiders' DVOA metric is a league-adjusted percentage that shows how efficiently a quarterback has passed the ball relative to the league. A rating of 0.0 percent would be roughly league-average.

Here is a year-by-year comparison of Luck and Manning. As you can see, Manning was consistently superior to Luck, despite similar raw totals. In fact, the gap between the two has been consistently large.

DVOA	1st year	2nd year	3rd year	4th year	5th year
Andrew Luck	-5.1%	4.6%	9.2%	-17.5%	8.0%
Peyton Manning	7.7%	36.9%	38.3%	14.7%	15.8%

stumbled to another 8-8 season, it was Luck's flaws that kept bubbling up.

The miracles that Luck produced so frequently early in his career melted away, replaced by late-game collapses and missed opportunities. By his sixth season, Manning was the league MVP. While Luck's sixth season has yet to be played, he's never seemed further away from such lofty accomplishments.

Obviously, Luck isn't Manning. No one is. No one could be. That fact notwithstanding, there are plenty of things that Luck is. He's perhaps the most entertaining player to ever wear the horseshoe. He's thoughtful and upstanding. He takes responsibility for his play. He's easy to root for.

And maybe, just maybe, he really is a kind of shackled superman, working to break free of the ties that have held him down. Before it's all over, he may just yet show us all what is truly possible.

He may not be Peyton. But he can still be the next-best thing.

Reggie Wayne: Out of the Shadows

I asked him what it was like to see Marvin Harrison's name go up in the Ring of Honor. His eyes misted.

I asked him what it was like to hear the fans chant his name the way they once chanted Reggie Miller's name. He laughed.

I shook his hand and thanked him for being the most classic of Colts. He smiled and said, "You're welcome."

It was January, 2012. I didn't think I'd ever see him play for the Colts again.

How wrong I was.

Reggie Wayne is used to being overshadowed.

At the University of Miami, Wayne put up record numbers but was better known for his teammates like Santana Moss and Andre

185

Johnson. By the time he was drafted to the NFL, he had fallen toward the back end of the first round.

When he arrived in Indianapolis in 2001, his rookie year was mostly spent watching Marvin Harrison catch balls. Harrison caught 252 balls and 26 touchdown passes in 2001 and 2002. Wayne caught just 76 for four scores. After two years in the league, people wondered if the Colts had made a mistake taking Wayne.

In hindsight, Wayne was one of the finest picks in a deep draft, but wide receivers need time to develop. For years, the Colts' offense struggled in the postseason in part because there was no true second receiver to help Marvin Harrison shoulder the load. Reggie Wayne's maturation changed that. Aided by a strong third season from Wayne (68 receptions, 838 yards, 7 scores), Peyton Manning won his first MVP award in 2003, and the Colts advanced to the AFC Championship game.

Wayne's breakout continued in the remarkable 2004 campaign. He posted his first 1,000-yard season and was part of the first trio of receivers[119] with at least 1,000 yards and 10 touchdowns. He graced the cover of *Sports Illustrated* after posting 221 yards and two scores against the Broncos in the playoffs. Wayne's huge day was the third-best receiving game in playoff history.

At first it was suggested that Wayne was lucky. He was lucky to be the number two receiver in a high-powered offense. He was lucky to play opposite an all-time great in Harrison. He was lucky to have Manning as his quarterback. The truth is that Wayne was not lucky at all. He was good.

Over the next several seasons, the league woke up to just how talented Wayne was. He put up six-straight 1,000-yard seasons. He caught at least 80 passes in five-consecutive years. He made four-consecutive Pro Bowls. In the Colts' Super Bowl victory, it was Wayne's 53-yard touchdown that got the team on the board after trailing early.

---

[119] Harrison and Brandon Stokely were the others.

Most importantly, Wayne took over as the team's top receiver. Harrison's injury in 2007 would have been more devastating, but Wayne responded by carrying the load. He led the league in yards and had his first 100-catch season. It was the changing of the guard for the Colts. Harrison's skills had faded by the 2008 season, but Wayne's were at their peak. After Harrison was let go by the Colts, some analysts foolishly wondered how the Colts would endure the loss of their number-one receiver. They had failed to realize that Wayne had already been number one for two years and was thriving in the role.

Wayne's status in the Colts pantheon took a major step forward in 2009. He showed up to training camp in a dump truck and wearing a hard hat announcing that the Colts had a "Super Bowl Under Construction." He embraced his role as top dog among the wideouts and went out of his way to mentor and train the younger Colts. Wayne's tutelage was frequently cited by Collie and Garçon as part of the reason they had so much success.

Wayne had a bevy of huge catches during the season. He had game-winning touchdown catches against the 49ers, the Patriots, and the Jaguars on the way to his second season of 1,200 yards, 100 catches, and 10 touchdowns. The only disappointing aspect of his season was the Super Bowl. Wayne struggled mightily and was involved in the Colts' lone turnover of the game. Indy's chances ended as Wayne let a touchdown pass slide through his hands on fourth down with seconds remaining.

Wayne rebounded from his devastating stumble to make his first All Pro team in 2010 thanks to a career-best 111 catches. He led the team through the difficult 2011 season, nearly gaining 1,000 yards with the likes of Curtis Painter and Dan Orlovsky throwing to him. In what promised to be his final home game as a Colt, Wayne led the Colts in a last-minute game-winning drive that culminated in a touchdown catch to beat the Houston Texans. His contract was up, however, and with so many great names departing, no one held much hope that Reggie would return.

When the Colts called the veteran receiver and asked him to return, it touched off a sequence that forever altered fans' perception of him. With Manning gone, Wayne was thrust into the role of franchise spokesman. He responded by emotionally carrying the team over his final three years in the league.

Wayne was the lynchpin holding the past and the future together. When his college coach Chuck Pagano was diagnosed with cancer, Wayne responded with an unforgettable performance to lift the team to an improbable victory. When Andrew Luck needed to be shown the ropes, it was Wayne who served as his comfort blanket, putting up 106 catches for 1,355 yards and his sixth Pro Bowl.

Before every game, Wayne ran to the end zone to soak in the cheers and as a promise to return once the game started. In the end, the afterthought, the bust, the second fiddle played more games as a Colt than any man in history.

He bridged Harrison and Hilton, Manning and Luck. When everyone else was gone, it was Wayne who made the Colts still feel like the Colts.

Robert Mathis

He was the last of his kind. With apologies to Adam Vinatieri, Robert Mathis was the last player from the golden age of Colts football to suit up. An unknown when he began, Mathis finished his career as the best-loved player on the field.

His rise from anonymity to stardom was abrupt. Originally a fifth-round selection out of Alabama A&M in 2003, Mathis forced his way onto the field with excellent special teams play and success as a situational pass rusher. By his second year in the league, he was already on his way to posting double-digit sack totals. Before long, he was entrenched as the starter at left defensive end.

Paired with Dwight Freeney, Mathis had a devastating knack for separating quarterbacks from the football. By the time he hung up his cleats, he had posted 123 career sacks, [120] but even more impressive

---

[120] Good for 17th on the all-time list. One half-sack ahead of Freeney.

were his 52 total forced fumbles. An astounding 47 of those came on sacks, an NFL record.

Despite his repeated dominance on the field, there were many who wondered if the soft-spoken Mathis was just a system player. Others attributed his success to the presence of Freeney on the other side of the formation.

All such doubts were laid to rest in 2007 after a Freeney injury. Even without his partner in crime to generate double-teams, Mathis continued to make a host of big plays, including a critical forced fumble on David Garrard against the Jaguars that helped Indy hold onto the lead in the division.

He had arrived as a player and a force to be reckoned with. During the 2008 season, Mathis made many memorable game-changing plays. His strip sack of Sage Rosenfels of the Texans helped the Colts pull off one of the greatest comebacks in history. He returned a fumble in the fourth quarter for a touchdown against Cleveland that proved to be Colts' only one of the day in a 10-6 win over the Browns. He was rewarded for his heroics with his first Pro Bowl nod, an honor bestowed again in 2009 and 2010.

In a testament to his worth, Mathis was re-signed even after the Great Purge. The brass understood that his value as a leader and a pass rusher would translate even to a new defensive system. No longer playing with his hand on the ground as a pass rusher, Mathis anchored the new 3-4 scheme Chuck Pagano brought to Indianapolis.

Though the scheme was never a good fit for Mathis, he rewarded the team's faith with two more Pro Bowl campaigns in 2012 and 2013. He was a top contender for Defensive Player of the Year in 2013 with a club-record 19.5 sacks.

Despite a suspension[121] and injury that cost him the entire 2014 season, Mathis finished his career with two productive seasons before retiring after the 2016 season.

In his final game as a Colt, he came up with a fourth-quarter strip sack in a tie game to help his team on to a victory. He stood on the field and soaked in the adulation of thousands of fans who knew that the next time they saw him, his name would be in the Ring of Honor.

The Comeback: Colts 45 Chiefs 44

When the Chiefs pierced the end zone again, I grabbed my son by the shoulder.

"Let's go, bud. This is disgusting." As we made our way to the aisle, the scoreboard read: Chiefs 38 Colts 10.

We meandered to the exit, and I told him, "Walk slow. Let's watch one last drive from the concourse. It's Luck, you know? You just never know with him."

Touchdown. Donald Brown.

"Let's hang back just one more minute."

Strip sack by Robert Mathis.

"Let's find a place to watch for a bit."

Two more touchdowns later and we were headed back to our seats. Not that we used them at all. No one sat the rest of the game.

It was my son's first playoff game. He'll never see another one like it.

---

[121] Mathis was suspended for four games for using a fertility drug that can serve as a masking agent for performance-enhancing drugs. Mathis claimed that the drug was prescribed by a doctor to aid with fertility issues. Mathis and his wife welcomed a baby girl to the family roughly nine months later, and Mathis claimed the suspension was worth it.

The 2013 Colts were as frustrating as any edition of the team had ever been. At various points in the season, they looked like world beaters.[122]

Other weeks they were non-competitive. They lost by 30 at home to St. Louis. They were boat raced by the Cardinals and Bengals. They laid an egg in prime time against the Chargers. Slow starts, uneven play, and uncharacteristic errors plagued a team that still managed 11 wins and a division title.

So when the Colts got off to a bumpy start at home against a Chiefs team they dominated just three weeks before, no one was entirely surprised. In fact, fan enthusiasm was so light before the game that Lucas Oil Stadium easily had 10,000 Kansas City fans present for the Wild Card game.

The mood was understandably sour as Alex Smith and company rolled through the Indy defense in the first half. After the Colts matched a 14-play touchdown drive by Smith with a nifty seven-play score of their own, the Chiefs kicked it into gear.

They scored on their next four drives of the half. The Colts made every conceivable type of mistake. A defensive breakdown allowed a 79-yard touchdown pass. A Trent Richardson fumble[123] set up a three-play touchdown, and after the Colts matched an earlier KC field goal, Kansas City ran the score to 31-10 with a 16-play drive that lasted over seven minutes. It capped easily the most complete and thorough systemic failure of a Colts' defense in decades.

Just for good measure, Andrew Luck threw an interception with 33 seconds to play in the half. Things couldn't get any worse.

Only they got worse.

With the Kansas City faithful roaring at the start of the second half, Luck got the Colts' comeback off to a halting start by throwing his second interception of the game on the first play after the break. The Chiefs wasted no time in converting the short field into a 28-point lead.

---

[122] They dumped the Broncos, 49ers, and Seahawks in notable upsets.
[123] His only carry of the game.

38-10.

Down four touchdowns, the Colts found a gear they had not shown all season. With Luck moving the team at near-warp speed, the Colts showed signs of a spark. In under two minutes, Luck moved the team in close for a Donald Brown touchdown run.

38-17.

Robert Mathis snuffed out the next Chiefs' drive by strip sacking Smith. Luck thanked him for his efforts by tacking on another score in less than a minute and a half.

38-24.

Even down 14, the Indy faithful had already started to believe. They were conditioned to expect dramatic comebacks from years of watching Harbaugh, then Manning, then Luck.

After a bobbled Luck throw was intercepted and turned into a short-field field goal for Kansas City with 4:17 to play in the third quarter, the crowd quieted briefly, but only long enough to catch its breath.

Luck atoned for his turnover with a six-play touchdown drive culminating in a 12-yard pass to Coby Fleener. In less than two minutes, disaster had again turned to hope.

41-31.

It felt inevitable now. Smith did his best to keep the Chiefs moving, but his ensuing drive stalled out at the Indianapolis 41. Chiefs' Coach Andy Reid ordered the ball punted back to the Colts, pinning them at their own 10-yard line with virtually an entire quarter to play.

If you ever wonder why Luck is revered in Indianapolis, look no further than the first four minutes of the fourth quarter of that game. The Colts relentlessly attacked, moving 90 yards after facing a third-and-10 from their own 10. Luck hit six-consecutive passes and scrambled for 12 yards to move the ball the KC 2.

With 10:45 to play, Donald Brown did something he had not done all season. He fumbled.

The ball squirted backwards into the waiting arms of Luck. He snatched the ball out of the air and dove head first, right arm fully extended, and leaped like he had been born on Krypton itself. He soared horizontally over Colts, over Chiefs, and over the goal line.

41-38.

Again, Smith did his best to rally his team. Having already lost All Pro runner, Jamaal Charles, to injury, he nevertheless mixed runs, scrambles, and short passes, chewing up nearly five precious minutes of the fourth quarter. The Indy D was only moderately better than in the first half, but it was enough to hold Kansas City to a field goal.

44-38.

The crowd buzzed. Normally Indy fans know to be completely silent when the team has the ball, but they couldn't help themselves. Everyone knew what was coming.

It took just four plays. It barely even took a minute.

Luck lofted a deep ball over the middle of the field to a wide-open T.Y. Hilton who streaked 64 yards for the score.

45-44.

If anything, the Colts had completed their comeback too quickly. The Chiefs still had 4:21 to work with, but needed just two plays to enter Colts' territory, needing only a field goal to win.

On fourth-and-11 with less than two minutes to play, Smith dropped back for one final pass. A first down would put the ball into field goal range and would likely lead to a Chiefs' victory.

Dwayne Bowe hauled in Smith's over-the-shoulder toss along the right sideline just as his foot nicked the chalk. Incomplete!

It was the second-largest comeback in playoff history. Luck finished the game with 443 yards passing and four touchdowns. Hilton piled up 224 yards receiving.

All down Capitol Avenue, you could hear fans shouting into the winter night, "Andrew Luck is the TRUTH."

Who could possibly argue?

The Feud

They almost had it too easy.

Chuck Pagano and Ryan Grigson were thought to be best friends, allies.[124] Their partnership had produced fantastic results on the field. Through three years, they had three post-season trips and three playoff wins on top of 33 regular-season victories. The team was considered the Super Bowl favorite in the spring of 2014. Success came early and often.

Then, out of nowhere, the stories started.

With the Colts positioned as media favorites heading into the 2015 season, strange columns appeared in the local press. Artificial outrage was generated over the fact that Pagano's contract was set to expire at the end of the year. The media began asking why he hadn't yet received an extension, and then when he was offered an extension, word leaked that the offer was insulting.

These were the first shots in what would become a multi-year saga. Despite an apparently successful collaboration up to that point, rumors of a rift between Pagano and Grigson made their way around town.

It made for great internet fodder. There was room for criticism on both sides. Grigson and Pagano had competing visions about how to win football games. The general manager muddled about in personal decisions, often favoring linemen who had fallen out of favor with the coaches.

Their personalities were incompatible. Pagano was charming with the media and well-loved by the players. Grigson, though not nearly as caustic as his predecessor, wasn't as accessible and was

---

[124] Pagano's book extoled the virtues of their relationship and the depth of their friendship.

privately despised by some corners of the locker room in a way that Bill Polian never was.[125]

By the time training camp rolled around, "the feud" was national news. While Pagano was operating on the last year of his contract, Grigson had one additional year. The impression was that Grigson had Jim Irsay's trust, while Pagano was forced to acquiesce at every turn.

Though both men denied it publicly, the chaos of the 2015 season further stressed the bond between coach and GM. At the heart of the problem was a structure that left both men reporting to Irsay. Without a clear chain of command, the working relationship deteriorated further.

On the field, the team tolerably weathered the loss of Andrew Luck to injury, managing to stay in contention until the final weeks. It was a disappointing campaign, but few teams make the playoffs after losing a quarterback like Luck. Under other circumstances, an 8-8 season would be seen as solid effort in a bad-luck year.

Pagano's contract status complicated the issue, however. The Colts couldn't do nothing. Irsay would have to take positive action to renew Pagano or to send him packing. The emotional conflict at the top of the chain of command had to be resolved first, however.

Speculation raged that Irsay had decided to part ways with one or both of them. There were public reports that Pagano would not be brought back, and despite a decided slant from the local press, his warts had been on full display.

Setting aside the complete undermining of Grigson by some in Pagano's camp, his skills as a coach were limited. Though Grigson had made serious blunders both via the draft and by trading for Trent Richardson, Pagano hadn't exactly clothed himself in glory either.

He remained an inspirational leader, but his tactical coaching skills were disastrous. His team routinely failed to start games well. His

---

[125] One of the great myths about Polian was that players didn't like him. He was genuinely well-liked by the vast majority of his players. He always took care of veterans and players spoke well of him.

understanding of how to structure a team was lacking, and his record as a developer of talent was non-existent.

With such obvious flaws in both parties, it was shocking when Irsay announced that he was not only going to give Pagano a new contract, but was also going to give Grigson a matching-length deal. At the press conference announcing the move, Irsay told of a long, honest meeting in which both sides aired their grievances.

The result was a press conference in which Irsay announced the Colts were moving forward in the same direction that they had been going. It was clear that behind the scenes, there would be a big difference. Pagano had gained the internal political advantage over Grigson. Their fates were now joined.

Of course, the 2016 season unfolded no better than the 2015 season had, and disquiet from the fans grew louder as December drew near. After a few months of quiet, rumors of Grigson's heavy hand again popped up in the media. Pagano was on the attack again.

As the season drew to a close, any number of stories leaked out. Peyton Manning was being pursued to run the Colts. No, it hadn't been discussed, but then, yes it had, and negotiations were taking place for him to buy part of the team, and Jon Gruden was being interviewed, and intrigue and drama and noise.

When word finally broke that Irsay had decided to part ways with Grigson but retain Pagano, it felt inevitable. Both men had equal shares in the slow disintegration of the Colts, but for the past 18 months, it had been Pagano that was the more aggressive in defending himself publicly.

In the end, Irsay decided the relationship between the two men was untenable, and the Colts fired their second-consecutive general manager due to personality issues.

It's hard to gauge Grigson's ultimate legacy in Indianapolis. There were periods of undeniable success, and the team never suffered a losing record during his tenure. His overall reliance on trades and free agency robbed the team of young talent, however.

196

In the end, his greatest sin may well have been not managing the media as effectively as his head coach did.

Or it was the trade for Trent Richardson.

Come to think of it, it was Richardson.

Definitely Richardson.

Classic Colts

Donald Brown: Running Back 2009-2013

Donald Brown never lived up to his draft status. He could never please the coaching staff. The fans spent most of his career complaining about him. One of the most memorable things he ever did was get Peyton Manning to curse at him during a play.

Still, when you look over the entirety of his career, it is easy to see why Brown became a Classic Colt almost in spite of himself. Brown had clutch performances in several games throughout his career, including a win over Jacksonville in 2010 that kept the Colts' playoff streak alive.

When Trent Richardson came to town, Brown was demoted, but kept his head down and worked hard. It only took a few weeks for fans and coaches to realize that Brown was the more successful runner. After Richardson fumbled in the playoffs against Kansas City, it was Brown who found himself on the field in the clutch.

He scored two touchdowns that day and averaged five yards a rush.

Brown was never a great player for the Colts, but he averaged 4.3 yards a carry over the course of his career, helped the team to two AFC Championship games, and acquitted himself well whenever he was called on.

T.Y. Hilton: Wide Receiver 2012-Present

For fans too young to remember Marvin Harrison, T.Y. Hilton is the next best thing. A late third-round pick, acquired via trade,[126] Hilton struggled to get on the field early in his rookie year, but every time he did, he made a difference. With 861 yards and seven scores in his first campaign, Hilton pushed less talented veterans for snaps on his way to one of finest rookie seasons for any Colt receiver ever despite only one start.

If that wasn't enough, he crashed the starting lineup six games into his second season, and crossed the 1,000-yard threshold for the first time. Over the next three years, he piled up three Pro Bowl spots and more than 240 catches, 18 touchdowns, and almost 4,000 yards receiving. In 2016, he led the NFL in receiving yards and averaged nearly 16 yards a catch.

In just five seasons, Hilton has already entered the top three in yards and receptions in Indianapolis history. He currently ranks fifth in touchdown receptions. No Colt has ever had more receiving yards through five seasons than Hilton. Only Harrison has more catches or touchdowns.

From his iconic "TY" touchdown dance to his game-winning heroics against Kansas City, Hilton has established himself as one of the most likeable, clutch, and productive receivers in the NFL.

Bruce Arians: Coach 1998-2000 2012

Bruce Arians didn't have a long stay in Indianapolis, but his impact on the two most visible quarterbacks in city history is profound.

---

[126] The Colts traded up five spots to take Hilton. It cost them a fifth-round pick.

He had the job of mentoring a young Peyton Manning as his quarterbacks coach in 1998, overseeing his development into one of the league's best in just a handful of seasons.

After a long and successful run as the Steeler's offensive coordinator, Arians came out of a brief retirement to take over offensive play calling duties for the Chuck Pagano regime in 2012.

When Pagano took a leave of absence to deal with cancer, Arians stepped in beautifully. He kept the light on in Pagano's office and a seat open for him on the bus, managing to inspire and rally the team without ever threatening Pagano's position.

The players responded to his brash personality and excellent tactics by charging to a playoff spot. Arians won NFL Coach of the Year for his efforts, before leaving to take the top job with the Arizona Cardinals, where he also won a Coach of the Year award.

His personality and influence will always be felt with the franchise.

Pat McAfee: Punter 2009-2016

There will never be another "Boomstick".

One of the largest personalities to ever grace an Indianapolis locker room, Pat McAfee is inarguably the best-loved punter in a city that has had several well-loved punters.

McAfee overcame an early-career incident that saw him take a drunken swim in the Broad Ripple canal. His sincere apology and general good humor led the fans to quickly forgive his youthful indiscretion. It also helped that he was one of the best punters in the league.

A two-time Pro Bowler and All Pro in 2014, McAfee had a devastating leg that saw him handle punting and kickoff duties throughout his time in town. He posted Youtube videos of himself draining 70-yard field goals, and regularly sent balls out of the back of the end zone on kickoffs.

McAfee was an excellent all-around athlete and made several highlight tackles on special teams, in addition to being a threat on on-side kicks and fake punts. His skill, good-nature, and accessibility made his jersey one of the most popular around town.[127]

He retired suddenly after the 2016 season while still in his prime. He plans to pursue media and comedy opportunities.

Vontae Davis: Cornerback 2012-Present

For most of his time in Indianapolis, Vontae Davis played on a defense that struggled to rush the passer. Normally, that makes life difficult for a cornerback, but Davis excelled where others failed.

Davis was acquired just before the 2012 season for a second-round draft pick after failing to live up to lofty expectations with the Miami Dolphins, who had used a first-round pick on him in 2009.

Davis found a home in Indianapolis and, in time, gained the consistency that had eluded him earlier in his career. Even during his first two years with the Colts, Davis was known for giving up big plays, but also for being a lock-down corner.

After signing a contract extension before the 2014 season, Davis came into his own, appearing in back-to-back Pro Bowls and snagging eight interceptions in two seasons. During this stretch, the Colts relied on blitzes to generate pressure on the quarterbacks. Davis's ability to cover without help made the scheme functional.

---

[127] McAfee's jersey was the 20th best-selling in the NFL at one point, and the second-best selling on the team behind only Andrew Luck. http://kentsterling.com/2015/12/29/indys-morning-sports-list-top-10-reasons-patmcafeeshow-has-earned-unprecedented-popularity-as-a-punter/ .

Post-Game Show

Indiana has changed.

Basketball will never be what it was, because Indiana is not what it once was either.

Oh, sure. High school basketball will always matter here. College hoops has made something of a comeback, and the Pacers currently are back to enjoying the same type of middling success they always have. Deep inside though, we know that while basketball hasn't left our hearts, it is no longer king in Hoosierland.

No, that throne belongs to the Colts now. After more than 30 years, they have roots in Indiana. There is a new generation of fans that never cheered for the Bears, Bengals, or Lions. This generation will have memories of Manning, Harrison, Freeney, and Harbaugh. This generation will have heard tales of glory from their parents who saw the team rise from the depths of the NFL to be dominant for more than a decade.

The Colts now have a waiting list with tens of thousands of people waiting to get season tickets. The Midnight Move is ancient history, and the Colts have been in Indianapolis for more years than they ever were in Baltimore. This team is Indiana's team now.

Peyton Manning has moved on to Valhalla, but fans love and cheer his replacement as fervently as they ever cheered for him. Hoosiers are now so accustomed to winning at football that they treat 8-8 seasons with disdain and demand a regime change because the team didn't win the division.

We are Hoosiers. We will always love basketball.

But the Colts are king.

Long live the king.

Appendix A
Regular-Season Indianapolis Colts Records[128]

Coaching Wins

Tony Dungy	85
Chuck Pagano[129]	40
Ron Meyer	36
Jim Mora	32
Ted Marchibroda	30

Games Played

Reggie Wayne	211
Peyton Manning	208
Eugene Daniel	198
Jeff Saturday	197
Robert Mathis	192
Justin Snow	192
Marvin Harrison	190
Rohn Stark	172
Dwight Freeney	163
Adam Vinatieri	162

---

[128] Records through the 2016 season. Stats reflect performance with the Indianapolis Colts only. Some players and coaches had stats that overlapped with the Baltimore Colts that were not counted for this list. Notably: Rohn Stark, Ray Donaldson, Donnell Thompson, and Ted Marchibroda.

[129] Pagano does not receive credit from me for wins gained by Bruce Arians during the 2012 season. Arians coached 12 games and went 9-3.

Passing Yards

Peyton Manning	54,828
Andrew Luck	19,078
Jack Trudeau	9,647
Jeff George	9,551
Jim Harbaugh	8,705

Rushing Yards

Edgerrin James	9,226
Marshall Faulk	5,320
Eric Dickerson	5,194
Joseph Addai	4,453
Dominic Rhodes	2,984

Receiving Yards

Marvin Harrison	14,580
Reggie Wayne	14,345
T.Y. Hilton	5,861
Bill Brooks	5,818
Dallas Clark	4,188

Touchdowns

Marvin Harrison	128
Reggie Wayne	82
Edgerrin James	75
Marshall Faulk	51
Joseph Addai	48

Tackles

Duane Bickett	1,052
Jeff Herrod	1,036
Eugene Daniel	720
Jason Belser	648
Antoine Bethea	569

Sacks

Robert Mathis	123.0
Dwight Freeney	107.5
Duane Bickett	50.0
Chad Bratzke	37.0
Jon Hand	35.5

Interceptions

Eugene Daniel	35
Mike Prior	27
Ray Buchanan	16
Nick Harper	15
Antoine Bethea	14

Appendix B

Games We'll Never Forget

October 21, 1984: Colts 17 Steelers 16

It wasn't the first win for the Indianapolis Colts, but it certainly was one of the most astounding. The Pittsburgh Steelers came to Indianapolis for the first time in October of 1984 to play the Colts, who were only 2-5. The Steelers were coming down from one of the great dynastic runs in history. Terry Bradshaw had recently retired, but they still had Franco Harris and Chuck Noll. They had made the playoffs in '82 and '83 and would again in 1984.

The mighty Steelers jumped out early, posting a lead of 13-0 on the Colts going into the fourth quarter. The Colts had to go with Mike Pagel at quarterback, thanks to an injury to starter Mark Hermann. Pagel helped the Colts to ten points, including a touchdown run by Alvin Moore with under six minutes to play to cut the Steelers' lead to a field goal. Pittsburgh rebounded with three points of their own, and the Colts were left to scramble with just 1:35 left on the clock.

Though Pagel got the team moving, all seemed lost as Indy faced a third-and-24 from the Indy 46 with 49 seconds to play. Pagel dropped back to throw, barely avoided a sack, and heaved the ball deep downfield in the direction of Bernard Henry. Pittsburgh defender Sam Washington reached for the ball, twice tipping it into the air where Colts receiver Ray Butler hauled it in at the Steelers' 30, then streaked into the end zone for the go ahead score. It was the Revenge of the Immaculate Reception. The floundering Colts suddenly had a lead in a game that they trailed until the final minute.

The drama was far from over as the Steelers hurried to try for a game-saving field goal. The game ended as Mark Malone hurled a deep ball that was again tipped by multiple players and into the arms of

Steeler Weegie Thompson. Thompson almost scored but was tackled at the Colts' 13-yard line as the clock ran out.

Mike Pagel, who had lost his starting job and was booed lustily by the fans earlier that day, became an instant hero, posting 13-of-17 passing for 178 yards and one unforgettable score.

The early days of football in Indianapolis did not feature many memorable wins. In fact, there were not a lot of wins of any sort. But no one at the Dome that Sunday will forget what they saw: the first miracle comeback by the Colts.

There would be many more to come. We just had to wait for them.

December 27, 1987: Colts 24 Buccaneers 6

The Colts in the playoffs? Just twelve months before, such a thought would have gotten you committed. But just a year after starting 0-13, the Colts needed only to beat the lowly Tampa Bay Bucs to claim the AFC East title. Ironically, it was the Bucs who had snaked the first pick of the 1987 draft, taking Vinnie Testaverde. The Colts parlayed their pick (and a few others) into super back Eric Dickerson. The difference was stark.

The defense relentlessly blitzed the rookie out of Miami, who completed just 8-of-31 passes on the day. Dickerson, on the other hand, did the heavy lifting. With 196 yards rushing and two touchdowns, Dickerson helped the Colts end the drama early. His big day also pushed him over the 1,000-yard mark in his nine games with the Colts. The game showed how quickly fortunes can change in the NFL as the Colts went from laughingstock to playoff threat in just one season.

January 9, 1987: Browns 38 Colts 21 Playoffs

The Colts' first playoff appearance in Indianapolis was not the glory-drenched march to victory that fans envisioned. All season the defense had kept the team in games and had made all the big plays. But on a cold January day, a relentless Cleveland run game proved too much to handle. The Colts held their own for a half, putting up 14 points, which was enough to keep the game tied. They marched the ball down to the Cleveland 9-yard line to start the second half, but penalties and an interception snuffed out the drive.

The Browns rattled off 17-consecutive points after that as Ernest Byner wore down the defense with 122 yards rushing. Indy scored a cosmetic touchdown late, but it was not nearly enough. The offense struggled most of the day. Dickerson was not able to get anything going on ground.

The Browns had been to the playoffs the two previous seasons and were simply the better team. Fans took consolation from the fact that the team was clearly on the rise, and that Indy would be back in the playoffs soon enough.

We had no idea it would take eight more seasons to reach the postseason again.

December 18, 1988: Colts 17 Bills 14

Some things just aren't meant to be. The Colts toiled through large stretches of the 1988 season, but coming into the last week they needed only to beat the Buffalo Bills, and get a little help from the Houston Oilers, to make the playoffs for a second consecutive year.

Despite great early news from Cleveland where Houston jumped out to a 23-7 lead, the Colts were floundering at home. The Bills were a good team playing for home field advantage throughout the playoffs and on the cusp of becoming a dynasty in the AFC. They stifled the Colts for most of the day, finally opening up a 14-3 lead early in the fourth quarter. Rookie quarterback Chris Chandler was ineffective against the Bills, completing just 4-of-11 passes before succumbing to an injury.

Veteran backup Gary Hogeboom entered the game with under 13 minutes to play. After getting acclimated, he led the Colts on one of the grandest comebacks in franchise history. First, he marched the Colts 80 yards downfield, hooking up with Matt Bouza with 5:36 to play to pull the Colts within 14-10. Hogeboom's entrance transformed the Colts' attack from an all-run based effort with Dickerson (who had 166 yards rushing on the day) to an efficient passing attack that saw Hogeboom complete 8-of-12 passes. After a Bills' punt, the Colts took over at their own 25 with just minutes to play.

The Colts ran the ball effectively on the game-winning drive, zipping upfield behind just two completed passes. On a key third-and-7 from the Buffalo 22, the Colts ran the ball with Albert Bentley for 12 yards. Bentley would later score the game-winning touchdown on a seven-yard pass from Hogeboom with only 1:18 to play. The Colts had won, and the Dome was jubilant. All the Oilers had to do was close out the Browns, and the Colts would be back in the playoffs.

The celebration was cut short some 20 minutes later as the news from Cleveland turned for the worse. The Browns had rallied with three-straight touchdowns, stunning the Oilers and devastating the Colts. Hogeboom's bitter-sweet heroics in his final game with the Colts were enough to win the game, but not enough to put Indy in the playoffs.

December 24, 1989: Saints 41 Colts 6

For a third consecutive season, the Colts' playoff hopes rested upon one final game. Indy needed only to beat the 8-7 Saints to clinch an AFC Wildcard berth. The Colts struggled in the first half, but kept contact with the Saints and trailed only 10-6. At the start of the second half, Donnell Thompson forced Saints' backup quarterback (and local legend) John Fourcade to fumble. The ball was recovered by the

Saints, however. After trading punts, the Saints executed a reverse handoff on a long punt by Stark. The ball was returned all the way to the Colts' 12. The Saints punched in the score, and at 17-6, the rout was on. The offense went in the tank, producing only three first downs in the second half.[130] Dickerson had another quiet day at a key time, rushing for only 54 yards.

The frustrating loss coupled with the poor play of Jack Trudeau (118-yards passing, one interception) forced the Colts to take drastic measures in the ensuing off-season.[131]

December 22, 1990: Colts 35 Redskins 28

It is easy to forget now, but there was a lot of hope brewing during the 1990 season. Jeff George's finest moment as a Colt came during his rookie season. On a nationally-televised Saturday Night game, the Redskins came to Indianapolis. The Colts were fighting to get to at least eight wins for the fourth-consecutive year and needed to capture the last two games of the season to do it.

Indy jumped out to an early lead thanks to a 42-yard strike by George to Stanley Morgan, but the Redskins took control in the middle of the game with 18-unanswered points. The Colts trailed 25-14 with a minute gone by in the fourth quarter when George went to work. In the final quarter, he was 10-of-13 for 117 yards and two of his three touchdowns. His 12-yard pass to Bill Brooks pulled the Colts even with the 'Skins at 28 with 1:21 left to play.

The Redskins tried to avoid overtime with a hurry-up drive, but nothing went as planned. They ran for a loss of three before Mark Rypien looked for Art Monk in the flat on second down. Donnell Thompson tipped the ball, and it deflected to rookie corner Alan Grant. Grant picked off the errant pass and sprinted 25 yards down the sideline for the game-winning score.

---

[130] Their second first down occurred with 2:10 to play in the game.
[131] They drafted Jeff George.

213

Though the Colts dropped the final game of the season and finished 7-9, George's career highs of 252 yards passing and three touchdowns gave Colts fans hope that greatness was in store for 1991.[132]

October 25, 1992: Colts 31 Dolphins 20

Steve Emtman's career was not memorable except for one unforgettable play and a lot of injuries. In a back-and-forth game with the Dolphins, it was Emtman who provided the defining moment.

The Colts entered Miami as two-touchdown underdogs, but battled the Dolphins close all afternoon. Clarence Verdin[133] atoned for an earlier fumble and kept the Colts in contention with an electric punt return of 84 yards for a score, but the Dolphins answered every point the Colts put up. Dan Marino gave the Dolphins a 20-17 lead with just six minutes to play.

Jeff George led the Colts on a run-heavy final drive that leaned on backup running back Ken Clark. George scored the go-ahead touchdown on a play-action-fake bootleg. He barreled over a Miami defender at the 1-yard line, and the Colts took the lead 24-20 with 1:32 left. No one celebrated yet. Dan Marino was still lurking on the other sideline.

The master of the two-minute drill went to work, zipping the Dolphins upfield. Marino worked the ball inside the Colts' 10-yard line and had four opportunities to steal the win from Indianapolis. As the clock ticked down under 30 seconds to play, Marino threw incomplete three times. On his fourth-down attempt, he fired the ball for the win, but Emtman, who was rushing the passer, reached up instinctively and

---

[132] It wasn't. The '91 Colts went 1-15.
[133] Verdin referred to himself as CNN because "I talk 24 hours a day."

snagged the pass from just a few yards away. The 290-lb. lineman pulled the ball down and rambled 90 yards for a dramatic touchdown, sealing a 31-20 win.

Two games later, Emtman blew out his knee and was never the same.

September 10, 1995: Colts 27 Jets 24 (OT)

This is the game that changed everything.

The week before, quarterback Craig Erickson had struggled early against the Bengals and was pulled in favor of Jim Harbaugh who nearly brought the Colts all the way back for the win. One week later, Coach Ted Marchibroda made the same move. He benched the newly acquired, highly-paid young QB and stuck in the aging veteran, Harbaugh.

A legend was born.

Despite trailing 24-3 in the third quarter, Indy roared back. With a 0-2 start looming, defensive tackle Tony Bennett returned a fumble for a score. Harbaugh's first two drives had ended with a goal-line fumble and a missed field goal, but in the fourth quarter, he hit Sean Dawkins and Marshall Faulk for touchdowns to force overtime. The Jets dropped some passes in the extra period, giving the Colts an opening. After Harbaugh hit Dawkins for 24 yards on third-and-10, Mike Cofer drilled a 52-yard field goal to win it, leaving the Jets stunned. Marchibroda decided that it was Harbaugh who best rallied the team behind him and quickly named him the starter for the rest of the year.

October 8, 1995: Colts 27 Dolphins 24 (OT)

Harbaugh did it again. Just weeks after his first miracle comeback, he pulled off a furious rally on the road against a divisional foe. Trailing 24-3 at half time, the Colts had little chance of upsetting the undefeated Dolphins. In a stunning turnaround, Harbaugh earned his nickname, Captain Comeback, by throwing three touchdown passes in the second half, the last with just a minute to go in the game. The Colts won the toss in overtime, and Harbaugh hit all five of his passes to set up a game-winning 27-yard kick by Cary Blanchard.

October 15, 1995: Colts 18 49ers 17

The very next week, the defending Super Bowl Champion 49ers came to Indianapolis, and a blowout loss was expected. Leading 7-6 late in the first half, the 49ers eschewed a field goal that would have put them up four points at the half and decided to go for a touchdown on fourth down. The Colts stopped the fourth-down play, and the game went back and forth the rest of the afternoon.

The Colts gave up the lead on a 51-yard field goal late in the game that made the score 17-15, 49ers. Harbaugh responded by driving the Colts into 49er territory where Cary Blanchard buried a 41-yard field goal. The 49ers had a chance to win the game with 41 seconds left, but Doug Brien missed a 46-yarder, and the Colts hung on.

The win improved the Colts to 4-2 and gave them much needed credibility. The Indianapolis Colts had never beaten any defending champion, so to knock off the 49ers was big news. At the time, it was considered perhaps the most significant win in 12 years of Colts football in Indianapolis.

December 23, 1995: Colts 10 Patriots 7

The Colts' run to the playoffs appeared set in stone as the lowly Patriots came to Indianapolis for the last game of the season. Indy only needed a win to secure the final AFC playoff spot. The Pats were 6-9 and had already lost at home to the Colts. But as it turned out, nothing that day would be easy.

The Pats posted a first-half touchdown, and the Colts could not move the ball at all as they lost Marshall Faulk to a toe injury. At half time, defensive tackle Tony Siragusa fired up the team. He threw a fit in the locker room, turning over tables and letting his teammates know their performance was unacceptable.

In typical Cardiac Colt fashion, they rallied in the second half. Harbaugh tied the game in fourth quarter as he hit seven-straight passes, ending with a 14-yard touchdown pass to Floyd Turner. Cary Blanchard then hit a big field goal with five minutes to play in the game. The Colts led 10-7, but the game was far from over.

The defense did the rest. With just over two minutes to play, Tony Bennett sacked Bledsoe to force the Patriots into a long field goal attempt that they missed. Jason Belser chipped in a clutch interception of Bledsoe with less than a minute to play. The game still was not over until Ashley Ambrose picked Bledsoe again with just seconds to play.

It took eight years, but the Colts were back in the playoffs for just the second time since coming to Indianapolis.

January 7, 1996: Colts 10 Chiefs 7 Playoffs

The Colts won their first playoff game at San Diego. It was exciting, but not necessarily a stunning victory. Their reward was a trip to frigid Kansas City to play the top-seeded Chiefs, who led the AFC with a 13-3 record. To make things worse, the Colts were without Faulk and Siragusa. Game-time temperature was 11-degrees with a wind-chill of minus-9. Kansas City boasts one of the strongest fan bases and best home-field advantages in the NFL. The 9-7 Colts were of little worry for the mighty Chiefs.

KC scored first on a Steve Bono pass to Lake Dawson, but those would be the last points that they would put on the board. Harbaugh hit Floyd Tuner to tie the game at 7-7 in the second quarter. Blanchard put the Colts ahead 10-7 in the third.

Desperation mounted for the Chiefs, and Marty Schottenheimer benched an ineffective Bono in favor of future league-MVP Rich Gannon, but it made no difference. The defense was stout and limited the Chiefs to field goal attempts. Fortunately for the Colts, kicker Lin Elliot had the worst day of his career and missed three different tries.

His last was a 42-yard attempt with 37 seconds left. As he lined up, everyone in every living room in Marion County swayed hard to the left, begging for the kick to lose its line. As Elliot slumped off the field in disgrace, the Colts danced openly on the frozen plain.

We were just one game away from the Super Bowl.

September 15, 1996: Colts 25 Cowboys 24

The Colts visited the Super Bowl champion Cowboys in one of the great "what if" games in history. Having narrowly missed a chance to play them in the title game the year before, the Colts responded by showing the world what a fantastic opportunity was lost. The Colts opened the game strong with a long drive, but had to settle for a field goal. The Cowboys answered with 21-straight points to take a 21-3 lead.

After a pair of field goals, the Colts opened the second half with a 48-yard catch-and-run by Marcus Pollard, whose first career touchdown cut the Dallas lead to 21-16. One drive later, Harbaugh found Ken Dilger to put the Colts on top 22-21.

The teams traded field goals as the Colts took the lead 25-24 with :51 to play. The Cowboys frantically drove down field but could only reach the Indy 40. As time expired, Dallas kicker Chris Boniol's 57-yard field goal carried as far as the crossbar but bounced off.

The Colts upset the World Champions on the road and opened the season 3-0. Harbaugh ripped off his helmet and ran up and down the sidelines in celebration yelling, "How 'bout them Colts!"[134]

---

[134] Mike Chappel, *Indianapolis Star*. September 16, 1996, C1.

October 6, 1996: Bills 16 Colts 13

This game may have cost the Colts a Super Bowl.

Indy marched into Buffalo at 4-0 and riding high after a tough Monday Night win over the Dolphins. In one of the most physically brutal games in years, the Colts suffered one injury after another. Jim Harbaugh was sacked six times and pressured on 16 other occasions.

After being down 10-0 in the second half, Harbaugh led the team on a clutch drive late in regulation to take the lead. Unfortunately, the Bills' defense was firm down the stretch, and the Colts' final two drives in regulation were not enough to run out the clock. Bills' backup quarterback Todd Collins rallied Buffalo for the game-tying field goal with 15 seconds to play.

In overtime, the Colts could not move the ball, and the Bills again drove for three points. During that game, the Colts suffered multiple injuries that would greatly affect the team the rest of the year. The Colts did win the next week, but a season that started so promisingly went south soon after. The team limped into the playoffs, but never really recovered from this game.

December 29, 1996: Steelers 42 Colts 14 Playoffs

The Colts got their rematch with the Steelers in the playoffs in 1996, but the result was no more pleasing the second time.

Indianapolis took the lead 14-13 on a Eugene Daniel interception return for a touchdown just before the half. What no one in the stands knew was that Harbaugh had broken a tooth, cut his mouth, and was spitting blood between plays.

The Steelers went on a bruising drive to start the second half and ran more than ten minutes off the clock. The Colts fumbled the ball in their only possession of the third quarter, and though they were only down seven points with 15 minutes to go, the Steelers were

219

already on the goal line, hoping to put the game away. They soon pounded in for a two-score lead. The Steelers poured on the points in the final period, resulting in a lopsided final score that belied how closely matched the teams were.

November 16, 1997: Colts 41 Packers 38

Few things went right for the Colts in 1997, but they did manage to upset the reigning World Champions for the third-consecutive year. The 0-10 Colts faced the Green Bay Packers. The crowd at the RCA Dome was comprised of at least 40-percent Packer fans, and the game started according to script. The Pack already led 14-3 when Paul Justin, filling in for an injured Harbaugh, drove the Horse downfield for a score.

The game was a wild affair. A pair of Brett Favre turnovers were returned for scores, the second on a nifty lateral from Lyle Blackman to Jason Belser. To everyone's surprise, the Colts inexplicably led 24-14. The Pack roared back with two-straight touchdowns to make the score 28-24. A Blanchard field goal cut the deficit to one at half time.

The Colts and Packers traded three points before a Lamont Warren touchdown early in the fourth quarter and a two-point conversion with just over six minutes to go gave the Colts a seven-point lead, 38-31.

Favre responded quickly to tie the game at 38, leaving the Colts just enough time for a game-winning drive. Justin moved the Colts downfield and picked up a key first down to Dilger at the 1-yard line with 1:22 left. The Colts then smartly killed the clock, kneeling on the ball until there were just seconds remaining.

Blanchard banged home the game-winning field goal as time expired. The devastated Packer fans left the dome with chants of "If you can't beat us, you'll never win the Super Bowl!" ringing in their cheese-clogged ears.

220

November 15, 1998: Colts 24 Jets 23

There was not much to excite the fans early in Peyton Manning's rough 1998 rookie season. However, his season turned the corner as the line improved and as the game "slowed down" for the young quarterback.

In mid-November, the Jets came to town. Up 16-10 just before half time, the Jets ran back a missed 63-yard field goal for a touchdown. The incredible 104-yard return put the Jets in control.

Facing their ninth loss in just ten games, Manning led the team back in the third quarter, throwing his second of three touchdowns. With just three minutes to play in the fourth quarter, the Colts had the ball with time for just one more possession and were trailing 23-17.

Manning led the team on a 15-play, 80-yard drive in only 2:40. The drive almost stalled at the 38-yard line, but he found running back Marshall Faulk for 18 yards on fourth-and-15. Manning then threw to Marvin Harrison for a first down at the Jet 14 with 52 seconds left. On second down, Manning hit Pollard over the middle. He was hit at the 3-yard line but desperately stretched out toward the goal line for the winning score. Though just a rookie, Manning gave us all an inkling of what was to come.

It was the first of Manning's record 52 game-winning drives.

October 10, 1999: Dolphins 34 Colts 31

The link between Peyton Manning and Dan Marino was obvious from the start. Manning squared off against the legend in his first career start, but it was a pair of contests in his second season that everyone remembers best. Both games were instant classics.

The first game should have been Manning's coming-out party as the Colts sought to start the season 3-1. Manning had a stellar afternoon, throwing for 274 yards and three touchdowns. Indy led 31-27 late, but Marino had the ball with one last chance to win the game. After moving the ball to midfield with 1:22 to play, he was sacked by Shawn King and fumbled. Indy recovered, and the game appeared over as fans in the dome went wild.

The play was reviewed, however, and despite visual evidence that Marino did in fact fumble, the ruling on the field was inexplicably overturned, and Miami was awarded the football after an incomplete pass.

Fans in the RCA Dome were irate because the in-stadium replay clearly showed the ball was pushed loose into Marino's face mask. Despite the fact that the correct call had been made, the official later claimed not to have received the same angle the fans in the dome saw. He over-turned the play based on incomplete evidence, violating the principle of the replay system. Miami finished off the late touchdown drive as Marino hit Oronde Gadsden in the corner of the end zone to win the game for the Dolphins.

December 5, 1999: Colts 37 Dolphins 34

Indy exacted revenge on the Dolphins in Miami just a few months later. The Colts entered the game with a chance to secure their hold on an AFC East division title, their first since 1987. The Colts jumped out to an early 17-3 lead thanks in part to an incredible run by Edgerrin James, who was playing near his boyhood home for the first time in his career. He would finish with 131 yards rushing and two touchdowns.

The Dolphins battled back, and the game see-sawed all afternoon with the Colts staying just a step ahead. The Dolphins tied the game at 31 early in the fourth quarter, but the Colts answered with a field goal by Mike Vanderjagt to take a 34-31 lead. With less than a minute to play, Marino put the Fins in position for an Olindo Mare field goal to tie the game at 34.

The Colts had blown a big lead, but Manning still had 29 seconds to play and two timeouts. Thanks to a couple of quick strikes, to Marvin Harrison, Manning deftly moved the team to the Dolphins 35-yard line. Vanderjagt banged home a massive 53-yard kick at the gun to win the game.

Manning and Marino had dueled twice and come out even. It was to be Marino's final season in the NFL, but Manning's legend was only just beginning.

January 16, 2000: Titans 19 Colts 16 Playoffs

This loss would haunt Colts fans for years. The Colts dropped their final regular season game of the 1999 campaign and in the process, lost starting linebacker Cornelius Bennett. His injury would shape the team's policy on resting starters before playoff games for seasons to follow.

The first ever playoff game in the Dome ended miserably as the more experienced Titans came into Indianapolis and won. The loss of Bennett was keenly felt when the Colts gave up a long touchdown run to Eddie George in the second half. It was the only Titans' touchdown of the day, but four field goals by Al Del Greco proved to be just enough points to upset the home team as 10,000 Titans fans cheered the upset.

The offense never got on track. Manning did hit a big play early, but receiver E.G. Green was carried off the field with a broken leg after the clutch 33-yard gain. This delayed the game about 15

223

minutes and brought the offensive momentum to a halt, forcing them to settle for the second of three field goals. The Colts had a potential game-swinging 87-yard punt return called back when replay showed Terrence Wilkins had stepped out of bounds in Indianapolis territory.

The Colts made a late play for the comeback, recovering an Eddie George fumble to set up the lone touchdown, a Manning keeper with less than two minutes to play. They could not recover the final onside kick, however, and the first playoff game in Indianapolis was a losing one.

As disappointed fans streamed out of the Dome, people could be heard yelling, "Go Pacers!"[135]

December 24, 2000: Colts 31 Vikings 10

Despite a rough patch in the middle of the 2000 season, the Colts caught fire late in the year. Still, they needed a small miracle in the final weeks of the season to make the playoffs. Eight different games broke Indy's way, and entering the final game of the year, they only needed a win against the powerful Vikings at home to qualify for the playoffs. The Vikings won the NFC North and would eventually advance to the NFC Championship game. The game was played on Christmas Eve, and the Colts made sure their fans had a happy holiday.

As was the case often in those days, Manning, Harrison (12 catches, 109 yards, three TDs), and James (207 total yards) carried the load for the club. Manning threw four touchdown passes, including three to Harrison and a 52-yard catch-and-run to The Edge. Indy jumped out to a 21-10 lead by the half, and the Colts cruised through the second half as the Vikings played their reserves.

The Triplets were the heart and soul of those teams, and in a virtual playoff game, all three came up large to lift the Colts back to the playoffs for a second-straight year.

---

[135] Rob Schneider, *Indianapolis Star*, January 17, 2000, A8.

224

December 30, 2000: Dolphins 23 Colts 17 (OT) Playoffs

The Colts were optimistic heading into their game with Miami just a week after beating the Vikings. After all, Indy had handled the Dolphins in Miami with relative ease just a few weeks earlier. The Colts started hot with Manning leading three-consecutive scoring drives to give Indy a 14-0 lead at halftime despite a failed fake field-goal attempt and a dropped touchdown by Jerome Pathon.

The second half belonged to the Dolphins, who punished the Colts with a relentless ground attack. Despite a strong push from Miami, the Colts still held a 17-10 lead with less than five minutes to play. Unfortunately, the defense wilted in the Florida sun and gave up a 14-play, 80-yard drive that resulted in the Dolphins tying the game with :34 left.

The Colts won the toss, and Manning put the Colts on the edge of field goal range before Jim Mora made a critical coaching error. Indy faced a third-and-12 from the Dolphins' 42-yard line. Manning hit Harrison for 11 yards, but there was a five-yard penalty called on the Dolphins. Mora had choices. He could take the penalty, moving the ball to the 37, setting up third-and-7. He could have elected to go for it on fourth-and-1. Instead, he decided to decline the penalty and kick for the game winning score, sending Mike Vanderjagt on to the field.

Vanderjagt shanked the field goal attempt, sending the ball well wide of the goal posts. The Dolphins took over on their own 38-yard line and proceeded to run right over an exhausted defense. Lamar Smith eventually scored the game-winning touchdown from 17 yards away.

The loss was Mora's record-tying sixth consecutive playoff loss.

November 24, 2002: Colts 23 Broncos 20 (OT)

The Colts invaded Denver on a snowy night in late November. Though later ignored by those who questioned the Colts' ability to win on the road in bad weather, the Colts and Broncos played a classic back-and-forth game that marked one of the best games of Mike Vanderjagt's career.

Denver jumped to a 13-3 lead in the third quarter, but the Colts responded with a pair of lightning-quick touchdown drives. After another Denver score, midway through the fourth, put the Colts down three, Indy failed on a couple of attempts to even the game.

The defense held serve throughout, and Manning and the offense took over at the 20 with 1:40 to play, still needing a field goal. Manning worked the ball downfield, finding Qadry Ismail for 16 yards on fourth down to put the team in range for a 54-yard try with just seconds on the clock. Vandy came out onto the snow-covered field and buried the tying kick.

In overtime, the Colts won the toss and marched for the win, stalling out around the Broncos' 34. Tony Dungy considered punting the ball back to the Broncos, but Justin Snow convinced him to let Vanderjagt attempt a 51-yard field goal. He hit the kick for the win.

January 4, 2003: Jets 41 Colts 0 Playoffs

The 2002 Playoffs were forgettable in every way for the Colts. The Colts had to play in the Meadowlands on a soggy field, and the offense never gained traction. After the Colts came up empty on their first possession, the Jets hit a 54-yard touchdown pass. Indy responded with a nice drive deep into Jets' territory, but had to settle for a 41-yard field goal attempt which Mike Vanderjagt promptly missed.

The Jets' answered with a field goal drive of their own and then kicked off to the Colts, up 10-0. Troy Walters fumbled the kickoff, and the Jets recovered. A few plays later, the Jets took a 17-0

226

lead, and the rout was on. The Indy offense never moved the ball effectively as Edgerrin James was held to 14 yards on nine carries.

October 6, 2003: Colts 38 Buccaneers 35 (OT)

The Colts opened the 2003 season with four-straight wins before traveling to Tampa to play the defending World Champion Buccaneers. The Bucs were Dungy's old team, and the game was played on his birthday. At first, it was an unhappy homecoming. The Colts trailed 21-0 at the half and 35-14 with just 5:09 left to go in the game. The Bucs had the best defense in football at the time and had dominated the Colts on both sides of the ball.

Out of nowhere, the Colts started to fight back. Brad Pyatt ripped off a long kickoff return. The Colts pounded it in for a quick score. The Colts then recovered an onside kick and drove the ball into Tampa territory. On fourth down from the Tampa 28, Manning hit Harrison for a touchdown to cut the Bucs' lead to 35-28. The Bucs barely recovered another onside kick but could not run the clock out on the Colts, garnering a bizarre personal foul call to stop the clock before the two-minute warning.

Unbelievably, the Colts had the ball with a chance to tie the game. Manning and Harrison hooked up yet again for 52 yards to set up a short TD run to force an extra period. The Horse survived an OT possession by the Bucs, and then Manning went to work. He carved up the Bucs on third down, moving the ball into field-goal range.

Instead of winning the game for the Colts, Vanderjagt shanked a 44-yard attempt. However, the officials stepped in with a "leaping" penalty on the Bucs[136] to give Vandy a second try. This time, he slammed it off the upright from 29 yards. The ball glanced through for one of the most improbable comebacks of all time.

---

[136] Leaping, the act of running up to the line, jumping in the air, and landing on other players, is a 15-yard personal foul.

Manning and Harrison were the heroes of the game. Harrison was called out by a "miked up" Keyshawn Johnson in the first half.[137] By the end of the game, Keyshawn was on the bench nursing an injury, and Harrison was triumphant with 176-yards receiving and two scores. It was the first time in NFL history that a team won a game when trailing by 21 points with fewer than five minutes to play.

November 30, 2003: Patriots 38 Colts 34

Few regular seasons games changed the history of the NFL like the Patriots and Colts' clash in Indianapolis in 2003. Both teams entered the game with records of 9-2. The Patriots jumped to an early 17-0 lead and appeared to take firm control after Bethel Johnson returned a kick 91 yards for a score just before the half. It quelled a rally by the Colts and put the Pats up 24-10. Another Pats' score put the Colts down by a normally insurmountable 21 points. On top of everything else, rookie Dallas Clark went out of the game with a knee injury. He was lost for the season.

Indy fans had learned earlier in the year not to give up. Manning rallied the team with three touchdown passes in the second half to tie the score. Johnson struck back with a 67-yard return to set up a go ahead score for the Patriots. Dungy faced a tough decision with just over three minutes to play. He sent in Vanderjagt who closed the gap to 38-34. The Colts defense held Brady, and the Patriots' punt traveled only 18 yards.

The Colts had a chance to win the game. They drove inside the red zone and had first-and-goal from the 2-yard line, but without Clark, the goal-line offense was ineffective. James was stuffed for a yard on two plays, and Manning threw incomplete to Aaron Morehead.

---

[137] The Monday Night Football crew put a microphone on Johnson the entire game. In the first half, he mocked Harrison for catching too many short passes.

On fourth-and-1 with 14 seconds to play, James was stone-walled for a loss by Willie McGinest. McGinest had faked an injury on an earlier play to stop the Colts from hurrying to the line. His miraculous recovery ensured that it was the Patriots and not the Colts who had home-field advantage in the 2003 playoffs. This same epic scenario would be played out two more times in Colts' history with Indianapolis winning both matchups,[138] but on this day the Patriots prevailed and went to the Super Bowl.

January 4, 2004: Colts 41 Broncos 10 Playoffs

As late as 2003, there were still rumors that the Colts might leave Indianapolis. The franchise needed a win at home to convince the locals to ante up for a new stadium. Manning had not won a playoff game. Much hung in the balance going into the 2003 playoffs, but with one spectacular game, Manning wiped it all away.

He assaulted the Broncos from all sides, throwing touchdown passes of 31, 46, 87, and 23 yards in the first half. Harrison had two touchdown catches, including a hilarious score when he caught a short pass, fell to the ground, realized that no Bronco had touched him, got to his feet, and ran into the end zone.

For the game, Manning was 22-of-26, 377 yards, and five touchdowns. It was the fourth "perfect" game[139] in NFL playoff history, and the first by a quarterback with at least 20 attempts.

January 11, 2004: Colts 38 Chiefs 31 Playoffs

The 2003 Chiefs were the top seed in the AFC, posting a sparkling 13-3 record and nine Pro Bowlers. The Colts rolled into

---

[138] It happened again in the 2006 Playoffs and in the 2009 regular season.
[139] 158.3 was Manning's rating under the NFL system. 158.3 is the maximum rating a quarterback can achieve in a game and is considered to be a "perfect" game.

Arrowhead Stadium, and fans enjoyed one of the most spectacular offensive days in history. The two teams combined for 69 total points and 842 yards of total offense with zero punts.

The Colts and Chiefs traded scores all game with Indy maintaining a steady lead throughout. The Chiefs simply could not stop the Manning-led attack as he torched their secondary for 304 yards passing and three touchdowns. Edgerrin James played an important role as well, running for 125 yards and two scores. Harrison chipped in 98 yards receiving. Many consider this to be Manning's finest game, considering the difficulty of doing it on the road in January in one of the NFL's most daunting stadiums. The defense had little success in stopping the Chiefs, managing to force just one missed field goal and an important fumble. The Colts had to score on every drive and did so, moving on to the AFC Championship Game.

January 18, 2004: NE 24 Colts 14 Playoffs

The Colts finally had a chance to go to the Super Bowl but faced a team that already had one title *and* sported an incredible defense. As brilliant as Manning was for the first two games of the playoffs, he was equally bad against the Patriots that day, playing unquestionably the worst game of his career. Manning ended the Colts' first drive of the day by throwing a terrible interception in the end zone with the Pats already leading by a touchdown.

After a Patriots' field goal, Manning threw a second interception that the Pats also turned into points. The Colts' third drive ended in a safety as a snap on a punt play went out of the end zone. Finally, the Colts finished the half with a Harrison fumble. They trailed 15-0.

Indy answered in the second half with a touchdown, but two more Manning picks killed any momentum the Colts had. Manning was given one final drive, trailing 20-14 with two minutes to play. Needing 80 yards to win the game, the Colts couldn't gain even one.

230

On both third and fourth downs, Marcus Pollard was grabbed by the Patriots. No penalties were called.

The Colts' Super Bowl hopes were dashed, but the ramifications of the slipshod way the game was officiated would resonate throughout the NFL for years.

September 9, 2004: Patriots 27 Colts 24

The league kicked off the 2004 season with a rematch of the AFC Championship Game. By now, the matchup was clearly the marquee rivalry in the NFL, as the debate about whether Brady or Manning was the better quarterback began to rage through internet chat rooms.

The game was played on a rainy Thursday night and was tight throughout. The lead changed hands several times, but the Colts had the chance to seize control of the game late. Trailing by just a field goal, the Colts had the ball first-and-goal at the 1-yard line with less than four minutes to play. James fumbled the ball while trying to reach out for the end zone, giving the Patriots new life. The Pats eventually punted the ball back to the Colts.

Manning hit a long pass to Brandon Stokley for 45 yards, and the Colts were in business inside the New England 20 with more than a minute to play. On third-and-8, Clark missed a block, and Manning was sacked for a 12-yard loss, forcing the Colts to attempt a game-tying field goal from 48 yards with just 24 seconds to play. Vanderjagt missed the critical kick, and the future was clear.

The Colts would have to go back to New England in the playoffs.

December 26, 2004: Colts 34 Chargers 31 (OT)

Peyton Manning's quest to break Dan Marino's touchdown record had come down to the final two weeks. The San Diego

231

Chargers came to Indianapolis for a game that would decide which of the two playoff teams would be the third seed in the AFC. Manning threw an interception in the red zone early in the game as Drew Brees helped the Chargers to an early lead thanks in part to a 74-yard catch-and-run by LaDainian Tomlinson.

Manning did manage to toss his 48th touchdown on a shovel pass to James Mungro, but the Colts fell further behind on the first play of the fourth quarter thanks to another LT touchdown. Trailing by 15 points, the Colts answered as Dominic Rhodes returned the ensuing kickoff 88 yards for a score. The Colts and Chargers traded empty possessions including a missed field goal by Vanderjagt, and Indy found themselves with the ball and just 3:42 to play. Fourth down came quickly, and it appeared the Colts would punt. Manning waived the punt team off the field and hit Reggie Wayne for 19 yards on fourth-and-4 from the Indy 26 as the clock hit the two-minute warning.

Buoyed by the bold move, the Colts offense clicked into high gear, moving the ball to the 21-yard line with a minute to play. Manning then hit Stokley in stride for a touchdown to break the record. Manning had drawn the play in the huddle. The 49th touchdown only drew the Colts to within two points, however. Edgerrin James snaked into the end zone to capture the two-point conversion, tie the game, and force overtime.

In the extra period, Indianapolis won the toss, and Manning wasted no time putting them in position to secure the victory. He hit Stokley and Wayne for a combined 55 yards, and Mike Vanderjagt pounded home the winning field goal. Manning had not merely broken the single-season touchdown record; he had done it in spectacular fashion.

January 16, 2005: Patriots 20 Colts 3 Playoffs

After dismantling the Broncos in the first round of the playoffs, the Colts traveled to Foxboro to face the hated Patriots once again. On a cold and snowy day, the Colts' offense struggled to get rhythm. The Colts went three-and-out on three of their first four possessions. The Patriots were not generating much offense, either, but did manage a pair of first half field goals. The Colts overcame a fumble by Dominic Rhodes and got inside the 5-yard line just before the half but had to settle for a 6-3 deficit. The game was played exactly to the style the Patriots wanted.

Early in the third quarter, the pivotal moment arrived. The Colts faced a third-and-4 from their own 48. Stokley gained three yards with a catch. On fourth-and-1 inside Patriots' territory, Dungy ordered the Colts to punt. It was the last realistic chance that they had to win the game. New England took the football and went on a 15-play, 87-yard drive for a touchdown. The Pats ran the ball 11 times and took more than eight minutes off the clock.

After another Colts' punt, the Patriots followed with another touchdown march that covered 94 yards and took more than seven minutes. Trailing 20-3, the Colts' final hopes were extinguished as Wayne fumbled in Colts' territory. The Patriots physically dominated the Colts on offense and defense as another promising season ended in defeat.

January 15, 2006: Steelers 21 Colts 18 Playoffs

January 15, 2006, is a day that will live in infamy for Colts' fans. The Colts had the NFL's best record and the top overall seed in the AFC. They were facing a Steelers team that they had soundly beaten just a few weeks earlier. Expectations were high, but everyone wondered how the team would respond to the tragic events in the Dungy family. The Steelers came out with a brilliant game plan, throwing the ball early in the game, and took a two-touchdown lead. The Colts could only manage a first half field goal as Manning faced a relentless Steelers' pass rush. A Tarik Glenn false start on the goal line pushed the Colts back on a key third down.

Late in the third quarter, the Steelers were leading 21-3. Again, Manning did what he could to bring the Colts back. Facing a fourth-and-2 from the Colts' 36, Manning once again waived the punt team off the field, converting the fourth down. Two plays later, he hit Dallas Clark for a 50-yard touchdown to bring the Colts within 10.

Later in the fourth quarter, the Colts scored another touchdown after a Manning interception was overturned by replay on a controversial call.[140] Manning took advantage and drove the Colts for another touchdown. The two-point conversion pulled the Colts to within a field goal at 21-18.

The Colts got the ball back with 2:31 to play, but Manning absorbed two more sacks, and it appeared the Colts' dream was over. The Steelers needed only to run the ball in from the 2-yard line with 1:20 to play. Then, a miracle happened. Gary Brackett popped the ball loose from Jerome Bettis, and it hopped into the arms of Colts' corner Nick Harper. Harper sprinted downfield and for a moment it looked like he might return the fumble all the way for a winning touchdown. Unfortunately, he was running on two bad legs,[141] cut the wrong way, and was tackled by quarterback Ben Roethlisberger who barely tripped Harper.

The Colts still had the ball at their own 42, however, and Manning drove the Colts inside the Steelers' 30. He tried to hook up with Wayne in the end zone, but the ball bounced off his hands. On a key third down, the two miscommunicated, and the Colts were forced to settle for a 46-yard field goal, well within the range of the most accurate kicker in NFL history.

Vanderjagt gave a poor effort, and the ball hooked to the right by a wide margin. It was never on line. He never gave it a chance. Instead of overtime, the Colts had been defeated.

---

[140] The referee misapplied the rules of possession and wrongly nullified a Troy Polamalu pick.

[141] He had suffered a knee injury but also had a knife wound in his leg. He had allegedly been involved in a domestic dispute with his wife the night before the game, and it was reported that she had stabbed him.

October 29, 2006: Colts 34 Broncos 31

"Last team with the ball wins" sounds like a cliché, but it summed up many games the 2006 Colts played. This late afternoon classic was no exception. Heading into the game, the Denver defense had been nearly impenetrable, allowing only 44 points through six games. Denver had specifically designed their defense to beat Manning and the Colts. The Broncos had the lead at the half, 14-6, but the Colts went on a long drive to start the second half and then converted a short field, after recovering a Jake Plummer fumble, for a 20-14 lead.

The infamous 2006 run defense completely collapsed. Indy gave up a rushing score at the end of the third quarter and trailed once again, 21-20. Vinatieri nailed a long field goal as the Colts answered, but the Broncos rammed the ball down the field for a 28-23 lead with less than seven minutes to play.

Manning and Wayne responded by completely abusing a young Denver corner named Darrent Williams, and with 3:56 to play, the Colts took a 31-28 lead after a touchdown and two-point conversion. With the 2006 Colts, no lead was safe. Linebacker Gilbert Gardner abandoned his responsibility on the next Denver possession, and the Broncos ripped off a 48-yard run. Fortunately, the defense stiffened, and they had to settle for a long field goal to tie the game with just 1:49 to play.

1:49 was too long to give #18 and, unfortunately for Denver, Williams was still on the field. Manning calmly moved the Colts downfield to set up a game-winning field-goal try from Vinatieri with just two seconds on the clock. By the time the dust had settled, the Colts were 7-0 for the second-straight season. Wayne finished the game with 138-yards receiving and three scores. Manning's offense beat the defense designed to stop him by posting 34 points.

January 13, 2007: Colts 15 Ravens 6 Playoffs

It was revenge time in Baltimore. The 2006 Ravens had the top-rated defense in football, and the fans had a serious grudge to settle. For the Colts, the question was whether or not the Indianapolis defense that had shut down Larry Johnson in the first round could re-emerge for a second week.

The game was a defensive battle from the beginning, as both teams took turns stifling the other. The biggest play of the game came mid-way through the second quarter with Baltimore on the Colts' 5-yard line. On third-and-four, Antoine Bethea intercepted McNair's pass at the 1-yard line, ending their scoring threat. Manning then led the Colts 65 yards in six minutes, capped by a monster 51-yard field goal by Vinatieri, giving the Colts a 9-3 lead.

The game was still in doubt until the fourth quarter. With Indy clinging to a 12-6 lead, the offense executed a 14-play, seven-minute drive. Facing a third-and-5 from the 45, Manning threaded the needle to Clark for a 14-yard gain. His clutch catch enabled the Colts to all but run out the clock before Vinatieri knocked home his fifth field goal of the game to seal a 15-6 win.

February 4, 2007: Colts 29 Bears 17 Super Bowl XLI

In a pouring rain, the Colts accomplished what so many doubters said they could never do. They won the Lombardi Trophy.

The Bears led early thanks to a game-opening kickoff return by Devin Hester. Manning put the Colts on the board later in the first quarter with a sensational 53-yard touchdown pass to Wayne. Despite yielding another score to the Bears, the defense played well and forced three first-half turnovers, including a forced fumble by Bob Sanders. Manning had a big first half, and the Colts were able to overcome their early deficit to take a 16-14 lead into halftime.

The Colts and Bears traded field goals into the fourth quarter when Kelvin Hayden picked off an errant Rex Grossman pass and ran

236

it back for a touchdown, barely keeping his feet in bounds. The Colts punished the Bears on the ground in the second half and walked home with a 29-17 win that was more comfortable than the score indicated.

Both running backs had huge days as the Bears were unnerved by Manning early in the game. They adjusted by trying to stop the pass and were stunned by Manning's willingness to call run play after run play. Addai and Rhodes had a combined 190 yards rushing, 74 yards receiving, and a touchdown. Sanders had a forced fumble and an interception, but the MVP award went to Manning for making the whole show work.

November 4, 2007: Patriots 24 Colts 20

Both the Patriots and the Colts were undefeated through the first two months of the 2007 season, and the hype machine cranked up to eleven for a titanic struggle.

The game was no disappointment. Indianapolis entered the game missing five starters and lost Anthony Gonzalez and Dallas Clark as the game went along. Joseph Addai provided one of the plays of the game at the end of the first half with a spectacular catch and run of 73 yards to give the Colts a 13-7 advantage as time expired.

For three quarters, the Colts' defense suppressed the vaunted Pats' offense, and Manning's one-yard run with 9:50 to play put the Colts up 20-10. Brady and Randy Moss would hook up repeatedly in the final quarter, however, and the Pats scored two quick touchdowns to take a 24-20 advantage.

The Colts struggled to protect Manning as the backup left tackle, Charlie Johnson, played poorly in the fourth quarter. Manning was sacked and fumbled on each of the last two drives. The loss gave the Patriots the pole position in the race for the number one seed in the AFC as they went on to have a perfect season. For the Colts, the mounting injuries would soon ruin a promising season.

237

January 13, 2008: Chargers 28 Colts 24 Playoffs

Despite a season full of injuries, Indy still claimed the second seed in the AFC. Hopes were high for a strong end to the season as several players, including Harrison, were slated to return for the playoffs. The Colts started the final game in the RCA Dome on fire. They quickly took a 7-0 lead on the Chargers before Kelvin Hayden intercepted Phillip Rivers. With the Colts driving in Chargers' territory, Manning found Harrison for a big first down. As Harrison scrambled for extra yards, the ball was popped loose. The rest of the game was a struggle.

Despite a 10-7 halftime lead, Colts' fans could see the season was in jeopardy. The Colts had no pass rush. Robert Mathis and Raheem Brock had returned to the lineup, but were still hobbled and ineffective. The lack of pass rush eventually sank the Colts as the Chargers put up two third-quarter touchdowns to take the lead.

With the Colts trailing 21-17 in the fourth quarter, Manning found Anthony Gonzalez down the left sideline for a touchdown, and the Colts had a 24-21 advantage. Manning had a spectacular day, passing for over 400 yards. He completed his first 14 passes of the day and did not throw an incompletion until the middle of the second quarter. The only blemishes were two interceptions both of which hit his receivers in the hands.

Despite an injury to Rivers, the Colts defense proved unable to hold the lead. The defense appeared to get a stop with just eight minutes to play, but the Chargers were given new life thanks to a facemask call against Marlin Jackson on third down. Billy Volek then burned the Colts with screen passes, and soon Indy trailed 28-24.

The Colts drove inside the Chargers' 10 but failed on four-consecutive goal-to-go plays as Shawne Merriman abused rookie left tackle Tony Ugoh, forcing Manning to throw incomplete on fourth down. The Colts got the ball back with 1:30 to play, but Clark dropped a fourth-down pass to end the Colts' hopes and deny everyone the coveted rematch with the undefeated Patriots.

September 14, 2008: Colts 18 Vikings 15

If you let Manning hang around in a game, he'll find a way to win it, even on one leg.[142]

The 2008 season got off to a rough start with a loss to the Bears at home, and the situation was bleak as the Colts had to go on the road to play a bruising Vikings team in Week 2. Indy had to play the game without several starters, including Clark and Jeff Saturday. The Vikings dominated the game early, but could not convert their drives into touchdowns. Five-consecutive field goals by the Vikings had the Colts staring at a 15-0 deficit in the third quarter. The Colts offense could not generate any traction as Manning simply did not look comfortable.

Gonzalez changed everything, however, thanks to a heady and crazy play. Facing a third-and-6, Manning threw a long bomb to Gonzo who made the catch deep in Vikings' territory. As he cut and weaved for extra yards, he spotted Wayne trailing him. Gonzalez lateraled the ball back to Wayne who hurdled Vikings as he tried to cover the final 18 yards to the end zone. Though he was tackled at the 1-yard line, it set up the Colts' first touchdown and gave them new life.

Both teams traded missed field goals before Manning locked in during the fourth quarter. He took the Colts on a two-play touchdown drive capped by a touchdown pass to Wayne and a two-point conversion by Dom Rhodes to tie the game with six minutes play.

---

[142] Manning was coming off of knee surgery at the start of the 2008 season.

The defense held fast, limiting the Vikings to just 17 yards in their final two possessions. Manning's offense took over at midfield with 1:07 left. On third-and-9, Manning threw one of the best passes of his career, hitting Wayne in stride over the middle for a 20-yard gain down to the Vikings' 29-yard line. After a spike to stop the clock, Vinatieri buried a 47-yard field goal to pull out the improbable win.

October 5, 2008: Colts 31 Texans 27

The 2008 season could have been a disaster for the Colts, but a series of incredible comebacks helped the team make the playoffs. No comeback was more improbable than the resurrection that took place in Reliant Stadium.

The Colts have owned the Texans from the creation of the Houston franchise, but with Manning ailing and several other starters hurt, the Colts came off their bye week at 1-2. They got off to a fast start against the Texans, but Houston answered a 10-point Colts' lead with 27-consecutive points of their own. Leading 27-10 with just 4:10 to play, the Texans were a lock to win their second game ever against the AFC South bullies.

The comeback began quietly. Manning found Tom Santi from seven yards out on fourth down to give the Colts a "cosmetic" touchdown. Indy's onside kick attempt failed, and the Texans took over at the Colts' 41, needing only to pick up a first down or two to ice the game. On third down, backup quarterback Sage Rosenfels broke the pocket and scrambled for what appeared to be a sure first down.

Raheem Brock and Dwight Freeney had other ideas. Rosenfels dove into the air, spun, and was hit by both defensive linemen. Freeney knocked the football loose,[143] and Brackett scooped it up, sailing 68 yards down the sideline to cut the Texans' lead to 27-24.

---

[143] The fumble was officially credited to Brock, but replays show that it was Freeney who caused it. This play also created the infamous "Rosen-

240

The pressure mounted on Houston. There was 3:36 to play, and the Colts still had a timeout. They had to come up with some yards or they risked giving Manning the ball one last time. Again, the defense stiffened, holding the Texans to just one yard on the first two downs. On third down, Rosenfels rolled away from pressure by Freeney and appeared to be in the clear. He never saw Mathis chasing him from behind. As Rosenfels cocked to throw, Mathis dove through the air like Superman, slapping the ball away. The ball bounced right to Mathis who fell on it.

The Colts were already in field goal range for the tie, but would not need their kicker. Addai ran for 15 yards before Manning found Wayne for an incredible one-handed spinning catch that put the Colts in front 31-27 with two minutes on the clock. In the span of just 2:10, the Colts posted 21 points. It was the Monday Night Miracle all over again. Melvin Bullitt picked off Rosenfels on the Texans' final drive, giving the defense three forced turnovers in the final four minutes.

January 3, 2009: Chargers 23 Colts 17 (OT) Playoffs

The 2008 Colts were a special group. They played hard. They never quit. They were also deeply flawed. In the final game of the 2008 season, their flaws caught up with them.

The Colts' reward for a 12-4 record was a cross-country flight to play the red-hot Chargers in San Diego. The game was typical of most Colts-Chargers clashes. It was close, hard fought, and decided in the final moments. Throughout the first half, the teams traded points, but the Colts' offense struggled thanks to terrible field position. Chargers' punter Mike Scifres had the game of his life, pinning the Colts inside the 20-yard line six times.

The Colts trailed 14-10 before Manning caught the Chargers napping. He hurried to the line and quick snapped the ball before they

copter" meme.

were set. Reggie Wayne strolled, untouched, 72 yards into the end zone to give the Colts a 17-14 lead mid-way through the third quarter.

The lead almost held. With 2:41 to play, Scifres again hit a perfect punt that stuck the Colts at their own 1-yard line. The Colts needed just one first down to end the game, but they could not get it. Two runs gained eight yards, but on third-and-two, tight end Gijon Robinson forgot the snap count. As Manning dropped back to pass, an unblocked Tim Dobbins sacked him back to the Colts' 2-yard line.

After a long return of a line-drive punt by Hunter Smith, the Chargers took over at the Colts' 38 and easily converted the good field position into a game-tying field goal. They won the toss in overtime, and the Colts never saw the ball. They had several opportunities to win the game, but a series of bad tackling and bad calls cost them. The Chargers' Darren Sproles eventually scampered home for the game-winning touchdown.

The Colts' defense never overcame the loss of linebacker Gary Brackett to a late-season injury. In the past, he had always helped to contain Antonio Gates, but without his coverage abilities, Gates burned the Colts for eight catches and 87 yards.

September 21, 2009: Colts 27 Dolphins 23

For several years, teams had been trying to beat the Colts by running the ball and working the clock. In Week 2 in Miami, the Dolphins worked the strategy to perfection…and still lost. When voters listed reasons to give Manning the MVP award, this game was at the top of the list. Manning opened the scoring with an 80-yard touchdown pass to Clark on the first play from scrimmage. The Dolphins responded with a nine-play touchdown drive of their own.

All game long, the Dolphins' unusual "Wildcat Offense"[144] caused fits for the Colts' defense. The Dolphins rushed for 239 yards

---

[144] The Wildcat Offense puts a running back in the quarterback position and tries to overpower the defense with an extra blocker.

242

and held the ball for more than 45 minutes of game time. Normally, that is the formula for total domination.

Manning had other ideas. He led the Colts to three touchdown drives, including two in the fourth quarter. Each drive covered at least 79 yards and lasted only 12 seconds, 3:17, and 32 seconds respectively. The final touchdown came on a screen pass to Pierre Garçon who put the Colts in front with 3:29 to play in the game. The Dolphins mounted a final drive, reaching the Indianapolis 30, but Antoine Bethea picked off Chad Pennington in the end zone to seal the victory. The game marked the first time in NFL history that a team won despite less than 15 minutes of possession.

The tight win on Monday Night Football became symbolic for the Colts' season. Throughout 2009, they found ways to win week-in and week-out no matter what the opponents attacked them with.

November 15, 2009: Colts 35 Patriots 34

The Colts and the Pats have played some of the greatest games of the decade of the 00s, but they saved the best for last. New England came into Lucas Oil Stadium in prime time desperate for a win that would vault them back to the top of the AFC. They came out of the tunnel scorching as the Colts simply could not cover Randy Moss. Tom Brady threw two second-quarter touchdown passes as the Patriots opened up a commanding 24-7 lead.

One thing is certain, however: Peyton Manning can never be counted out. Though the Patriots dominated much of the game with leads of 31-14 with 13 minutes to play and 34-21 with less than four minutes remaining, Manning attacked the Patriots relentlessly. He posted two quick touchdown drives of just 2:04 and 1:49 to pull the Colts within 34-28 as the clock neared two minutes. If the defense could stop the Pats one last time, the offense would get a chance to steal a win.

After rookie Jerraud Powers nearly intercepted Brady on third down, Patriots coach Bill Belichick was faced with a difficult decision.

There was only 2:08 on the clock, and the Colts only had one timeout left. The Patriots had fourth-and-2 from their own 28-yard line. The conventional choice would have been a punt, but Belichick knew his defense could not stop Manning and the Colts. In one of the most shocking coaching decisions ever, Belichick ordered his offense back onto the field.

Brady hit running back Kevin Faulk with a short pass that would have been good enough for a first down, effectively ending the game. Instead, Faulk slightly bobbled the pass and was hit immediately by Melvin Bullitt. The contact knocked Faulk back behind the first-down line, giving the Colts a first down just 28 yards from a go ahead score.

Instead of hurrying up, the Colts wisely worked the clock, patiently running the ball down to the 1-yard line. On second-and-goal with just 16 seconds to play, Manning rifled a pass to Wayne on a slant. Wayne caught the back half of the ball. The extra point gave the Colts a miraculous 35-34 victory. Belichick was roundly criticized for the decision not to punt, but given the way the Colts' offense was playing, he was right to go for the win with his offense.

On that night, Manning was just too good for the Patriots' defense.

December 17, 2009: Colts 35 Jaguars 31

Despite having clinched home-field advantage throughout the playoffs, the Colts decided to treat a midweek clash at Jacksonville as an important game. The Jaguars' franchise had struggled with attendance all season but managed to sell out the Thursday night affair with the 13-0 Colts. Many in Jacksonville saw the game as a referendum on the viability of the Jaguars' franchise. The Jags came out ready to play, and the two teams put on an offensive show.

With Freeney and Mathis only playing limited snaps, the Jaguars were uncharacteristically explosive on offense. They put up 17 first-half points against the Colts, but each time the Horse answered.

244

Manning did not throw an incomplete pass in the first half, and Chad Simpson contributed a kickoff return for a touchdown to give the Colts a slim 21-17 advantage.

The Jaguars gave themselves an excellent chance to win by scoring touchdowns on both of their first two possessions in the third quarter, and the Colts trailed 31-28 with less than six minutes to play. On third-and-5, Manning grabbed the MVP award by the throat thanks to a 65-yard bomb to Wayne to give the Colts a 35-31 lead. Manning's 308 yards and four touchdowns provided evidence of the kind of dominance he possessed in 2009.

The Colts' defense did its part to seal the victory as well. Despite early struggles, the defense allowed no points in the fourth quarter in part because Freeney and Mathis played virtually every down. The Jags last-ditch drive ended at the Colts' 33-yard line as rookie corner Jacob Lacey intercepted David Garrard. The win pushed the Colts to 14-0 on the season and ensured a perfect 6-0 record against the AFC South.

January 24, 2010: Colts 30 Jets 17 Playoffs

It was the mother of all rematches. To make the Super Bowl, the Colts had to beat the team that they had allowed into the playoffs. The upstart New York Jets, fresh off their upset of the Chargers the week before, boasted the best defense in football. Though the Colts were heavy favorites, the Jets were well-coached and extremely confident. Their confidence only rose as they expertly executed play fakes and trick plays to take a 17-6 lead.

Just when it appeared that the Jets might have Manning's number, he solved their complicated defense. With 2:11 to play in the half, Manning drove the Colts for a touchdown in just four plays. The incredible 80-yard drive featured three-consecutive passes to rookie Austin Collie, including an immaculate 46-yard pass that hit the young wideout in stride. Manning's quick strike pulled the Colts to within four points at the half.

In the second half, the Colts' defense shut down the vaunted Jets' running game as the Colts took the lead back on their first possession of the third quarter. The Colts' lead was not safe at 20-17, but Manning drove the Colts downfield for 10 points in the fourth quarter to give the Horse a comfortable margin of victory. Thanks to Manning's 377 yards and three scores and a 151-yard game from Garçon, the Colts won their second AFC Championship in Indianapolis.

November 7, 2010: Eagles 26 Colts 24

Even though this game came down to the wire, fans will remember it most as the beginning of the end for Austin Collie's promising career. Half-way through the season, the second-year wideout was a break-out star and among the league leaders in receptions and yards.

Late in the second quarter, he was the victim of a savage hit by safety Kurt Coleman on a deep ball over the middle. Collie lay motionless on the field for several minutes while the crowd booed and several Eagles danced gleefully about. Collie left the game, and played only two games the rest of the year. In both, he was forced to leave with head injuries.

The stunned Colts led at halftime, but faded in the third and fourth quarters. A furious Manning rally came up yards short, as his pass for fill-in receiver, Blair White, was intercepted at the Philadelphia 36 with 18 seconds to go. The Colts went on to lose four out of five games as dreams of a follow-up to the 2009 AFC Championship evaporated.

November 21, 2010: Patriots 31 Colts 28

It was just your typical Colts-Patriots game in the Brady-Manning Era. The Colts trailed at various points 21-7 and 31-14, as

246

Manning interceptions helped set up 10 points for the New England side. To add injury to insult, the Patriots targeted Collie's head in his return from the concussion he suffered in Philadelphia. By the middle of the second quarter he was out of the game.

With injuries mounting and the Patriots all but assured of victory, Manning did what he always did. He willed the team back into the game. Trailing by 17 with 10 minutes to play, the Colts clawed back, thanks to two Manning-to-White touchdowns. For a few brief moments, the calendar rolled back to 2009 again.

After a defensive stop, Manning took over with 2:26, and marched the Colts down to the New England 24. With just over a half-minute left and the offense already in field goal range, Manning lofted a ball down the right sideline between Garçon and Jacob Tamme. James Sanders picked it off to seal the game for New England. The comeback was dead, and it was clear something was seriously wrong with the Colts.

December 5, 2010: Cowboys 38 Colts 35

The horror that was late fall of 2010 reached its crescendo as the reeling Colts stumbled at home to the Dallas Cowboys, dropping their record to 6-6.

It was a wild game of back-and-forths, as the Colts overcame interception-fueled deficits of 17-0 and 27-14. Aided by a Taj Smith blocked-punt touchdown, the Colts took the lead early in the fourth quarter 28-27, but the Cowboys responded with a 19-play, ten-plus minute drive for a touchdown that required multiple third-down conversions and a field-goal-erasing leaping penalty on Eric Foster.

Despite the setback, Manning again rallied the Colts for a game-tying touchdown with just 33 seconds to play. His heroics were short-lived however, as his fourth interception of the game and his 13th in four outings set the Cowboys up in field goal range in overtime. It was one of the darkest moments of the Manning era.

December 19, 2010: Colts 34 Jaguars 24

As bleak as things had looked for the Colts two weeks before, a pair of AFC South contests lifted them right back into playoff contention. In a reversal from their usual roles, the Jacksonville Jaguars came to Indianapolis needing only to beat the Colts to secure their first-ever division title. A loss spelled playoff elimination for Indy.

Donald Brown and Collie would have none of it. Collie returned from his concussion-plagued hiatus by catching eight passes for 87 yards and two scores in the first half before tragically succumbing to yet another vicious hit that ended his season.[145]

Brown finished what Collie started, putting up the best day of his career to that point. He finished with 129 yards rushing on just 14 carries, aided by an early 49-yard run and a second-half touchdown scamper of 43 yards.

A late Jaguars' touchdown cut the Indianapolis lead from 24-10 all the way down to 27-24 with less than two minutes to play. Before fans could get truly nervous, however, Tyjuan Hagler pounced on the onside-kick attempt, scooping it up and running it back 41 yards for a game-sealing touchdown. Once again, Jacksonville failed when it mattered most. The Colts held serve down the stretch, winning their final four games in a row to clinch their final playoff berth of the Manning era.

January 8, 2010: Jets 17 Colts 16 Playoffs

We didn't know it at the time, but this heart-breaking playoff loss was to be Manning's final game in an Indianapolis Colts uniform.

It was a typical slug-it-out affair with the Jets, and the Colts managed a 7-0 lead at halftime. Recently re-acquired running back

---

[145] Collie finished the year with a catch rate of 81.7-percent on 58 receptions. He would have only 61 more over his final three years in the league.

Dominic Rhodes split carries with Joseph Addai, and though much beloved, Rhodes' best days were behind him. The Jets limited him to just 33 yards on 14 carries as both offenses ground out long, painful drives in the second half. Donald Brown scarcely saw the field.

Indianapolis and New York each scored on their first two possessions of the second half, but the Jets put up touchdowns to the Colts' field goals, and clung to a 14-13 lead as Manning took over at his own 20 with just 2:36 remaining.

His final drive in blue was masterful, as he guided the team to the New York 32-yard line to set up Adam Vinatieri for a go-ahead 50-yard field goal with less than a minute to play.

From that moment on, everything that could go wrong for the Colts, did. Antonio Cromartie returned the ensuing kickoff into Colts territory. The Jets had a fumble bounce right back to them, and Mark Sanchez completed a pair of passes to the Indy 32. With 29 seconds left, Jim Caldwell, reasoning that the Jets were already in field goal range, called a timeout.[146] He was hoping to force the Jets into a sack or turnover, but instead Sanchez hit Braylon Edwards along the sideline for 11 more yards of cushion. Nick Folk buried a 32-yard kick as time expired to end the tumultuous season.

September 25, 2011: Steelers 23 Colts 20

"Keep Calm and Kerry On" was the tongue-in-cheek response to the loss of Peyton Manning, but by the third game of the 2011 season, no one was in a laughing mood.

Already 0-2 and sinking fast, the Colts hosted the Steelers and their thousands of uninvited towel-waiving party crashers to Lucas Oil

---

[146] Caldwell took immense criticism for this decision, but the odds of Folk hitting a 49-yard field goal indoors were likely 70- to 80-percent. By allowing Dwight Freeney and Robert Mathis one more crack at the uneven Sanchez, Caldwell gave the Colts the only real shot they had at winning.

for a prime-time game that had already lost most of its luster. Pittsburgh wasted little time in jumping out in front by 10 points.

Despite the foreboding sense of doom that hung over the season, neither the crowd nor the team was interested in rolling over. Two field goals and a Freeney-induced sack/fumble returned for a score staked Indy to a tenuous 13-10 halftime lead. The defense, led by Pat Angerer's double-digit tackle effort, did their best to compensate for Kerry Collins' increasing ineptitude.

By the start of the fourth quarter, Collins was out for the game, the season, and his career with an injury, and the Curtis Painter Era was upon us. Despite the full-throated encouragement of the Purdue faithful in attendance, Painter's terror was palpable even in the 600 level. As the clock slid under six minutes to play in a tie game, Painter dropped back to pass one too many times. He was obliterated by James Harrison, then fumbled, and Troy Polamalu scooped up the ball to give the Steelers the lead.

To his credit, Painter peeled himself off the turf and led the Colts on a game-tying touchdown drive, culminating in a Joe Addai score with 2:15 to play. For the 2011 Colts, it was their high-water mark. The sold-out crowd roared its approval.

As it turned out, two minutes is, of course, too much time to leave Rothlisberger, who marched the Steelers down the field against an exhausted Indy defense, setting up a chip-shot field goal as time expired.

It was all downhill from there.

October 23, 2011: Saints 62 Colts 7

The most public of the Colts' many humiliations in 2011 came in Week 7. Most fans forget that up until they traveled to New Orleans, the Colts had been largely competitive with Curtis Painter at quarterback. Aside from the heart-breaker against Pittsburgh, they had also blown games against the Bucs, Chiefs, and Bengals. They had the ball with the chance to tie or take the lead in the fourth quarter in each
250

game. The Colts were not the uncompetitive nightmare every week that people remember.

The reason people think of that team as being a complete train-wreck is because of the prime-time ass kicking they took from the Saints.

The coaching staff, unable to cope with the reality that Manning would not return in 2011, trotted Painter out to play in Manning's no-huddle offense on the road in a dome.

Painter threw an interception and also fumbled, ultimately posting a passer rating of 38.1 for the game. He generally looked like a confused child playing against monsters.

The Saints scored virtually at will, reeling off 31-consecutive points to start the game, and then responded to the lone Colts' touchdown of the night by ripping off another 31 points for good measure.

Local reaction to the loss was outrage and humiliation. Blood was in the water, and for the first time, the media sharks began circling, eager to take their pound of flesh from Bill Polian.

December 22, 2011: Colts 19 Texans 16

Though they had eked out a forgettable win over a bad Titans team the week before, the pre-Christmas mood around the Colts was anything but festive. With a 1-13 record and a near certain lock on the first-overall pick in the draft, the Horse entered its final home game facing the reality that many great stars would no longer be with the team the following season.

Wayne was front-and-center among those likely to be shown the door in the offseason, and it was lost on no one that he could be saying farewell to the city. As a parting gift, he delivered one of the great performances of his career against the playoff-bound Texans.

Trailing by four points with two minutes to play, Indy took over on the wrong 22-yard line. Despite generally looking lost, Dan

Orlovsky hit Wayne for a long gain on third down, moving the Colts all the way to the Houston 20. As the clocked ebbed away, the team inched closer to the end zone, aided by three Texans' penalties in a five-play span. Without completing a pass, the Colts had moved to the 1-yard line. With 24 seconds left, Orlovsky found Wayne again to give the Colts what would be their second and final win of the year.

Wayne finished with eight catches for 106 yards and a score and stood exultant in the end zone, soaking in the adoration of fans not yet ready to part with him.[147]

October 7, 2012: Colts 30 Packers 27

The news that Chuck Pagano had been diagnosed with cancer rippled through town, but the NFL is not a forgiving league. Even as the team grappled with the significance of losing their head coach, the schedule called for them to take on Aaron Rodgers and the Green Bay Packers.

The 1-2 Colts were heavy underdogs and in the first half showed no signs of winning one for their coach. They trailed 21-3 at the break, and the game hadn't even been that close. It felt like the entire season was on the verge of coming apart.

Wayne had other ideas. Led by the veteran receiver who posted 212-yards receiving on 13 catches,[148] Indy scored 19-consecutive points to take a 23-21 lead.

Even with Rodgers driving the Pack for a go-ahead score in the final five minutes, the Colts kept hope alive through the remarkable play of Andrew Luck. Luck bounced off would-be sackers and repeatedly found Wayne for big gains. On the Colts' final drive, he hooked up with Reggie for gains of 14, 12, 15, and 18 yards before

---

[147] I interviewed Wayne a month after the season ended and shook his hand, thanking him on behalf of Colts fans for that moment. Even at the time, it looked unlikely that he would return to the Colts.
[148] Including a one-handed miracle grab that defied logic and physics.

connecting on a four-yard strike that saw Wayne frantically lunge for the end zone, breaking the plane of the goal by sheer force of will.

Despite only having 35 seconds to play, Rodgers moved the Packers to the Indy 33, but a 51-yard field goal try by Mason Crosby missed, leaving the emotionally spent Colts to celebrate through their tears.

October 28, 2012: Colts 19 Titans 13 (OT)

By all accounts, the Colts were lucky to be 3-3 midway through the season. They had won three close games thanks to Luck's encouraging play, but with the streaking Houston Texans running away with the AFC South, Indy would have to fight their way to a playoff berth via the Wild Card. Everyone circled their first division road game of the season against the Titans as a litmus test of their aspirations toward contention.

Indy's offense sputtered most of the day as the teams traded field goals, punts, and missed kicks that amounted to a seven-point lead for the Titans in the fourth quarter. Taking over with 10:26 to play at their own 20, the Colts ground out a 14-play drive that saw them convert a fourth-and-1 from the 8-yard line[149] before Delone Carter plunged ahead for the tying touchdown.

The Colts won the toss in overtime, and Brown took over. Brown carried the ball on the first six plays, moving the ball 44 yards into Titans' territory. After a long gain to Wayne moved the ball into the red zone, Luck dumped a screen to rookie Vick Ballard who rumbled toward the pylon, diving, and spinning in the air with the ball outstretched for his first career score. As he tumbled out of bounds, the signal went up.

Touchdown.

Another week, another miracle.

---

[149] Replays showed that the Titans played both third and fourth downs in that sequence with only ten men on the field.

December 2, 2012: Colts 35 Lions 33

Luck has been responsible for some of the most amazing comebacks in Colts' history, but none were quite as improbable as his Houdini act against the Detroit Lions in his rookie season.

It hadn't been his finest afternoon, as three interceptions helped to dig a 12-point fourth-quarter hole for the Colts, but, with the clock winding down, Luck found a new gear. The Lions punted to Indianapolis with just over four minutes to play, giving an uneven offense one final shot to tighten up the game.

Luck managed to convert a fourth down with an eight-yard scramble before eventually connecting with LaVon Brazill for a 42-yard touchdown with 2:47 left to cut the deficit to five.

Despite having two timeouts and the two-minute warning to work with, the defense initially faltered thanks to a pass-interference penalty on Cassius Vaughn. In fairness to Vaughn, Matt Stafford was targeting Calvin Johnson, who finished the game with three scores and 171 yards receiving. Grabbing him and pulling him to the ground was as legitimate a defensive technique as the team had against him.

Despite the penalty, the Lions couldn't quite put the game away, shanking a punt that gave Indy the ball with just 1:07 to play, no timeouts, and 75 yards away from the end zone. Over those final 67 seconds, the full promise of everything Luck could become was on display.

He completed short passes and long passes, baffling the Lions' defense with laser strikes. He also scrambled like his life depended on it, trucking smaller defenders who stood in his way. Of course, it's silly to describe a man playing a child's game as "heroic," but for that minute and change, Luck was a veritable Hercules in blue.

His furious rally moved the ball to the Detroit 14 with 14 seconds to play, but three incomplete passes later bled all but the last dregs of hope and the clock. With three ticks left, Luck surveyed the field on fourth down, dumping the ball to his fifth option. Donnie Avery snagged it on a crossing route and turned up field at the five.

With Luck streaking, arms raised into the end zone just behind him, Avery scored, touching off a mad celebration just in front of the Detroit fans who sat in dejected disbelief in the stands.

October 20, 2013: Colts 39 Broncos 33

We all knew the day was coming. Peyton Manning was returning to Indianapolis. He was putting up MVP-numbers and looked to lead his new horse to the Super Bowl. He was on enemy soil in the house that he had built.

Before the game, the Colts played a video tribute to Manning and gave the fans the chance to offer up a deafening ovation. Every man, woman, and child present gave him their heartfelt thanks.

The game itself was a thrilling contest that saw Indianapolis rip off 23-straight points before holding on for a six-point win. Mathis provided one of the indelible images in franchise history with a savage strip-sack safety of Manning.

Luck managed the game brilliantly, but no one felt safe with a nine-point lead with less than six minutes to play. Manning had burned too many other teams with epic comebacks. He drove the Broncos to the 2-yard line with 3:15 left when Eric Walden forced Ronnie Hillman to cough up the ball, functionally sealing the victory and preventing Manning from becoming the first quarterback to defeat all 32 NFL franchises.[150]

December 7, 2014: Colts 25 Browns 24

Throughout his first three seasons, Luck would often put the Colts in near-impossible holes, then dig them right back out of them. Such was the case on a chilly day in Cleveland in 2014.

---

[150] A distinction he obtained later in Week 1of the 2014 season when the Broncos beat the Colts in Denver.

Three Luck turnovers (two immediately returned for touchdowns) helped stake the Browns to a 21-7 third-quarter lead.

T.Y. Hilton (150 yards receiving on 10 catches with two touchdowns) did his best to keep Indy in the game, but the team's propensity for turnovers ensured Cleveland maintained a steady advantage. After a series of abortive drives, the home team clung to a 24-19 lead with 3:46 to play.

Starting at his own 10 before taking a sack back to the 6-yard line, Luck picked away at the Browns as the closing moments waned. A long pass to Donte Moncrief and a 35-yard pass-interference call against Cleveland moved the Colts from the shadow of their own goal line all the way to the Cleveland 25 in just four plays. It would take eight more plays to move the final yards as the Colts drove down to the 1-yard line, thanks in part to a Luck scramble.

With three downs to get that elusive final yard and just over a minute to go, Dan Herron was unable to make progress on either second or third down. Finally, with 36 seconds to play and the game literally resting on the goal line, Luck managed a quick hit to Hilton for the game-winning score.

As has so often been the case with visits to Cleveland, the game was ugly, if unforgettable.

January 11, 2015: Colts 24 Broncos 13 Playoffs

Manning and the Colts just couldn't avoid one another. After easily dispatching the Bengals in the first round of the playoffs, the Colts faced an old friend in his new home with a berth in the AFC Championship game on the line.

The Broncos started fast, ripping through the Colts' defense, but after an opening-drive touchdown, it became apparent that Indy was trying a technique rarely ever employed against Manning. Both corners pressed up on the wideouts, practically begging Manning to throw deep balls.

In his younger days, Manning would have made quick work of that plan, but he had been hobbled with a leg injury throughout the second-half of the 2014 season. He was unable to connect with his receivers and the Broncos could only muster six points the rest of the game. Meanwhile, the Indy defense teed off on a passer unable to move in the pocket and unable to punish the defense for aggressive gambles. Rookie Jonathan Newsome rang up a vicious sack-fumble to set up an Indy score.

Two touchdown drives put the Colts up four at the half, and after a three-and-out by Denver, Luck went to work securing the victory. Luck was resplendent on a 12-play drive on which he accounted for 68 of the 72 yards by the Colts. The biggest play was a phenomenal 32-yard pass to Coby Fleener on third-and-16 to set up a first-and-goal at the Bronco 8.

With a 21-10 lead, the defense only had to keep Manning from escaping. They continued to harass him, picking up two three-and-outs over the next three drives, allowing only a field goal to history's greatest comeback artist.

With 12:20 to play and clinging to an eight-point lead, the Colts methodically put the game out of reach. With 13 clock-grinding plays, Dan Herron and Zurlon Tipton played Keep Away from Denver. Though the drive eventually stalled inside the Denver 10, by the time Adam Vinatieri's field goal found the back of the net, more than eight minutes had evaporated.

It was painful to watch the once-great Manning struggle so egregiously against the Colts, but with Luck's steady-as-she-goes play, Indianapolis had once again booked a date with the New England Patriots with a chance to go to the Super Bowl on the line.

October 18, 2015: Patriots 34 Colts 27

Trailing by six points late in the third quarter, the Colts had a fourth-and-3 at their own 37. With the entire punting unit lined up to one side of the field, Griff Whalen snapped the ball to Colt Anderson who was swarmed under by the entire Patriots team.

Chuck Pagano still has a job.

November 2, 2015: Panthers 29 Colts 26 (OT)

Luck took a lot of criticism for his play in 2015, but no one ever questioned his toughness or heart. He put his will to win to the test on Monday Night Football on the road in Carolina and nearly pulled off one of the year's great upsets.

The rain-soaked debacle was more than a little sloppy, especially for the Colts. Quan Bray muffed the opening kickoff, then two plays later, a blown exchange between Luck and center Jonotthan Harrison, set the Panthers up for a quick field goal. Three more plays later, Luck threw an interception to set the Panthers up to take a 10-0 lead.

The Colts' defense performed admirably enough to keep the game close, and the Horse chipped away with a pair of field goals. As the game moved to the fourth quarter, however, the Panthers asserted control, putting up two touchdowns that sandwiched another Luck pick, giving Carolina a 17-point lead with under 11 minutes left.

With the game dripping away, Luck picked up the pace. He hit six of seven passes to pull the Colts within 10. The defense, aided by a Carolina penalty, forced a three and out. After missing on a couple of throws, Luck again found his range, nailing six-straight tosses to four different receivers, including three in a row to Coby Fleener to slice even further into the Panthers' edge.

After yet another stop by the Colts, Luck took over at his own 40 with 2:02 left. He drove the Colts all the way down to the Carolina

258

6-yard line with nine seconds to play, but couldn't come up with the game-winning touchdown. A chip-shot field goal forced overtime.

Indy won the flip, and a long return by Bray and a couple of short completions set the Colts up for a go-ahead field goal. They had ripped off 20-consecutive points to take the lead on the road against the eventual NFC Champions.

The upset was not to be, however. Cam Newton tore through the Colts' defense for a tying field goal. The Colts received the ball with a chance to win outright on a field goal, but Luck's second-down pass was picked off deep in Colts' territory. The Panthers didn't even need a first down. After three plays, they banged home the game-winning kick.

November 8, 2015: Colts 27 Broncos 24

Following the crushing loss to the Panthers on Monday night, the Colts dismissed offensive coordinator Pep Hamilton before facing the best defense in football on a short week.

For once, the Colts roared to life early in the game, putting up 17 points in a row to start. Still, they couldn't stay out of their own way, as Pat McAfee failed to get a punt out of bounds with 15 seconds to play in the first half. Omar Bolden picked it off and ran it back 83 yards to give Denver a little fight.

Manning was in the middle of the worst season of his career, and age had clearly caught up to him. He labored against Indy's press coverage as his arm strength had all but left him. Still, he found a way to push through the few cracks the Colts gave him. A 64-yard catch and run by Emmanuel Sanders pulled the Broncos to within a field goal, which Denver picked up on their ensuing drive.

With the game tied, Luck led the Colts on a touchdown drive that spanned the end of the third and beginning of the fourth quarters. He took an especially vicious hit while scrambling for the goal line, but managed to keep himself composed enough to guide the team in. Of course, Manning responded with an 80-yard drive of his own to tie the game with less than nine minutes to play.

The Colts eked out a couple of first downs, but it was just enough for Adam Vinatieri to slam home a 55-yard kick to give the Colts a tenuous three-point advantage.

With the ball and a chance to break the hearts of his former team, Manning threw a bad interception on first down, giving the Colts the ball right back with a chance to run out the final six minutes of the game.

The offense was deliberate. Three runs equaled a first down. Luck converted to Griff Whalen on a third-and-10 to move the ball deep into Broncos' territory. As the clock meandered under three minutes, the Colts pounded away at the Denver line. Aided by two personal foul calls, they kept the ball away from Manning entirely, securing an upset win.

It was to be Manning's last game in Indianapolis, and the last game of Luck's 2015 season. He suffered organ damage on his fourth-quarter scramble. Though he stayed in the game, he wouldn't return the rest of the season.

December 20, 2015: Texans 16 Colts 10

Without Luck, the Colts still managed to win a game here and there, and with two weeks left to go in the season, they played a virtual playoff game at home against the Houston Texans, who had never won in Indianapolis. A win would have put the Colts in the driver's seat for another AFC South title.

Veteran backup Matt Hasselbeck had performed admirably in relief of Luck, but a season behind the patchwork offensive line was taking a toll. The Colts' offense was nonfunctional over the last few games.

Hasselbeck did manage to turn two short fields into ten points early, but those were the only points the team would muster. Houston closed the first half with a field goal and added another in the third quarter. They had their own quarterback issues, but kept the pressure on the Colts defense. With 12:45 to play in the fourth quarter and trailing by four, Houston went for it on fourth-and-1 from the Colts' 45. Alfred Blue controversially converted, and Houston went on to take the lead for good at 13-10.

Hasselbeck wouldn't last another drive. After hitting Donte Moncrief for 21 yards, he left the game thanks to a brutal hit. Charlie Whitehurst came in and couldn't get the Colts deeper than the Houston 44-yard line.

After the teams traded punts, Hasselback re-entered the game with the ball just across midfield and 3:07 to play. The Colts only needed three points to force overtime, and realistically could get those points with just 15 more yards. Instead, Griff Whalen fumbled the ball back to the Texans.

The Texans put up a quick field goal for a six-point lead, but still left Indy 1:52 to put up a last-ditch touchdown drive. Hasselbeck launched a desperation heave on first down right into the arms of A.J. Bouye to functionally kill the Colts' season.

September 11, 2016: Lions 39 Colts 35

Luck was back from injury and hopes for the 2016 season were high. Those hopes would not survive the first game.

In what had become their signature move, the Colts fell behind a mediocre Lions squad 21-3 in the first half as the offense struggled to protect the quarterback and the defense had no answer for Matt Stafford.

Luck did his best to keep the Colts competitive, stringing together consecutive touchdowns to bracket halftime, cutting the Lions' lead from 21-3 to 21-18. But for every Indy score, the Lions roared back. They had six players with at least three catches on the day as injuries in the Indianapolis secondary and a non-existent pass rush left Stafford with open men all over the field.

Still trailing by six with four minutes to play, Luck took the Colts on a 75-yard drive deep into Lions' territory. After a completion to Hilton took the ball to the opposing 12-yard line with 1:15 to play, Pagano called an inexplicable timeout with the clock running. Instead of burning the clock down to the final seconds, the Colts scored the go-ahead touchdown two plays later, leaving 43 seconds for the Lions to respond.

Stafford had all three timeouts, and in just five plays moved his team 50 yards. Matt Prater hit a 43-yard field goal with eight seconds remaining to steal the home opener.

Luck's masterful 385-yard, four-touchdown effort was wasted in a game that served as a microcosm for the season and indeed the entire Pagano era.

October 16, 2016: Texans 26 Colts 23 (OT)

The Texans were division champions but had serious problems at the quarterback position. Brock Osweiler had been signed to a huge free-agent contract, fresh off a Super Bowl ring as Peyton Manning's backup in Denver, but struggled despite his team's first-place record.

The Colts had the opportunity to shrug off a disastrous start to the season and lay claim to first place in the AFC South by winning a Sunday-night contest in Houston.

For more than three quarters, Indianapolis demonstrated that they were the most talented team in the division. The Texans' offense languished as Indy built up a 23-9 lead with just over seven minutes remaining in the fourth quarter.

Unfortunately for the Colts, the Texans changed tactics late in the game. Osweiler switched to short passes and picked away at the Colts who were content to let Houston string together a 12-play drive with just minutes remaining. After all, a Texans' score still left the Colts with a seven-point lead and the ball with under three to play.

Needing one first down to end the game, the Indy offense stumbled badly. An ugly series netted negative-11 yards[151] and only managed to burn 32 seconds, leaving Houston two minutes to tie the game.

Osweiler did just that in three plays and just over a minute, thanks to sloppy tackling by a defense that was confused about how to close games. If there was any silver lining, it was that Houston scored so quickly, Luck had a chance to put together a winning field-goal drive.

Luck responded, moving the ball to the 50 on the first play of the ensuing drive. The next three plays were chaotic, as Luck burned two timeouts and managed just a two-yard scramble. With no points to show for the promising start, the game moved to overtime.

The Colts won the toss in the extra period, and picked up a first down before a sack at their own 38 cut short the drive. They punted back to Osweiler and company who wasted no time in putting together their third-consecutive scoring drive, needing just four plays to move into range for the game-winning field goal.

December 11, 2016: Texans 22 Colts 17

Despite an up-and-down year, the Colts entered their Week 15 game against the Texans needing a win to move into first place in the division. This time around, it was Luck that let them down.

After an interception setup the first Houston touchdown, Luck's offense sleepwalked through the first half, as the Texans flipped up a string of field goals to build a 16-3 lead.

Thanks to Osweiler's own ineptitude, what should have been a blowout, became tight as Luck found Frank Gore for a touchdown to cut the lead to six points mid-way through the third quarter.

---

[151] Run for two, false start, sack for a loss of seven, run for a loss of one.

After a Houston three-and-out, the Colts marched to the Houston 3-yard line, before a third-down sack-fumble of Luck by Jadeveon Clowney snuffed out a prime scoring opportunity.

Houston sandwiched a later Luck touchdown throw with a pair of field goals, giving the Colts 2:47 to pull out a win and the chance to go to the playoffs.

Like the first game against the Texans, Luck hit two quick throws out to the Indy 49-yard line, and it looked like the Colts were in business. The next three plays netted just nine yards, however, and with 1:24 left, Luck faced a fourth-and-1 from the Houston 42. The resulting screen attempt fell incomplete as penetration by the Texans disrupted the play from the start and ended any playoff dreams for the 2016 Colts.

The 2016 season was defined by the two games against Houston. The Texans finished the season one game ahead of the Colts after beating Indy twice in games that the Colts had every opportunity to win. Despite a strong statistical season, Luck's final-drive failures against the Texans doomed the team.

Appendix C

Bonus Content

Original Essay About Jim Irsay[152]

Irsay is the best owner in football. He is classy. He is respected. He is beloved. He has a wonderful relationship with the community. He is unfailingly generous and one of the influential voices among NFL owners.

There was a time when such words would never have been uttered. Two decades ago, outside of Marion County, the Irsay name was something of a national joke. Now "Irsay" is held in high esteem alongside names like Rooney and Mara.[153] In many ways, the story of the Indianapolis Colts is the story of Jim Irsay's quest for excellence and for the redemption of his family's reputation.

Jim Irsay was around football from a young age. His father bought the team when he was just 12 years old, and Jim began working at nearly every level of the organization. From the ticket window to the front office, Irsay the son had the privilege of learning football from the ground up. His father was a wealthy man who happened to buy a football team, but Jim Irsay grew up a football man who understood what makes a franchise tick.

Fresh out of college, he was handed the reigns to the newly-minted Indianapolis Colts. His father named him General Manager of the team in 1984. It took Jim some time to find his footing. It is easy to criticize him for some of the early failures on the field, but the team he took over was already in shambles. Irsay had to draft effectively for

---

[152] This is included in order to preserve the spirit of the original book.
[153] The Rooney family has owned the Pittsburgh Steelers for decades. The Maras own the New York Giants. They are considered the most respected, successful, and classy families in football.

several years before the Colts were finally on the cusp of contention in 1987.

One thing has always marked Jim Irsay, regardless of his role with the team: he does what it takes to win. As general manager, his trade for Eric Dickerson instantly transformed the Colts into a playoff team and made the team relevant to Indianapolis. He did what he could to make the Colts into a winner quickly. In those early years, he often traded away first-round picks for players who could make an immediate impact.

Jim Irsay was committed to the Colts staying in Indianapolis and becoming part of the local fabric. His deal to bring Indy hero Jeff George to the Colts was not just an attempt to give the Colts a franchise quarterback, but was also about giving the people of Indianapolis an icon who would help the city take emotional ownership of the team.

Despite the best of intentions, the numbers show that Irsay was not an effective GM. His trade for Fredd Young[154] cost the Colts two first-round picks. He agreed to give Eric Dickerson a new contract after his best days were behind him. Ultimately, the Jeff George experiment ended in acrimony. What matters is not the results of individual decisions, but the wins and losses that resulted from them. Jim Irsay was the general manager for ten seasons, posting just three winning records, one playoff appearance, and never more than nine wins.

Perhaps his lack of success as a team builder led him to exercise such tremendous restraint when it became his turn to run the team. Bob Irsay was famous for meddling in the day-to-day operations of the team. He routinely inserted himself into game day coaching decisions. His son has been the opposite. Despite taking over 100-percent ownership of the team at the relatively tender age of 37,[155] he

---

[154] Young played three seasons with the Colts, collecting just two sacks and two interceptions.

[155] He was the youngest owner in the league. As recently as 2010, he was still the fourth-youngest owner in the NFL, despite owning the team for 13 years at that point.

266

has shown remarkable restraint and maturity. Since Jim took over the team, the Colts have had just two general managers and only three head coaches.

One of his first actions upon taking over as owner of the Indianapolis Colts was to hire Bill Polian from the Carolina Panthers. Polian had worked with Jim on the Dickerson trade and was renowned as the best personnel man in the business. Jim Irsay gave the reigns to Polian and then stayed out of his way. That is not to say that he has been an absentee or disinterested party to events. As owner, Irsay has chosen to be the guiding influence and the emotional center of the franchise. He was closely involved in the process of drafting Peyton Manning and urgently sought to bring Tony Dungy on board as head coach of the Colts.

Irsay deserves credit for breaking with his father in other ways as well. As the RCA Dome became an increasingly obsolete home for an NFL franchise, Irsay never once threatened to move the Colts out of Indianapolis. Rumors swirled in the background that Los Angeles was interested in bringing the Colts out west, but Irsay was careful to maintain his commitment to the city. His greatest accomplishment was the construction of Lucas Oil Stadium. The public/private collaboration cost him $100 million, but ensured the Colts would stay in Indianapolis long enough that memories of the Midnight Move from Baltimore would fade into the past.

As owner, Irsay has promoted a vision for a special kind of NFL franchise. Tony Dungy recalled his conversations with Irsay about the identity of the Colts this way:

"We talked about the Colts family, about values, about community. He said he wanted to win, but he wanted to win the right way. And if we ever did win the Super Bowl, he wanted Indiana to feel a personal connection, for it to be *their* team and *their* trophy."[156]

It has been his goal to make the Colts an elite franchise that feels as if it belongs to the people of Indiana. His success as an owner

---

[156] Tony Dungy, *Quiet Strength* (Carol Stream, IL: Tyndale Momentum, 2008), 203.

is indisputable. Under his watch, the Colts have posted 14 winning seasons and a Super Bowl victory. All over the state of Indiana, Hoosiers bleed blue and white.

His vision has come to pass.

He has redeemed the Irsay name.

It's time to talk about Luck[157]

Andrew Luck is the consensus choice to be the first overall pick in the NFL draft.

The Indianapolis Colts are likely to be in the running for the worst record in the NFL.

Given that the Colts just signed Peyton Manning to a five-year deal, everyone wants to know: if they get the first overall pick, will they take Luck?

Before looking at the situation, let's lay the groundwork:

1. The best draft philosophy is to take the best available player. For the remainder of this piece, I'm operating under the assumption that Luck is the best available player. If he isn't, then none of this applies.[158]

2. We are assuming the Colts will have the first overall pick.[159] If they don't, the equation is entirely different. Trading up to get Luck only makes sense in a world where Peyton Manning is going to retire or the Colts don't believe he's likely to play in 2012. In that case, Indy should go hard after Luck and pay what it takes to get him.

3. We are assuming Peyton Manning is healthy. If Manning is not healthy, there is <u>no choice</u> to be made. If the odds of Manning playing in 2012 are anywhere south of 70 percent, the Colts MUST cut him and move on. They cannot be on the hook for his whole deal. For the purposes of this exercise, we are assuming Manning will be ready to play.

---

[157] This piece was written September 20, 2011 for 18to88.com. It has only been edited for formatting and typos.
[158] As it turns out, he was.
[159] As it turns out, they did.

Many have wondered why the Colts would bring Manning back at all in 2012 if they draft between second to tenth or something similar. The reason is simple: they have to find out if he can still play. I've come around on this point. Indy has to know definitely if they can count on Manning. If they can't, they have one window of escape, and they must take it. If Peyton can play in 2011, he should. The Colts have to get a better idea of what they have in him going forward. If he takes over a 1-10 team (yes, it could be that bad),[160] and wins the last four games of the year with them (which he would if he's healthy), then they can feel much better about him going forward.

The Colts will be faced with a difficult choice when it comes to Luck. They have four primary options.

1. Take Luck first overall and let him develop behind Manning.

I hate this choice. It's intellectually lazy. Taking Luck does not make the Colts better in 2012. If the Colts think Luck is a once-in-a-decade prospect, they should take him, obviously. However, if he's that good, then it's time to move on.

However, many people love to "develop" quarterbacks. I think this leads to animosity and ugliness. People point at the Packers' situation as an ideal, but forget that they wasted a season recovering from the Favre/Rodgers fiasco. They went from a Super Bowl caliber team to 6-10 in 2008. Yes, they won the Super Bowl in 2010, but they could have won it in 2008 or 2009 if they hadn't screwed around. Beyond that, Rodgers was the 24th-overall selection, so it wasn't nearly as costly to have him sit and wait for a few years. Doing that with the first overall pick isn't nearly as attractive an option.

Indy was always going to have to endure a miserable season at the end of the Manning era. If 2011 has to be it, so be it. The problem with the "keep both" plan is that then you've occupied tons of cap room on quarterbacks, and eaten up most of Luck's "cheap" years sitting on the bench. Then, you have to decide whether not to give him

---

[160] It was that bad.

270

a huge second contract (which he'll want even if he sat for three years), without really knowing if he can play.

If Manning is healthy, he's going to play for four to five more years.[161] It's too soon to take Luck to "learn" from Manning. This option makes the least sense. It's probably the most popular among fans and pundits, but it's pure, unadulterated stupidity. It will ruin the franchise.

2. Take Luck first overall and trade/release Manning.

The first-overall QB selected is basically ready to lead a team by his second season. If the Colts take Luck AND keep Manning, they weaken their team moving forward. You can't play them both. Keeping Luck means parting ways with Peyton. The Colts have an out in Manning's contract, and to keep both would cripple them cap-wise moving forward. It's a coward's play.

If Luck is the man, then he's the man. Manning should be dealt (Indy could at least get a first- and a second-round pick for him),[162] or cut. It's hard to know what the market will be for him given his contract and health.

From 1987-2008 there have been 25 quarterbacks taken in the first five picks. Eleven of those have been successes (Peyton and Eli, Aikman, Palmer, McNabb, Bledsoe, Ryan, McNair, Rivers, Sanchez,[163] Kerry Collins). Three have had some success (Vick, Testaverde, Vince Young), and Matt Stafford has battled injuries, but looks like he might be successful. The other ten have been beyond terrible (Carr, Alex Smith,[164] Meier, Harrington, Shuler, Akili Smith, Ryan Leaf, George, Couch, Russell). Of the players who hit, all of them but McNair (5) and Rivers (3) were in the playoffs by Year Two.

---

[161] Nailed it.

[162] The Redskins traded for the second pick and the rights to draft Robert Griffin III. They functionally gave up two firsts and a second.

[163] Move him down a tier in hindsight.

[164] Alex Smith probably qualifies as a "success," but not for the team that drafted him.

271

By taking Luck and moving on from Peyton, the Colts have a coin-flip chance of being back in the playoffs by 2013 and on the road to a new dynasty. They also have a coin-flip chance of Luck busting and the team being horrible for five years.

3. Trade the pick.

The first-overall pick this year will merit a king's ransom. The Colts could deal the pick and infuse the team with a wealth of young talent that would set them up for a nice three to-four-year run at the top of the AFC. You take this choice if you are 100-percent convinced that Manning is healthy. If Peyton is right, you are essentially saying, "We have three-to-four years of being a guaranteed Super Bowl contender (because Peyton makes you that), and we'll take that over a 50-50 chance that we've landed the next franchise QB in Luck."

This is the "bird in the hand" strategy. The pick for Luck cannot go for less than first rounders in both 2012 and 2013 and a second rounder in 2012 and change. That's a lot of talent to bring into the franchise in the next two years.

4. Take Luck and then deal him after the 2012 season.

A variant of #1 and #3, the Colts could take Luck as insurance for Manning in 2012, and then deal him once it looks like Peyton can play. It's better than option #1 because you aren't paying two quarterbacks for four years. It's also worse than option #2, because it keeps the team on the hook for Manning's full signing bonus moving past this year. Still, it's a middle path. I favor bold action, personally, and respect positions two and three the most because they show clear thinking and a definite course of action.

Conclusion

Which is better: Three years of being elite or a 50-percent chance of earning another decade of relevance? It's a tough call, for sure. Hopefully, the Colts get the chance to make the call. It only matters if Peyton Manning is healthy enough to play in 2012. If he's not, there's no choice.

Personally, I'd rather trade the pick and go all in with Peyton for three or four years. I think you take the sure thing, even if it's short lived. Options 1 and 4 don't make the Colts a better team in 2012. You can't play two quarterbacks, and there's no reason to carry two expensive ones.

If the Colts decide to part ways with Peyton, it will be a sad time in my life. If they do so boldly, however, believing Luck is the next elite quarterback, I'll be able to respect and defend the decision.

*****

Should he have done it? If Jim Irsay could do it all over again, would he have cut Peyton Manning?

This essay is included because long before the Colts had secured the top pick, I argued that if Manning was going to be healthy, the Colts had to keep him and trade the pick that became Andrew Luck. Or they could dump Manning and take Luck. The only bad choice was no choice.

Despite what some in the media reported, the Colts could have kept Manning and stayed under the salary cap.[165] In fact, all they had to do to accomplish that feat was to release Dwight Freeney. They would have saved more than enough to absorb Manning's deal, and they still could have re-signed Robert Mathis, and Reggie Wayne and had money left over.[166]

Knowing what we know now, that Manning was healthy and that he had MVP seasons left in him, I wish they could have kept him. As I argue in this piece, taking Luck wasn't a mistake, and there's no denying that he has provided Colts fans some amazing memories.

But nothing would have compared to the joy of seeing 18 in blue again.

---

[165] This is the most oft-repeated "wrong fact" in Indianapolis history. It was never true. Too many people failed to do the math and took the regime's word for it.

[166] And no, Manning would not have "gotten killed" by the terrible Indianapolis line. The 2012 line was better than the 2008 line. Manning doesn't take the sacks or hits Luck does because he was simply a better quarterback than Luck is.

Stealing the Thorny Crown[167]

Indiana is a simple place, really. You can size it up quickly. There's no complicated topography. There're some hills in the south and some lakes in the north, but for the most part, what you see is what you get. It's flat.

Flat can be deceiving.

Flat makes distance hard to judge. Objects are always further away than they appear. Nothing sneaks up on you in Indiana. You have a feel for that water tower a mile or so before you get to it. Of course, you can't read the graffiti until you get up close.

Hoosiers are like so many water towers. You see them; you size them up, but don't expect to read them from afar.

Michael Weinreb came to Indianapolis recently.[168] Our lack of flash mobs disappointed him.

His conclusion after talking to the editor of NUVO, a museum curator, Bob Kravitz, and a professor was that Hoosiers don't really love Peyton Manning.

"He could have been the king of this town, if he wanted to be," said David Hoppe.

The carpetbaggers never plagued Indiana the way they invaded the South. It's ironic, because Indy has always lusted after their attention, or at least their money. For as long as I can remember, Indianapolis was a city that craved the spotlight, the chance to show the world that we were just as good or better than anyone else. We begged and cajoled the carpetbaggers to come, to notice us. We

---

[167] This piece originally appeared on ColtsAuthority.com on February 28, 2012. I was awarded the 2013 Dick Conner award for blog writing by the Professional Football Writers of America in part for this piece.

[168] The piece referenced can be found here:
http://www.grantland.com/story/_/id/7620692/indianapolis-meaning-peyton-manning

relished the Pacers and Knicks for all the reasons many have mentioned before. At least they were paying attention to us.

After reading Weinreb's piece, however, it is clear to me how little New York understands Indiana. Maybe we are just too flat.

According to Weinreb's exhaustive interview of a handful (and clearly representative sample) of people living in Indiana (most not even Hoosiers), Peyton Manning isn't really beloved, never lived up to expectations, doesn't own the city, was too down-home and personable, and should never have made all those funny commercials because now no one takes him seriously.

I don't want to mock or ridicule Weinreb. His piece wasn't malicious. It was just so profoundly wrong and out of step with the way people around here feel, that I marvel at how badly he missed the essence of what Peyton Manning means to Indiana.

Comparing Manning to Bob Knight or even Reggie Miller is utterly beside the point. Knight was always hated by a good chunk of the state, and he was ultimately ushered out by his own doings after his considerable talents eroded past the point where we could overlook his flaws. As for Reggie Miller, as beloved as he was, even in the late 90s, there was not a 31 jersey hanging in every closet. Reggie was special and electric, but he was never transcendent. He did not change Indiana. He wasn't even the greatest basketball hero the state has ever had. Not by a long shot. He hasn't been gone ten years, and now we shower his chant on a football player.[169]

Peyton Manning *changed* Indiana.

What people like Bob Kravitz have never understood is what this state was like before he got here. I'm not going to rewrite Blue Blood here and now,[170] but after a decade of Peyton Manning, high school football outdraws high school basketball.

Peyton Manning isn't king of Indianapolis?

We built the man a football palace.

---

[169] Reggie Wayne.
[170] I mean, I am doing that now. Just not then.

His number hangs in every closet and on every back come Sundays in the fall. People love everything about him, ESPECIALLY his commercials. Fail to take him seriously? The whole city has been in mourning for the past eight months. What Weinreb read as disinterest is just emotional exhaustion. People have been dying inside since August. No, I'm not taking to the streets in February. I broke down in September and cried at my desk in December. I'm spent. We all are.

There was a pocket of people that blamed Peyton that there was "only" one Super Bowl. That much is true. Those people also shut up permanently after the 2011 season. What dissenters remained were forever silenced by watching the same team that had made the playoffs in 2010 completely implode without Peyton. There are no doubters left. There are plenty of people who actually blame the Colts for failing him.

So no, no one's taking to the streets to protest. There's nothing to protest. No one even knows if Peyton is healthy. We've been battered by rumors of impending retirement, secret surgeries, last-ditch attempts to take the field. We've no angst left for a flash mob. At this point, most Hoosiers just hope he's ok. Yeah, we are pragmatic. How else can we feel at this point? He's going to leave. Everyone hopes he'll stay, but this is Indiana. No one really believes it possible that he'd choose us over Miami or New York. No one ever does. People want the best for Peyton. It's hard to see how that's Indianapolis at this point. Just writing those words tears me apart. It's like admitting defeat.

The Peyton Manning Saga has been dragging on since August. It's been hard on the city watching our greatest hero just vanish. He was here with us every week for years, and with little warning he was just...gone. Can you imagine, even IMAGINE, what it would be like if Peyton showed up in public? He'd be swarmed. He's the most recognizable face in town. People hang on his every word. Peyton Manning couldn't be any more the king of Indianapolis if he started wearing a blue robe, crown, and pranced about calling himself the "Prince of Catfish" (we don't really have whales around here. We make do with what we've got).

276

There's no point in trying to express how deeply this city feels about Peyton Manning. You either get it or you don't. Yeah, I have four Peyton Manning jerseys in my closet. Who doesn't at this point? No, I'm not the least bit impartial when it comes to Peyton Manning. No Hoosier is. How can anyone interview a guy who grew up in Minnesota rooting for John Unitas and think his opinion is indicative of how Indiana feels about Manning? It baffles me.

NUVO? Really? I mean...really?

Weinreb came to Indianapolis and saw what he expected, or didn't see what he expected. Either way, he packed his notepad, recorder, and type-writer in his shag-lined satchel and went back to New York to spin his yarn about how the yokels like their southern-white savior, but they don't like-like him.

I mean, all they do is name their kids after him.

About the Author

Nate Dunlevy is an Indianapolis native and a graduate of Pike High School. He holds a Masters of Divinity in the area of Intercultural Studies from Grace Theological Seminary in Winona Lake, IN. He currently resides in Indianapolis with his wife, Deborah, and three children.

Dunlevy was the founder of the Colts-centric website 18to88.com, his work has been featured on several national platforms, and he was named the 2013 Dick Connor Writing Award winner for the Blog Category by the Professional Football Writers of America.

He currently writes for ColtsAuthority.com. His 2011 novel, *Invincible, Indiana*, also available from Madison House Publishing, was selected for the Next Indiana Bookshelf by Indiana Humanities as a book "to encourage Hoosiers to think, read, and talk about the present and future of Indiana."

Works Cited

The author would like to recognize the following sources for their contributions to this book:

Arizona Republic

Bleacherreport.com

Colts.com

Coltsauthority.com

Footballoutsiders.com

Grantland.com

HuffingtonPost.com

Kentsterling.com

Profootballreference.com

Sports Illustrated

The Indianapolis Star

The Toronto Star

WTHR

Bill Hudnut, *The Hudnut Years* (Bloomington, IN: Indiana University Press, 1995).

Chuck Pagano and Bruce A. Tollner, *Sidelined: Overcoming Odds through Unity, Passion and Perseverance* (Grand Rapids, MI: Zondervan, 2014).

Mike Chappell and Phil Richards, *Tales from the Indianapolis Colts Sideline* (New York: Sports Publishing, 2004).

Phillip B. Wilson, *100 Things Colts Fans Should Know & Do Before They Die* (Chicago, IL: Triumph Books, 2013).

Ron Jaworski, *The Games that Changed the Game* (New York: Random House, Inc. 2010).

Terry Hutchings, *Let 'Er Rip* (Dallas: Masters Press, 1996).

Tony Dungy, *Quiet Strength* (Carol Stream, IL: Tyndale Press, 2007)

Printed in Great Britain
by Amazon